THEOLOGY IN RECONSTRUCTION

THEOLOGY
IN RECONSTRUCTION

T. F. TORRANCE

*Professor of Christian Dogmatics
in the University of Edinburgh*

Wipf & Stock
PUBLISHERS
Eugene, Oregon

Wipf and Stock Publishers
199 West 8th Avenue, Suite 3
Eugene, Oregon 97401

Theology in Reconstruction
By Torrance, Thomas F.
Copyright©1996 by Torrance, Thomas F.
ISBN: 1-57910-024-4
Publication date 12/19/1996
Previously published by Eerdmans, 1996

To
J.B.T.
and D.W.T.

CONTENTS

8   *Contents*

PREFACE

THE essays gathered together in this volume have been produced in the course of dialogue with modern thought as during my day to day work in the teaching of Christian theology I have struggled to develop modes of inquiry and exposition that are appropriate to the nature and logic of God's self-revelation in Jesus Christ. They have been written under the conviction that we must allow the divine realities to declare themselves to us, and so allow the basic forms of theological truth to come to view and impose themselves on our understanding. Theology is the positive science in which we think only in accordance with the nature of the given.

Perhaps the most difficult part of theology is the struggle we have with ourselves, with the habits of mind which we have formed uncritically or have acquired in some other field of knowledge and then seek with an arbitrary self-will to impose upon the subject-matter. We have to remind ourselves unceasingly that in our knowing of God, God always comes first, that in a genuine theology we do not think out of a centre in ourselves but out of a centre in God and his activity in grace toward us. Hence when we are engaged in dialogue with modern thought in its science and philosophy we must not try to bring knowledge of God down to the level of man's natural understanding, for we may not formulate our understanding of God on any ground lower than that which he has provided in revealing himself to us. Moreover, when we make use of modern tools of thought and speech we must beware of subjecting knowledge of God to an alien frame-work by adapting it to the patterns of thought which we rightly develop in our investigation of the world of nature in its contingent existence. Rather must we let our understanding be raised up to what is above so that, human though it is and must remain, it may yet suffer adaptation under the impact of God's self-revelation and acquire new habits of thought appropriate to God himself.

Theology of this kind is possible only because God has already condescended to come to us, and has indeed laid hold of our humanity, dwelt in it and adapted it to himself. In Jesus Christ he has translated his divine Word into human form and lifted up our human mind to understand himself. Hence in theological inquiry we are driven back upon Jesus Christ as the proper ground for communion and speech with God. Because he is both the Word of God become Man and Man responding to that Word in utter faithfulness and truth, he is the Way that leads to the Father. It is in him and from him that we derive the basic forms of theological thinking that are appropriate both to divine revelation and human understanding.

We live in an era of sharp theological conflict and yet of genuine advance. 'Theological solipsism' (to borrow an apt expression from my brother, J. B. Torrance) is rampant, breeding disagreement—hence the need is all the greater for a rigorous and disciplined inquiry that will not let us think in the way we want to think but only in the way we have to think if we are to do justice to the 'object' we are investigating. On the other hand, when we actually engage in a critical and scientific approach to the basic forms of theological thinking and are ready for positive reconstruction in accordance with them, unity and logical simplicity re-emerge, theological disagreements begin to fall away, and a steady advance in coherent understanding takes place in continuity with the whole history of Christian thought. It is one of the most heartening features of our time that we can begin to see something of the lines of this advance.

Since terminological misunderstanding has contributed so much to recent confusion in theological writing I would ask my readers to be patient with my use of technical terms, refraining from putting a meaning upon them merely according to their own habits of thought. Need I say that 'scientific' is never restricted to the mode of rationality that obtains in natural science, or that 'objective' never means 'objectivist'?

Essays of this kind thrown up by debate here and there inevitably overlap when brought together. I hope the reader will pardon the repetition and that instead of causing *ennui* it will help toward clarification of the questions at issue.

I am deeply grateful to the various publishing houses who have allowed me to reproduce here essays that have appeared elsewhere under their imprint. I owe a particular debt of gratitude to D. L. Edwards and M. C. King of the SCM Press for their selfless labours and unfailing courtesy. My thanks are also due to my nephew, Robert T. Walker, of Edinburgh University, for helping me with the proofs.

T.F.T.

New College, Edinburgh, Martinmas 1964

ACKNOWLEDGMENTS

Grateful acknowledgment is made to the following for permission to reproduce essays in this volume.

New College Bulletin for 'Theological Education Today'

Theologische Zeitschrift and *Dialog* for 'The Influence of Reformed Theology on the Development of Scientific Method' and 'The Problem of Theological Statement Today'

Dr A. J. Philippou for 'The Logic and Analogic of Biblical and Theological Statements in the Greek Fathers'

Lutterworth Press for 'The Word of God and the Nature of Man' and 'The Place of Christology in Biblical and Dogmatic Theology'

Scottish Journal of Theology for 'Justification: Its Radical Nature and Place in Reformed Doctrine and Life' and 'The Foundation of the Church'

Eastern Churches Quarterly for 'The Roman Doctrine of Grace from the Point of View of Reformed Theology'

Oekumenische Rundschau and *Verbum Caro* for 'The Relevance of the Doctrine of the Spirit for Ecumenical Theology'

Revue d'Histoire et de Philosophie Religieuses for 'Knowledge of God and Speech about him according to John Calvin'
Revue d'Histoire et de Philosophie Religieuses and *Theologische Zeitschrift* for 'Come, Creator Spirit, for the Renewal of Worship and Witness'

The London Quarterly and Holborn Review for 'A New Reformation?'

PROLOGUE

I

Theological Education Today[1]

THIS is not an essay about the content of theological courses, nor is it another attempt to argue for reform in the training of the Ministry. Its aim is to open up a few of the perspectives within which theological education in the modern world must be carried out, and to single out some of the main issues that have to be considered at every point by teacher and student alike, if only because they have to think and speak within the same room in which others are also at work, scientists, philosophers, literary critics, historians, sociologists, physicians, etc. By its very nature theological activity must involve a dialogue with those at work in other fields, for it cannot avoid the questions they raise and cannot but pose for them other questions demanded by inquiry into its own subject-matter. Moreover, the articulation of theological knowledge, and therefore its communication, must make use of the forms of thought and speech that are current in the world, but for that very reason it must wrestle hard with them, for if they are to be used properly and scientifically they must be adapted to the nature of the material content of theological knowledge.

Four lines of thought are pursued a little here, those forced upon theological education today by the dominant place of *science* in modern life, by the widespread attention to the medium of *language* which all knowledge must employ, by our ineluctable involvement in *history*, and by the demands of sheer *human need*.

(i) There cannot be any question about the fact that the whole of future life and thought will be dominated more and more by pure and applied science. It is within this perspective that theology must learn to think with its own kind of precision and its own disciplined controls. Apart from the benefit this will bring to theology itself, we must understand the world within which we live, and really live in it through engagement with its thinking, if we are to fulfil our Christian mission.

[1] Reprinted from *New College Bulletin* I/1, 1964.

Modern science is by no means divorced from our historical cultures, as some would have us believe. It would be more true to say that it acquires its basic habits of thought from the cultural traditions that derive from the Greeks and the Romans, and indeed from the Hebrews. Let us consider them in that order.

The Way of the Greeks. In all their thinking, in philosophy or science, the Greeks were intent upon discerning the shape and pattern of things. Thinking for them was ultimately a kind of *seeing*, and truth was discerned in terms of *form*. Greek culture stands for the primacy of vision. That is one strand that contributes to our modern understanding of science through observation, although nowadays it is not only with the eyes that we observe things; we make use of electronic probes or radar telescopes to 'observe' what goes on millions of light-years away on the outer fringes of the universe. Yet we still speak of this as 'observation'.

The Way of the Romans. The great genius of the Romans was for law and order, for administration. They were concerned with ways and means, with getting things done, with management and control of resources, armies and supplies, and of public life. These Latin modes of thought have left their mark in the legal structures, and social and political institutions of the West.

In many ways it is the combination of these two ways, the Greek and the Roman, that gives us the habits of mind which we use in modern science, *observation* and *control*. We claim to know only what we observe and control. Along these lines modern science has made immense progress, but only within the limits of what can be observed and controlled. If the latest developments in nuclear science have taught us anything, they have taught us the limited range of the criterion of perceptibility, with the result that scientists today are in many ways humbler than they were a few decades ago, for they have discovered that this kind of science can offer only a limited way of knowledge.

The Way of the Hebrews. This is far more important for science than many people think. It is the kind of thinking which we find in the Bible, where we learn and know through *listening* and *responding*, by *serving* and *obeying*. As one example of this kind of thinking in science one can point to Albert Einstein who used to speak of the *awe* and *humility* that one must have before the secrets of the universe and its amazing rationality—something that could be learned only by giving ear to it.

This is the way of learning that the modern world even in its natural science has learned largely through the Reformation, with its emphasis upon hearing the Word of God, and letting it speak to us out of itself, and upon the obedience of the mind in response to it. When Francis Bacon started empirical science upon its new methods, he deliberately transferred Calvin's method of interpreting 'the books of God' to the interpretation of 'the books of nature', as he expressed it. Nature is to be understood only by humble learning, by serving it, following the clues it gives us of its own secrets, without attempting to force our own patterns upon it.

The principle involved here can be stated in this way: we know something in accordance with its nature, when we respect it and consciously behave in terms of it. This Hebrew and Christian way of thinking, as John Macmurray has so often said, has made a major contribution to modern science, for it is here that we have our concern for *objectivity*, our determination to know something out of itself, unhindered by what we think of it *a priori*, and undistorted by any previous notions we may claim to have about it.

These three ways of thinking, the Greek, the Roman and the Hebrew, have to be put together if we are to get the three main ingredients in our modern habits of thought. We are being forced to recognize, however, that while we can never do without any one of them in true human knowledge, the emphasis changes in accordance with the nature of the object of inquiry. In some fields of knowledge observation and description are all-important, in other fields they have a minimal place; in some control must be exercised, but in others control of the object would prevent us from learning, although disciplined self-control is always essential; in others again the meek, listening approach is more appropriate, and a different but more implacable objectivity than that which is yielded by determinate objects faces us. It belongs thus to the refinement of scientific activity to discern the nature of what is being investigated, to adapt not only our questions but our mode of questioning to its nature, and at every point to let ourselves, with our preconceptions, be called into question that we may really know what is there as it ought to be known.

In our day, however, another element of great importance has entered into our habits of thought, and is everywhere making an immense impact upon the thinking of men and women. It has arisen out of the sheer success of the experimental method in natural science, and out of the magnificent achievements of applied science. In experimental science we not only direct our questions to nature, but we have to use violence in order to extort from nature its secrets. We make nature answer questions according to our own stipulations, and so to a large extent control the answers it gives us. Hence it is argued that it is we who determine the shape and pattern of the universe we know by applying to it our scientific methods. We are not concerned with some order in a nature 'out there' independent of us, but with the order we ourselves impose upon it by our scientific thinking.

This is the line of thinking for which Mr Wren Lewis stands and which he expounds so clearly and persuasively. According to him the modern world is in the midst of a great revolution in which the mastery is passing from pure science to technology, for it is the technologist, who invents things, who imposes his will upon nature, who more and more is able to control human destiny, that supplies the purest example of scientific activity. The modern technological mind, he claims, is more and more reaching ascendancy, for it is creatively at work in the world around us, giving nature its true form and order and determining its course.

The whole of this argument, however, depends upon the validity of its initial step: from the violence of the experimental method to the imposition by the scientific and technological mind of patterns of its own determining upon nature. That is manifestly not a valid conclusion. All that one is entitled to draw from this view of the experimental method is that the knowledge it yields is a compromise between thought and being, between scientific questioning and nature. In other words, the knowledge gained is severely limited by the human observer, experimenter, or theorist. Not to recognize this amounts to a trespass upon rigorous scientific thinking. Yet it is here that we have one of our deepest tensions within the academic world of today, the tension between the masterful claims of many technologists and the rigorous adherence to objectivity on the part of pure scientists.

This is not something from which theology can stand aloof, if only because it has already been drawn into it by writers like Dr J. A. T. Robinson, who certainly relies heavily upon Mr Wren Lewis, but whose habit of thinking is more akin to that of the artist than that of the technologist, and who appeals, accordingly, to the world of the 'arty' as Mr Wren Lewis appeals to the world of the 'crafty'. But theology cannot stand aside for other reasons: it has a mission to fulfil in the world of technology and art as much as anywhere else, and must engage in dialogue with all the masterful movements of the times if it is to be faithful to the Gospel entrusted to it. Here theology does not find itself alone, today, for it is inevitably thrown into close dialogue with pure science, since the problems that arise between pure science and a masterful technology are not unlike those between theology and technology. This dialogue with pure science can do theology nothing but good, for it will help theologians to clarify their fundamental methods in the light of their own peculiar subject-matter, and to wrestle again with the implacable objectivity of the Word of God until they learn to distinguish objective realities more clearly from their own subjective states. This is the task both of 'Dogmatics' which corresponds in theological studies to 'pure science' (we recall that Husserl's term for an exact science like physics was 'dogmatic science'), and of the 'Philosophy of Theology' which corresponds in theological studies to the 'Philosophy of Science' (and which everywhere today tends to displace the old-fashioned 'Philosophy of Religion').

This does not mean that the content of theological education requires to be changed today, but rather that the whole content must be thought out and articulated within this universe of scientific discourse.

(ii) The problem of language and its relation to thought has been raised in a new way in the modern world by the mathematicians, who find themselves forced to use ordinary language in mathematical statement and who are faced with the great difficulty of disentangling their thought from the countless ideas and images that keep on obtruding themselves from the ordinary language they have to use. From the mathematicians it has entered philosophy, and thinkers of great power such as Wittgenstein, Russell and Heidegger have been wrestling with it in very different ways. It was inevitable that the debate should be carried into the fields of linguistic and philological science, and that different semasiological theories should be advanced in accordance with different philosophical preconceptions. It is thus obvious that serious thought about the nature of biblical and theological language is more necessary than ever in theological education, where we are intensely concerned with questions of interpretation and communication. Theological studies find themselves today in a situation very like that of the sixteenth century when mediaeval physics and metaphysics began to break up under the attacks of a highly sophisticated linguistic philosophy, and when a nominalist view of language and grammar in its turn came under the attack of the humanists who sought to rehabilitate the classical languages through a re-examination of the ancient cultures out of which they arose. In the midst of this upheaval the Reformers had to address themselves to the questions of interpretation and communication, without avoiding the problems posed from different sides. Because they had to deal with the relation of words to the Word, they

TIR B

found themselves thinking out the relation between significant language and the realities signified, and developed a method of interpretation of biblical statements in which the language employed was understood in the light of the *subjecta materia*, as Calvin expressed it.

The basic problem that has been raised again in our time is *the relation of language to being*. Naturally, that takes on a different form in accordance with the kind of being one is concerned with, creaturely being or the Creator of all being, for example; but whether the question is raised in theology or in physics, it is the relation of language to being that has to be considered. The upshot of this for theological education today, as at the Reformation, is the need for a disciplined grasp of the basic languages, not only the classical languages but our own native language, which we must always use, and for a critical training in the relationship between language and explanation within the context of an articulated grasp of the subject-matter. Thus it would be immense folly, particularly at this stage in the development of modern thought and in view of the very difficult problems that are posed, to yield to the obscurantist demand to cut down the study of Hebrew and Greek, not to speak of Latin and even English, or to divorce the problems of interpretation and communication from the disciplines of dogmatic and philosophical theology.

It will be sufficient for our purpose to indicate two of the main problems that have arisen in recent years which theological education, if it is to maintain its integrity, must think through.

(*a*) The problem created by a *damaged relation* of language to being. As Heidegger sees it, this is the major problem with which we are faced in hermeneutics, for as soon as the relation of language to being is damaged, the language becomes obscure. How, then, is it to be interpreted, if it is to make some kind of sense? At least two ways may be and are being taken.

On the one hand, the language may be correlated with the subject and interpreted from the life-relation or affinity that exists between the subject of the interpreter and the subject of the writer. This is the line taken by Dilthey and Bultmann, but while it does have the advantage of exploring the relation of language to culture, it cannot but make all the wider the cleavage between language and being. In theological studies this has the effect of positing a radical dichotomy between historical writing and historical events, and behind that a radical dichotomy between 'this-wordly' realities and 'other-wordly' realities, but both of these involve the recasting of theological statements into statements of human concern which, as Alasdair MacIntyre points out, is a form of atheism.

On the other hand, the language may be treated quite independently as something having significance in itself, and interpreted through the interrelations of words and statements and the syntactical patterns of continuous discourse, and not by reference to the realities beyond to which they direct us. This is the line taken by James Barr, but while it has the advantage of helping to counteract the subjectivism inherent in existentialist hermeneutic, it also inevitably widens the gap between language and being by reducing the semantic function of language to the relations linguistic units have with one another. This is a peculiar form of nominalism which rejects the relation of language to culture (reminding us of the 'new barbarism' of the nominalist grammarians of Paris attacked by Erasmus in the sixteenth century), and which to get any kind of sense out of theological language treats it merely as a description of religious phenomena. It is not surprising that by denigrating the objective reference of language Barr should find so many people 'obscure', for he fails to deal faithfully with their language in accordance with their intention in using it.

(b) The problem created by positing a *mimetic relation* between language and being. This is the line taken by J. A. T. Robinson, who insists that he 'will always think and theologize in pictures'. This has of course a long history, for behind it lies the Greek habit of thinking by seeing. It was the Greeks that used to teach that words are images of realities, and that a mimetic or imitative relation gives meaning to our statements. That is why the Greeks employed *myths*, artistic forms, to express the transcendent realities of the intelligible world which they called the *forms*, and could think of God only through *eidetic images*.

Now if the relation between theological language and God is mimetic, if it involves a pictorial relation, then of course we are led to identify God by some picture we have in our mind, and are forced to think of theological language as essentially descriptive. Thinking in pictures thus creates desperate problems, as we can see in Robinson's book *Honest to God*—his remedy is to keep changing the pictures and images, lest one image should harden into some idolatrous form and become substituted for God. This has the advantage of reminding us that all our theological statements fall short of the divine reality to which they direct us, for God, as Anselm used to say, is greater than we can ever conceive, but in the nature of the case Robinson is unable to extricate himself from picture-thinking, and so can only substitute one image for another.

What is basically wrong here is the assumption that theological language is essentially descriptive, that the relation between sign and thing signified is a mimetic relation, for it is that basic assumption that is always productive of idolatry.

This drives us to fresh examination of biblical language and to the biblical rejection of images applied to God. The Bible certainly uses many dramatic and vivid images, but these are employed as pointers to realities beyond themselves, and are not thought of as imaging them. They are symbols but not myths, they are signitive but not eidetic images. Or, to express it in another way, the connection between the sign and the thing signified is the Word; it involves an acoustic and not a mimetic relation.

We must not enter more fully into this, but let us recall the fact that the Roman Church abolished the second commandment from use, on the ground that it applied only to Jews. It is not difficult to see that there is an inherent relation between Roman images and Roman errors, for pictorial thinking of God can only lead to error. It is strange that the Lutherans should have followed Rome in their rejection of the second commandment, but this may help to explain to some extent the preoccupation of many modern Germans with mythology and demythology.

Calvin and the Reformed theologians, however, rehabilitated the second commandment in the Church, and returned to the biblical rejection of all images of God, even the plastic images of the mind, for the mind, as Calvin said so often, is a perpetual factory of idols inasmuch as it is always seeking to bring God within the grasp of its imagination. Thus Reformed theology operates with concepts that are formed through the Word in which pictorial thinking, while it has a rightful place for we are inescapably involved with earth and history, is never primary. It is not surprising that after the rise of representationalism in philosophy and theology once again, Spinoza and Hume in different ways found themselves questioning and rejecting all 'imaginative' ways of thinking of God. Theology has still a great deal to learn from Jewish and Reformed criticism in this respect. One thing is increasingly apparent, that when our children are taught to find in the Bible dramatic and picturesque 'stories', with perhaps only a moral application, then our failure to give them their proper *theological* content, forces them to treat the Bible as a book of myths and fairy-tales, as soon as they come of age to think for themselves. Sooner or later they find themselves losing confidence in the Church, for merely pictorial or descriptive language is discerned to be empty of reality.

So far as theological interpretation and articulation are concerned, whether it be in the field of biblical or dogmatic studies, a damaged relation, or a mimetic relation, between language and being, not only makes language obscure, but transfers the real difficulty of theological understanding from the nature of the object, God himself in his revealing and reconciling activity, to the language used. Nothing could be worse in theological education than such a confusion between theological and linguistic difficulties, for it would be false both to the nature of theology and to the nature of language. So long as our students are not very proficient with their basic languages, no doubt they will be tempted to transpose theological problems into merely linguistic ones, but they ought to be given such a training in the basic languages that they can use them as transparent media for the interpretation and communication of the Word of God.

(iii) It is not by chance that history has become a great problem to us today, for radically different interpretations have arisen which correspond in their way with the differences between pure science and technology. Nowhere is this felt more keenly than in the so-called quest of the historical Jesus.

Historical science, as we have developed it in the West, is dominated by the primacy of vision, as our word history (ἱστορία) shows—the way of thinking it involves can be described as *controlled and tested observation*. In the nature of the case the application of this mode of historical investigation, particularly with the kind of criteria it ordinarily develops in secular historiography, can only be quite baffling when applied to Jesus Christ. Nowhere are the eye-witnesses concerned with describing Jesus; rarely do they tell us what they actually saw and observed in him. But that was surely part of their faithfulness in *reporting*, for the reality they speak of was one whom they knew primarily through hearing and serving and obeying. What they have left us, therefore, to use their own language, is by way of ἀκοή (cf. the Hebrew *shᵉmuah*, Isa. 53.1) requiring on our part a ὑπακοή for its understanding. What is required of us, therefore, is a mode of historical investigation appropriate to the nature of this Reality, but so far that has not been really possible, for the only kind of historical investigation we have developed operates for the most part through the criterion of perceptibility.

This problem has been seriously aggravated, however, by the gradual assimilation of historical science to the patterns of thinking that obtain in the natural sciences, with the result that there has taken place within it a cleavage rather like that between pure science and technology. This tension is sometimes, and confusingly, described by some Germans as that between *Historie* and *Geschichte*, the former representing a positivistic approach to history, the latter representing the constructive and interpretative approach in which it is claimed that history is looked at from the point of view of man's responsibility for it. Here, for example, Gogarten draws the same kind of false conclusion as Wren Lewis draws from the experimental method, in arguing for the view that it is we who by our decisions give the world the particular form which makes it relevant to ourselves. All that is real for man is what he is able to accept for himself and thus understand historically. Man is himself the creator of history, and in historical investigation he is seeking to meet himself and understand himself. As Gogarten insists, this view of history rejects the objective attitude with which science is concerned, and indeed transcends the subject-object relation altogether.

The application of this to the New Testament has very radical consequences, for it rejects *ab initio* any attempt to interpret the events recorded by the New Testament writers as 'objective' and 'really factual', as actually having taken place in an ascertainable way, and insists on interpreting them as modes in which the creative nature of the early Church was at work making 'history' through its responsible decisions. What we are to concern ourselves with, then, in reading St Mark's Gospel is not with what Mark claims to be talking about, but rather with what went on in Mark's soul and what his editorial creations tell us of his attitude to existence. We need not pursue this further, for the views of Gogarten and Bultmann in regard to history are so well known, but enough has been said to show that what we are concerned with here is indeed in another form the conflict between a rigorously scientific approach that respects the nature of what it investigates, and another in which the artistic, technological mind of man claims to be at work creating and fashioning for himself the only reality he will or can accept and appreciate. And what makes it particularly difficult and indeed impossible, is that it combines in one both the errors we noted above, a damaged relation and a mimetic relation of language to being, with all the philosophical presuppositions that lie behind them.

This new view of history appears to kill interest in the past, for the main concern throughout is with the future, with what we can create in our own day. This emphasis is accentuated by Bultmann's (rather Roman) thesis that the meaning of past events is only disclosed in the future, and that it is only as we make them understandable to ourselves within our own situation that they can be given any reality at all. The effects of this attitude to history are very apparent in German students, among whom one finds a pronounced disregard of the history of thought. No doubt that is also influenced by the trauma left in the German memory by two world wars and the disastrous defeats they brought. But nothing can be more disastrous than a refusal to take stock of one's position through historical inquiry, for then one's thinking is apt to be quite rudderless, and one is at the mercy of all the winds that may blow from this or that direction. The immense value of church history and of the history of doctrine is the dimension of historical depth it gives to one's understanding of the faith, and the balance it brings into one's judgments. Did ever the Church stand in greater need of this?

Three further aspects of historical study and their importance for theological education may be mentioned.

(*a*) Historical study is an invaluable correction to our thinking in the present. That is apparent for example in the history of exegesis, for it is the study of how a passage was interpreted throughout the centuries that helps to deliver us as far as possible from interpretations unconsciously and arbitrarily governed by the *Zeitgeist*. This was the method pursued by the Reformers, for instead of adopting the Roman view of tradition that the truth of a thing is what has actually become of it in history, they traced the understanding of a thing back through history, and claimed to understand the errors of the present by seeing the actual steps taken in arriving at it, which is very akin to some modern methods of verification. Too many people forget today that there is hardly anything new under the sun, and that new theories and discoveries are so often but old errors dressed up in new forms. Certainly where there is no knowledge of the history of thought it is difficult for people to escape the delusion that they have really discovered something new. It is the pursuit of objective historical investigation that supplies us with constant correctives and makes us critical of our own elaborations.

(*b*) On the other hand, historical study makes us appreciate tradition and value its contribution to understanding of the truth in the present. Sometimes that takes the form of bringing to its fruition immense efforts that have taken place for centuries in which the Church has been struggling to achieve clarification of some aspect of the truth, by distinguishing it from time-conditioned elements that have tended to obscure it. But sometimes it takes the form of new building upon foundations that are already well laid in the prior understanding of the Church. No scientist ever begins his work *de novo*; while he works with a methodological questioning of what he has already known he builds on knowledge already achieved and engages in a movement of advance. But it is one of the worst characteristics of theological study, whether in biblical interpretation or in dogmatic formulation, that every scholar nowadays thinks he must start all over again, and too many give the impression that no one ever understood this or that until they came along.

In the introduction to his epoch-making work, *The Foundations of Arithmetic*, Gottlob Frege writes of the sad and discouraging observation that discoveries once made are always threatening to be lost again, because we allow the crudest of views to keep on obtruding themselves upon us from the realm of popular knowledge. That is accentuated in theology because of the constant and proper demand to communicate the truth to uneducated people, but we must beware of using the layman's understanding as the criterion of what is truth. There are many ministers in the Church who think they understand the Gospel so well that they need not bother to engage in theological activity, but that is precisely the kind of arrogance against which Frege complained, and he is certainly right in insisting that in this way much work promises to have been done in vain. True thinking takes place within a frame of continuous historical development in which progress in understanding is being made. Sometimes it is extremely important and very necessary to get outside that frame of continuous historical development if we are to undertake the self-criticism that is always necessary for real leaps forward in understanding. This is extremely difficult to do, but it is something that happens today in ecumenical encounter between different historical traditions, for in such encounter we may be sufficiently freed from ourselves to recognize the limits as well as the possibilities of our own tradition. Nevertheless, no constructive thinking that is worth while can be undertaken that sets at nought the intellectual labours of the centuries that are enshrined in tradition, or be undertaken on the arrogant assumption that everything must be thought through *de novo* as if nothing true had already been done or said. He who undertakes that kind of work will inevitably be determined unconsciously by the assumptions of popular piety which have already been built into his mind.

(*c*) Another aspect of historical study that must be raised in theological education is the relation between church history and secular history. Is church history simply the secular history of the Church, and can church history be written with precisely the same canons of interpretation and verification that are used in political or social history? This is the scientific question as to the appropriateness of church-historical investigation to the nature of the Church as the Body of Christ, as the sphere in which the risen Lord is present through his Spirit and mightily active through his Word. Everything will depend again upon whether we operate with that radical dichotomy between the two worlds which we find in different ways in Schleiermacher and Bultmann, which makes them think of this world as a closed continuum of cause and effect and of all historical events as falling within that closed concatenation. But if the acts of God in Israel, and if the Incarnation mean anything real at all, surely that will effect our understanding and telling of church history, for we will not be able to leave out of it the eschatological and even the apocalyptic element which by definition must be left out of all secular historiography. If in the theological faculties we feel our historical writing falling under the pressure of secular historical writing, that may be but the sign that we require to think out far more deeply the problems of scientific method appropriate to our own subject-matter. This cannot mean, of course, that church history must be pursued in its own private corner in some sort of pietistic isolation from the rest of the university. On the contrary it means a real engagement between church history and secular history which will be all the more acute for church history overlaps so much with secular history and must therefore submit also to the kinds of criteria that have been developed for its understanding and writing, yet never in such a way as to compromise its own proper subject-matter.

What is needed today is a closer integration between church history and the history of exegesis on the one hand, and the history of doctrine on the other hand. In that way church history will be drawn more deeply into the centre of the problems we have been discussing where alone it will be able to clarify and formulate its own proper procedure and method. It is one of the distinguishing marks of the theological faculty that the work done in different departments is much more closely integrated than in any other faculty, and that is as it should be.

(iv) There is space to write only very briefly about the fourth main perspective in which theological education must be carried out, that which is set by the demands of sheer human need.

It must ever be kept in mind that what we are concerned with in theology is the understanding and proclamation of the Gospel that is directed to human need. This involves both the bringing of the Gospel to man and the bringing of man to the Gospel, but in no circumstances can man and his need become the criteria for what the Gospel is or ought to be. We may express this in a more epistemological way by saying that in all knowledge of God we are concerned with the divine Truth and with a human knower. The communication of the Truth must take into account the nature of the receiver, and the mode of communication will be conditioned also by the mode of the reception, but that does not mean that the human knower or receiver may determine the content of the Truth.

On the other hand, the content of the Gospel is found in the Word made flesh, and in the Truth of God which is not only communicated to man but received by man and translated into human life in Jesus Christ. It is the nature of this Man that conditions both the content of the Gospel and the mode of its communication and reception by those to whom he is proclaimed and ministered. In Jesus Christ the Truth of God has already been made relevant to man and his need, and therefore does not need to be made relevant by us. Because God has already accommodated or adapted his revelation to human nature and human understanding in Jesus Christ, the closer theological instruction keeps to the *humanity* of Jesus Christ, the more relevant it is to the humanity of the receiver. Thus in all theological activity, whether it be in the education of the Ministry or in the teaching of the people, we are concerned with two basic factors: with the nature of the Truth of God as it is in Jesus Christ, and therefore with a mode of communication appropriate to his unique nature; and with the nature of the human receiver, and therefore with a mode of reception appropriate to his human nature. These must never be separated from one another, for in the very nature of the Gospel they belong together, and indeed it is because they do that the Truth of God as it is in Jesus is really Gospel, good news to man in his need.

All true theology is thus intensely practical. That is why all theories purporting to show how the Gospel can be made relevant to man, even modern man, in his need, are by their very nature impossible, for they are substituting an intellectual relation for the practical relation which God himself has established in Jesus Christ. That is the epistemological relevance of justification by grace alone—no works of ours, carnal or mental, can establish a bridge between our understanding and the Truth of God. Knowledge of God is in accordance with his nature, that is in accordance with *grace*, and therefore takes its rise from God's *action* in revealing himself and reconciling us to himself in Jesus Christ. The relation between our statements about God and God himself in his own Truth is not one that we can either forge or describe in statements, but one that we can only allow to happen to us through sub-mitting obediently and gratefully to his saving and revealing acts. Full place for that action must be given in theological knowledge as in evangelical proclamation. Thus unless dogmatic and philosophical theology can be geared into practical theology they are pretty wide of the mark.

We must be content with three further observations only.

(a) In all theological knowledge a proper balance must be maintained between the divine Subject and the human subject, that is, between the divine Object and the human knower. Theological knowledge is after all a *human* activity, human knowledge of God, but of God in accord-ance with his revelation of himself to man. If the human factor is eliminated, then the whole is reduced to nonsense, but unless the divine element is dominant, then man is in the last resort thrown back upon his own resources and an impossible burden is laid upon him. We can see the importance of this balance in pastoral counselling, for that is theology in action. It is the task of the minister to listen, to respect the humanity and personality of the man seeking help, but if in the last resort he throws the man back upon his own resources demanding of him a responsible decision as the *condition* for healing or forgiveness, then he is being terribly cruel, for he has no Gospel to meet the man in his need. Rather must he direct him to Christ as he who has already borne his burden and taken his cause upon himself, and so declare to him freely and unconditionally the grace of God in forgiveness and healing, for only on that basis will it be possible for broken and despair-ing humanity to be rehabilitated and made new. It is not otherwise in theological education, where, while we must respect one another in our rational human natures, we are cast finally upon God himself, for we may know him only as we are known by him, or respond to him in faith only on the ground of his self-communication to us in his Incarnate Word. The Gospel never asks of us the impossible thing, to make real or make relevant to ourselves what it has to offer, rather does it offer us a Word that is already made relevant to us, flesh of our flesh, full of grace and truth. It is out of that fulness that we receive.

(b) Michael Polanyi reminds us in his Gifford lectures that we cannot convince others by formal argument, for so long as we argue within their framework, we can never induce them to abandon it. 'Formal operations relying on one framework of interpretation cannot demon-strate a proposition to persons who rely on another framework' (*Personal Knowledge*, p. 151). That applies to theological communication as much as scientific controversy, and yet this is precisely the erroneous line taken so often by apologetics, whether by the theologian or the preacher. Whenever we take that line we are simply reducing ourselves to be servants of public opinion or popular ideas of science and religion, and in that event we have nothing at all to offer to people which they do not already know or cannot tell to themselves much better than we. Moreover by taking this line we eliminate from theological knowledge its real meaning, for we deprive it of its proper message. That is why theological statements inevitably appear meaningless and impossibly paradoxical if we claim for them validity within a frame of reference which is the correlate of ordinary observable and empirically verifiable experience.

When we are faced with the problem of communication between two different frames of reference separated by what Polanyi calls a 'logical gap', then the first step in understanding is to explore the nature and the depth of the difference. The only proper road to take at that point is to persuade those operating from the other frame to look away at the realities we seek to indicate, and to persuade them to take, in face of it, the kind of 'heuristic' step forward which we always have to make in any genuine scientific discovery, for only then will they discern and know for themselves what we are speaking about. That is to say, in theological language, we have to bear witness to the divine Truth, and try to get from others a genuinely open hearing, but if they take the heuristic step which they must if they are really to know, it will involve on their part a self-critical act in reconstruction of their prior understanding, i.e. what the New Testament calls *metanoia*.

The important point to be noted here in theological instruction is the realization that theological language is not descriptive, compelling assent, but persuasive, challenging conversion. Theological statements are primarily not coherence-statements which carry their truth or meaning in themselves, but existence-statements which have their truth beyond themselves and their meaning in directing us beyond themselves. To borrow language from David Hume, they are not susceptible to demonstrative reasoning merely through the correlation of ideas, but are susceptible to 'moral' reasoning through their persuasiveness, and are accepted as true only when we ourselves discern the realities they point out to us. That is to say, in the last resort theological communication is practical, and that means it takes our human nature seriously instead of treating us like intellectual machines.

(*c*) We have spoken of a tension between two different frames of reference, but the problem is deeper than that, for we are accustomed to *live* in our frames of reference; we and they belong together. Thus to cross from one frame of reference to another involves an act of radical self-denial on the one hand and radical reconciliation to the new frame of reference on the other hand. This is another way of stating that theological communication and understanding always involve a movement of *reconciliation*.

That is the real difficulty about the Truth of God as it is in Jesus, not a difficulty about language or history in the last resort, but an *offence* which reaches its climax in the Cross. No one can understand very well what he resents or opposes, especially in the realms of personal or theological knowledge. That failure is all the deeper when we are up against the fact that man is severed from the truth, 'existentially' (in Kierkegaard's sense) severed from it, and can only know it when he is reconciled to the Truth in his own being. Thus once again we are led to state that theology is at bottom essentially practical, for the epistemic relation is grounded upon atoning acts and is completed in the reception of forgiveness. Persuasion has its fruit in reconciliation.

If this is so, the last thing we must ever attempt to do is to eliminate the real difficulties that confront us in the nature of the Truth itself, and so try to make it easy for people to believe and understand—in so doing, we make it next to impossible for them. That is apparent in biblical interpretation—the point at which we are pulled up with a halt, the point where we really reflect upon the meaning, and finally understand what is intended, is the point where we are offended. If there were no offence, we would find nothing new in the Scriptures, hear nothing we could not and have not already been able to tell ourselves. That which challenges us, which calls us in question, is the radically new, the element we are unable to assimilate into what we already know, without a logical reconstruction of all our preconceptions and a repentant rethinking of what we already claim to know. But that is the element in the Scriptures which makes them the means of bringing Good News—yet in the nature of the case it is Good News, not of some cheap grace that heals the hurt of God's people too lightly, but of radical and complete reconciliation to God through the Cross of Jesus Christ. That is the only message that really strikes home to the human heart and meets at last the desperate plight of man.

2

The Logic and Analogic of Biblical and Theological Statements in the Greek Fathers

AN examination of the theological writings of the Greek Fathers from Irenaeus to the great Alexandrians or Cappadocians reveals three basic insights running throughout their thinking whenever they interpret biblical statements or formulate theological statements of their own: (i) The unapproachableness of God which calls forth from us the attitude of worship and reverence. God's nature and glory are ineffable and his Name, as the Hebrews taught, is unutterable. This means that in our understanding of him, particularly in the forming of conceptions and the formulating of propositions, we must break off our activity and let it remain incomplete, for the ineffable and unutterable is to be honoured, as St Basil says, by silence (*De Spiritu Sancto* 18.44). (ii) Only by God is God known—that was an insight that Irenaeus early injected into patristic theology, recalling the biblical statements that only God can finally bear witness to himself. This was taken up later by Athanasius and Basil in their doctrine of the Spirit, for as it is only the Spirit of God who knows the things of God, it is only in the Spirit and by his power that we may really know God and apprehend his Truth. The revelation of the unknowable is the peculiar function of the Spirit. But even in revelation what is revealed remains mystery for it is not the kind of reality that can be brought under our human controlling or dividing and compounding—it transcends us and remains exalted far above us even in being revealed and apprehended. (iii) The application of our ordinary language to speech about God involves a fundamental shift in its meaning. We cannot but use language taken from our common experience in this world when we make theological statements, but even so it is the subject that must be allowed to determine the meaning. It would be inherently wrong to use expressions like 'right hand' or 'bosom' or even 'father' and 'son' as if they meant when applied to God the same thing they mean when used of creatures. It is thus one of

the most important elements of theological activity to discern the basic
change in meaning which our ordinary speech undergoes, lest we should
speak in merely human terms of God or speak in unwarranted ways of
creatures. This was one of the major issues in the Arian controversy, for
the Arians fell into error by refusing to admit the limitations of creaturely
images and notions, and by pressing them improperly into use beyond
their creaturely reference, and so they distorted the knowledge of God
through the misapplication of human and earthly analogies.

The Catholic Church took its stand on the biblical teaching that God
is beyond comparison (as Athanasius expressed it, θεὸς μὲν ἀσύγκριτόν
ἐστιν πρᾶγμα, *C. Arianos* 1.57), and rejected the epistemological principle
of the Arians that what men cannot understand cannot be true (see
Athanasius, *Ad Serapionem* 1.17; 2.1). Catholic theology is bound to
recognize that there is a measure of impropriety in all human language
of God, and therefore must ever be ready to call a halt in its speaking
of him, in humble acknowledgment of the fact that our human thought
cannot travel beyond a certain point, and be ready at the same time to
let the human speech used by the Holy Spirit in the Scriptures point
far beyond itself to the sheer reality and glory of God who alone can
bear witness of himself and create in us, beyond any capacity of our own
to achieve it, genuine knowledge of God.

This does not mean that for Athanasius or any of the Greek Fathers
rational, that is logical and coherent, thinking has no place. On the
contrary, it means that our minds are not to be engrossed like the Arians
with themselves, but are directed away toward their proper object
(*skopos*) in God to be governed by his Word (*logos*). Consistent thinking
in that way involves thoroughly rational procedure which is reflected
in the disciplined mode of theological articulation. It does mean, however, that the primary reference of theological statements is to the Reality
of God infinitely beyond and above us, and that, though secondary, the
reference of our statements to one another in logical sequence (*akolouthia*)
cannot be neglected. Hence in arguments with the Arians the Alexandrians and Cappadocians demolish their errors by exposing their
intrinsic illogicality and by showing that they are the result of human
devising, and without objective foundation in the Reality of God himself. Correspondence to objective reality and internal coherence in
thought and statement are thus the criteria employed in theological
argument.

The twofold reference of religious language must be kept clearly in
view in the interpretation of biblical statements. If we let Athanasius

be our guide again here, we may speak of biblical statements as *ostensive* for they employ expressions and relations taken from this world to point beyond to God, and as *sequential* for they function within a coherent pattern of discourse determined by its specific subject-matter. Thus expressions like 'fountain', 'light', or 'begetting' are used in the divine Scripture, by way of relieving the impossibility of explaining and apprehending these matters in words, as *paradeigmata* to point us to the Truth of God and give us something for our minds to lay hold of in order that we may think legitimately of God (*C. Arianos* 1.20; 2.30; 3.3, 10; *De decretis* 12; *Ad Serapionem* 1.19f. etc.). Apart from this divine act that lays hold of some of our expressions, images, etc. changing them and making them sufficient and suitable for God's self-revelation, even biblical statements would be empty of objective content or without reference to any given reality. On the other hand, because these statements and the words and images they employ are made to point beyond to a given reality, they manifest among themselves a coherent pattern of reference determined by their common point of reference (*skopos*). Thus the sequence or coherence (*akolouthia*) they have between one another as human statements is not just a grammatical or formal-logical sequence, but one that is imposed upon them by the subject-matter itself. Hence in interpreting the Scriptures the fathers use *skopos* in two different but allied senses. On the one hand *skopos* refers to the object to which biblical statements are directed, but that creates a context or a perspective which all biblical statements share and which can be described as their general intention or tenor. Athanasius can speak of Christ himself as the *scope* of the Scriptures, that is, the primary object of their witness even in the Old Testament, but he can also speak of the *scope* of the Scriptures as the fundamental slant given to the Scriptures by their essential theme, as the perspective within which alone their statements are meaningful and understandable.

This way of regarding and interpreting biblical statements holds good for all the great fathers in the East, not merely for the Alexandrians such as Athanasius and Cyril but also for the Antiochene expositors such as Chrysostom, who constantly appeals to the *skopos* and *akolouthia* of biblical statements in order to make clear their meaning. If we put to them the question as to the logic and analogic of biblical statements, they constantly say that they have to be interpreted *kat' eusebeian* or *kata sunetheian*. That is to say, the language of the Scriptures is to be understood in accordance with the habitual mode of scriptural usage, in which common speech is directed away from ordinary experience and made to serve the self-revelation of God—the logic of that, however, derives from the reference of these words and statements back or upward (*ana*) to God, and it is only when we get inside that God-ward and godly relationship that we may properly discern their reference or meaning. It is thus in the context of worship and godliness alone, which means within the communion of the Church, indeed within the mind of the Church (*to ekklesiastikon phronema*), that the Scriptures are rightly to be interpreted in accordance with their inner and real meaning.

Theological statements, that is reflective statements as to the message and content of the biblical statements, are made, however, not just by stringing together biblical citations, but rather by hard exegetical activity in which we interpret biblical statements in the light of the Truth to which they direct us from all sides. In this activity we compare the different biblical *paradeigmata*, gathering together from them what they have to say, and summarizing them in exact and disciplined propositions by which we point to the basic pattern of truth in the objective reality and at the same time allow that objective reality to impose its own rationality upon our thinking and articulation of it. The supreme example Athanasius gives of that exegetical and theological activity, is the *homoousion* formulated by the Fathers of Nicaea (*Ad Afros* 6, etc.). The *homoousion* represents, then, the basic logical economy or logical simplicity which is exposed to our scientific inquiry and which we then allow to govern the pattern of our doctrinal formulations, assured that, in this way, our theological statements about God will be made in accordance with the pattern which his own self-communication to us has actually taken in the Incarnation. The *homoousion* is thus an exceedingly dense or compressed statement, a fundamental dogma, which once it comes to view becomes normative for all faithful theological statement, for it enables it to be made in true correspondence with its proper object and in consistent relations with other faithful statements.

We have referred to the patristic use of *kat' eusebeian* as expressing the God-ward and godly relationship within which we may properly discern the meaning of biblical statements and go on to make theological statements. But *kat' eusebeian* has a deeper meaning. It refers to the mystery of godliness, God manifest in the flesh (I Tim. 3.16), a passage to which the fathers referred again and again in their controversy with Sabellians and Arians alike. The basic logic with which we are concerned is not just some sort of church piety but the logic of God's grace in the Incarnation of the Son. Theological statements can be made truly when they repose upon that foundation and when they manifest in themselves a logic that corresponds with the actual way which the Word of God has taken in becoming flesh amongst us, and so raises us up to communion with the eternal God. That is the basic logic that the Fathers of Nicaea sought to express in their formulation of the *homoousion*.

In order to grasp the epistemological significance of the *homoousion* and its continuing importance for theological statement, we must examine more carefully two lines of thought which we have in the fathers—and here I am thinking particularly of Athanasius and Basil, although one could follow through the thought of others at this point in the same way, such as that of Hilary of Poitiers.

(*a*) The epistemological significance of the *homoousion* becomes clear when we see it against the background of the radical disjunction between the *kosmos aisthetos* and the *kosmos noetos* which in different ways lay behind Origenism and Gnosticism, and gave rise to the problem of mythology. *Once this disjunction is posited*, as it was quite axiomatically in the secular culture of the second and third centuries, the following questions must be asked. How are we to understand the biblical statements about the acts of the eternal God within the history of Israel, that is, within the *kosmos aisthetos*? And, how are we to regard the *Logos*: does he belong to the eternal side of that disjunction, the *kosmos noetos*, or is he ultimately to be regarded as a creature and therefore as belonging to the *kosmos aisthetos*? Then in answer to the first question, it would have to be said that biblical statements about the acts of God himself within space and time can only be interpreted as mythological ways of speaking of something that is eternal and timeless. This is a world of change and decay, of shadow and unreality, but it is the other world, that of the noumenal, that is real and changeless. How can God who is impassible and changeless be thought of as entering into our changing world, and living within contingent and temporal existence? It is unthinkable. Yet if we remember, so the Greeks tended to think, that this world partakes of reality in so far as it is a passing reflection of the eternal, then we may interpret the biblical doctrine of the Incarnation or of the crucifixion of the Son of God as a passing image of some timeless truth in God.

Then, too, in answer to the second question, it would have to be said that the *Logos* belongs to the creaturely side of the disjunction—even if he be regarded as an angelic being and the highest of all angelic or spiritual powers, he is nevertheless a created power. In his own being he belongs to this side of the radical disjunction (*chorismos*), to the world of changing, contingent actuality. The *Logos* is thus to be regarded as detached from the being of God (*diairetos, choristos*), and as changeable (*alloioumenos, treptos*). But if we remember, so the Greeks tended to think, that there is a mimetic relation between true thought and speech and the eternal forms of the real world, then we would have to interpret the *Logos* or the Son as somehow imaging, albeit in a passing and changeable way, the nature of the eternal Deity. But since (on this assumption) he belongs ultimately to the side of the creature, rather than the side of the Creator, and is not therefore identical in his being with eternal God, he could only provide us with one of many *logoi* or *eikones* (images) of God—there must in fact be myriads of them, as Arius affirmed. Thus in the last resort Jesus Christ cannot be regarded as the eternal *Logos* inherent in the Being of God become Man, and as providing us with the one and only and exclusive Image of God, who is at the same time his Reality, but only as a form of man's imaging of God, one of the conceptions he forms in his own mind as he tries to think of God.

Two things may be said in reply to these answers, and here we are still following the great Athanasius. First, this Arian or semi-Arian way of thinking converts statements about God into statements of human concern; that is, converts statements that derive from God and really refer to him for they have God himself as their object, into statements that have only this-worldly reference, and so in the last analysis have only human or earthly meaning. As such they could be given some kind of religious meaning if they are treated as mythological speculations about God or made to yield 'spiritual meaning' by allegorical interpretation. Secondly, this way of thinking is an objectifying way of thinking, not an objective way of thinking, to use modern terminology; but to use the old patristic terminology, it is a way of thinking *kat' epinoian* in which our thoughts and statements are related to God only *thesei*, by convention, and not a way of thinking *kata dianoian* in which our thoughts and statements are related to God *kata physin* and *alethos*. What happens here is that we obtrude ourselves into the place of God and never rise above ourselves, for we only continue to imprison our thoughts within ourselves. This way of thinking has an element of madness (*mania*) about it, for it means that we are so engrossed with ourselves that we are unable to distinguish objective realities from our own subjective states, or to distinguish God from ourselves.

However, the proper line to take in answer to this whole way of thinking is to call in question its initial assumption of a radical dicho-

tomy between the *kosmos noetos* and the *kosmos aisthetos*. It is significant
that although Athanasius was brought up within the Alexandrian
tradition he rejected from the very start this assumption although it
was held so strongly by both Clement and Origen who contributed so
much to that tradition. This did not mean that the distinction between
God and the creature was abolished, far from it, but that it was regarded, as it is in the biblical witness, as a distinction between the
Creator and the creature to whom the Creator gives reality in relation
to himself. This reality of the creaturely world was affirmed by the
Incarnation and further established by the resurrection of Jesus from
the dead. Thus while maintaining the distance between the Creator
and the creature, the Christian faith taught that God in his own divine
Being, God the Word, God the Son, became flesh, and entered into
creaturely being for our sakes, without ceasing to be God. The doctrine
of the Incarnation thus both maintained the distinction between God
the Creator and the creature, and taught that God is yet active within
our creaturely existence in space and time in Jesus Christ, revealing
himself to us, and reconciling us to himself.

That is the fundamental essence of the Christian Gospel to which the
fathers penetrated in their exegetical and theological activity at Nicaea
when they formulated the *homoousion*, the doctrine of the consubstan-
tiality of the Incarnate Word and Son of God. The epistemological
significance of that lies in the rejection of the Valentinian and Arian
dichotomy that made the *Logos* in the last resort a creature of God and
so recast theological statements into statements with only this-worldly
reference, and lies in the insistence that in Jesus Christ we have a *Logos*
that is not of man's devising but One who goes back into the eternal
Being of God for he proceeded from the eternal Being of God. The
Incarnation means that God has really given himself and communicated
himself in his eternal Word to man. It is out of that Word and in
accordance with the way which that Word has taken in the Incarnation
that genuine theological statements are made. They are genuine statements in so far as they *derive from* that Word and *refer back* to it: that is
their essential *ana-logic*. Theological thinking is thinking of and on the
ground of a given Reality, hard objective thinking *kata dianoian*,
thinking that must be rigorously tested along the line of the twofold
reference which we have already discussed. What God is to us in Jesus
Christ he really is antecedently and eternally in himself—that is the
ana-logical reference. But if in Jesus Christ and only in Jesus Christ do
we have the one *Logos* of God, his one self-revelation, so that **Jesus**

Christ is the Way and the Truth and the Life, without there being any other way to the Father, then all true theological statements will be consistent with one another in so far as they have this *Logos* as their centre of reference, and through this *Logos* speak of all God's acts in creation and redemption, in recreation and sanctification, and therefore not only in the Son but in the Spirit.

The importance of this can been seen in the rise of the doctrine of the Spirit and in the way that it arose. As Athanasius insisted (and the Cappadocians no less than he), it is from our knowledge of the Son that we must take our knowledge of the Spirit (*Ad Serapionem* 3.1-3). If the Incarnation of the Son is the one point where the *Logos* of God has come through to us, then it is at that point too that we establish true knowledge of the Holy Spirit. Hence Athanasius built up his doctrine of the Spirit from the foundation laid in the doctrine of the relation between the Father and the Son and the Son and the Father. The Holy Spirit is not independently cognoscible—he is very God in all his unapproachable majesty and glory, and is only known on the ground of the Incarnation of the *Logos*, but then really known, and known in himself, although of course inseparably from knowledge of the Son and of the Father. Thus from the *homoousion* of the Son the Greek Fathers went on to affirm the *homoousion* of the Spirit, and because they rejected the radical *chopismos* of the Valentinians, Origenists and Arians, they rejected also the impious doctrine that the Spirit is a creature and affirmed the doctrine of the Spirit as *homotimos*, he who is to be worshipped equally with the Father and the Son as himself very God.

(*b*) The other line of thought regarding the *homoousion* we must now examine is that which inquires into the actual way that the grace of God took in incarnating his Word for us in Jesus Christ, and in raising us up to knowledge and communion with himself through Jesus Christ—this is a line of thought we find in Irenaeus and Hippolytus before Athanasius, but we shall follow the form it takes in the *De Spiritu Sancto* of Basil the Great, in which he relates together the economic condescension of the Son of God to be one with us and his growth and advance in our human nature whereby he provides for us in himself a way up to God (8.18f.).

In himself God is incomprehensible to us, and unapproachable in thought, but he has condescended to come down to our weakness to reveal himself to us and to redeem us in and through the humble ministry of Christ. This is the patristic doctrine of the economy (*oikonomia*) which refers to the self-humbling of God the Son in becoming man and being made a servant for our sakes. It is important to note that the Greek fathers understood this realistically. Later on the term 'economical' came to be used in a different sense, as when an act of God was spoken of as *'only* economical'—*oikonomia* then has the sense of *reserve*, on the part of God, for he is not to be taken as being in himself quite what he appears to be in the economic act in question; and so *reserve* also, on the part of man's understanding of the act of God, for he is not to understand it strictly in the way it appears. Unfortunately this later notion is very often read into earlier patristic teaching (e.g. by J. H. Newman), but that amounts to a serious falsification of their thought. In Irenaeus, for example, economy is understood strictly in the Pauline sense of Ephesians, and in Athanasius *kat' oikonomian* may be used as the equivalent for *alethos* and even sometimes for *kata physin*. It is in that sense that we are to take it here in St Basil's account of the action of God which he speaks of as 'the economy through the Son'. In his economic condescension God really imparts to us knowledge of himself as he is, for he is antecedently and eternally in his own Being what he reveals of himself in his Incarnation and humiliation in Christ. The economic condescension means, then, that the Eternal *Logos*, without ceasing to be *Logos*, has adapted himself to us in our weakness and lack of ability in order to effect real communication with us.

But this economic condescension has its counterpart in a movement of *prokope*. The fathers have in mind here the Lukan account of the obedience and development of the child Jesus who 'cut his way forward' (*proekopte*) as he grew in wisdom and favour with God and with man (Luke 2.52). In other words Jesus' growth in wisdom was regarded as opening up a way for man to rise to true knowledge of the Father. Jesus Christ is not only the Truth who has accommodated himself to us in order to reveal himself, not only the Word become flesh, but he is also Man hearing and obeying that Word, apprehending that Truth throughout his life on earth, so that he provides for us in his own obedient sonship within our human nature the *Way* whereby we are carried up to knowledge of God the Father. 'We understand by Way that *prokope* to perfection which is made stage by stage, and in regular order, through the works of righteousness and the illumination of knowledge, ever longing after what is before, and reaching forth unto those things which remain, until we shall have reached the blessed end, the knowledge of God, which the Lord through himself bestows on them that have trusted in him. For our Lord is an essentially good Way, where erring and straying are unknown, to that which is essentially good, to the Father. For no one, he says, comes to the Father but through me. Such is our way up to God through the Son' (*De Spiritu Sancto* 18.18).

Along with this Basil combines another line of thought. Christ became incarnate through the operation of the Holy Spirit, and it was through the power of the Spirit that he made that advance or *prokope*, as it was through the power of the Spirit that he wrought miracles, and was raised from the dead. This he speaks of as 'the economy of the Spirit', for every operation of God in the economy of our salvation was wrought with the co-operation of the Spirit (*De Spiritu Sancto* 16.39). The operation of the Spirit is spoken of here as 'the perfecting cause', which brings creatures to their fulfilment in God and so consummates their creation (16.38). That operation of the Spirit is what we see taking place in the *prokope* of Jesus Christ, for since he came to share our human nature and we are united to him through the Spirit which he gives us, it is through the power of the same Spirit that we participate in *prokope*, and so rise through the Son to true knowledge of, and communion with, God the Father. Moreover this is a movement that continues to take place in the power of the Spirit from our creation to final judgment and renewal, when God's works of creation and redemption will be brought to their ultimate completion (16.39).

Now we are able to see what the nature of theological activity, as the fathers engage in it, really is. In theological activity we do not only engage in exegesis, interpreting biblical statements, but we penetrate behind the statements themselves (*ta gegrammena*) to the actions (*ta genomena*) of God, and in the light of what they are, we articulate our understanding and formulate our statements of the Truth of God as it is in Jesus Christ. Theological activity is one in which, by the power and communion of the Spirit, we know God through conformity to the economic condescension of his Word and through following the Incarnate Word in his advance up to the Father. In this way theology not only operates with a divinely given Truth, but apprehends it in accordance with its own mode of activity in condescension and ascension, and articulates it in accordance with its own interior and active logic, the movement from grace to glory. The hinge of that movement, and therefore the actual hinge of meaning and apprehension, is the Incarnation and in the Incarnation the identity between the Being of Christ and the Being of God—that is, the *homoousion*. Apart from the *homoousion* there is no real and objective connection between our human knowing and speaking of God, and God himself in his own reality and nature.

Hence in formulating the *homoousion* the fathers were penetrating down into the depth of the divine logic of grace, and tracing its reference or ana-logic back to its source in the eternal *Logos* in the Being of God.

We must now return to the fact that the *homoousion* was gained through hard exegetical activity. It is not itself a biblical term, but it is by no means a speculative construction, an interpretation put upon the facts by the fathers of Nicaea; rather is it a truth that was forced upon the understanding of the Church as it allowed the biblical witness to imprint its own patterns upon its mind. We can see the same thing happening in the formulation of the doctrine of the Spirit. The biblical writers nowhere provide us with clear-cut propositions as to the Deity of the Spirit but acknowledgment of the Deity of the Spirit and his inseparable connection with the Father and the Son in the Holy Trinity is forced upon the Church as it penetrates into the interior logic of the biblical witness and through it allows the inherent order and pattern of the divine Reality to impose themselves upon its mind. Theological activity, then, is not concerned merely with biblical exegesis or with a biblical theology that builds up what this or that author in the New Testament taught about the Faith; it is concerned with the Truth at a deeper level, in the necessary and coherent thinking of the Apostles as they mediated the divine revelation in Jesus Christ to the world of historical understanding and communication. Thus in formulating the *homoousion* the Fathers of Nicaea were penetrating into the interior logic of the apostolic witness, and allowing the truth that was embedded there to come to view in an orderly and articulate way. They allowed the fundamental nature of the subject-matter to shine through to them and to take, in their thought and speech of it, a form through which its truth could be accurately and clearly and unambiguously acknowledged. The *homoousion* is thus an articulation of what the Fathers of Nicaea *had to* think and say when they set themselves to a disciplined and objective inquiry into the biblical witness to Christ, for its basic formulation had already been given by the Apostles themselves. Hence true theological thinking is basically and inescapably apostolic, for it is determined by the form in which the Apostles handed on the Word which they themselves had received.

This is the point which we must now explore more fully: the transition that took place within the apostolic foundation of the Church from the self-witness of Christ to witness to Christ as the Son of God. It was the special task of the Apostles to effect that transition, and so to hand on the divine revelation mediated in Christ in such a way that it was a historically communicable Word capable of being heard and understood from generation to generation. The historical Church took shape as in and through the apostolic mission the living Word began to grow and multiply among men. In other words, in the apostolic foundation of the Church testimony to the Word of God was given in such a way that through that testimony the Word of God continued to operate, and so went on to fulfil among men what God had begun to do in the historical Jesus Christ.

He with whom they had to do was the *Logos* and Son of the living God. He was both Word and Person, Word in the form of personal Being, and Person who was himself the Word communicated from God to men. If he were Word only, we would be thrown back upon our own resources to authenticate him; if he were Person only, we would be thrown back on our own resources to interpret him. But as One who is both Word and Person, he interprets and authenticates himself. He is the self-communicating, self-authenticating Word; the *Autologos*, *Autozoe*, *Autexousia*, *Autobasileia*, as the fathers spoke of him.

Now when we consider the apostolic witness to this Word, we find that two relationships are involved which are inextricably woven together, corresponding to the twofold nature of Christ as Word and Person.

(*a*) There is a relationship in word to Christ as Word. The apostolic witness is by its very nature a *report*—it derives from and reposes upon the Word of Christ in which he interpreted and communicated himself. The apostolic statements are thus by their nature recognition-statements which at one and the same time point away from themselves to Christ as alone the Word and Truth of God and communicate information about him in such a way that others hearing or reading their report are themselves directed to look away to Christ, and indeed meet him and know him through the apostolic witness. Through the testimony of the Apostles they are brought under the objective revelation and power of the Word and are summoned to testify to the Word and formulate their own understanding of him. As they do that, they find that they are driven back upon the basic recognition-statements of the Apostles themselves, for it is the form in which they handed on that Word in tradition that determines the form in which the historical Church continues to grasp and apprehend the Truth. The mission of the Apostles was not just to reproduce the *ipsissima verba* of Jesus, but under the compulsion of his teaching and his actions, as they illuminated one another, to communicate a faithful report of him, by means of which others in historical tradition could be brought under his power, and find their minds compelled to think of him and speak of him in the same basic way.

(*b*) There is a relationship in person to Christ as Person. Because the Word is in the form of personal Being, relationship to the Word cannot be in word and understanding only but must itself be intensely personal. Hence just as through the apostolic witness the Word created understanding of Christ in the mind of the Church, so through the Apostles the Person of Christ creates the community which receives him and which he compacts around himself as his own Body, the Church. Knowledge of Christ and union with Christ went hand in hand together, so that relation to Christ was grounded and mediated through personal and living communion, within which he himself was present, and within which his Word was effectively operative in the lives of men.

We have spoken of the Apostles and their mission in the transition from the self-witness of Christ to witness to Christ—but in order to effect that through the Apostles Christ sent to them the Holy Spirit and inspired them to give the Word they heard from him the form which he meant it to have in their knowledge of him and in their witness to him. Christ himself was not a Christian. A Christian is one saved by Christ, one who is reconciled to God and united to him *through the mediation* of Christ—hence a *Christian* knowledge of God is one mediated by Christ, the knowledge sinners have of God in and through Christ's revealing and reconciling work. The Apostles were not sent therefore to hand on the Word in the precise way in which Christ himself uttered it or communicated it, but to hand it on in the way in which they, as sinners saved by Christ, whose knowledge of God was mediated and transformed by Christ, had to understand it. The apostolic knowledge of the Word was *Christian* knowledge, and the apostolic understanding of Christ was *Christian* understanding, for that was the knowledge and understanding that Christ meant the whole Church to have of himself and of God through himself. The Apostles were the primary, the foundational Christians (they were chosen, appointed and trained as such), and it is upon their knowledge and understanding of the divine revelation that the whole Church rests, so that the apostolic mind is determinative for all theological activity within the Church.

We have been speaking of *Christian* knowledge and understanding, but the fathers for the most part used another expression. They spoke of *ecclesiastical* knowledge and understanding in this way, as identical with, because built up on, the apostolic mind. Thus, for example, we find Athanasius using 'apostolic mind' and 'ecclesiastical mind', or 'apostolic tradition' and 'ecclesiastical tradition', quite interchangeably. Hence he can say that theological statements have to be in accordance with the basic piety (*kata ten eusebeian*) of the Apostles and of the Church, and have to be in accordance with the mind of the Church (*to ekklesiastikon phronema*), if they are to be true and faithful to Christ.

The importance of this we may elucidate in the following way. If the apostolic witness can be said to have a twofold reference, a vertical reference to Christ, and a horizontal reference to others to whom witness is being communicated, then we may speak of the Apostles themselves in their unique relation to Christ as the 'hinges' or 'cardinals', where the vertical and the horizontal references meet, or where the vertical is folded out into the horizontal in such a way that throughout history men and women on the ground of this witness communicated to them horizontally and mediately on the plane of history may be directed vertically, as it were, and immediately to the Lord to meet and know him for themselves. When the New Testament speaks of the Church as founded once and for all upon the Apostles and Prophets, and insists that no other foundation can be laid, then that means that the Apostles are the only 'cardinals' of the faith, the only 'hinges' in which the vertical and the horizontal meet together, or in which the vertical is folded out into the horizontal. In that sense, the Apostles in the nature of the case can have no successors, for it is not given to anyone else to receive the Word directly from Christ and to translate it into Word about Christ in such a way that through their witness the whole historical Church may be directed and determined in knowledge of Christ and of God through him. Hence, it would be difficult to imagine any error more far-reaching than that of trying to be one's own apostle. This is the difficulty that the whole non-Roman Church has with the Church of Rome, it is also the difficulty that the one Catholic Church must always have with scholars who try to penetrate behind the apostolic witness to some set of *ipsissima verba* of Jesus or some Christ divested of the theological clothes the Apostles are alleged to have put upon him. It was a form of the same basic difficulty with which the Greek Fathers wrestled in encounter with the Gnostics and Arians. That is why they laid such emphasis upon *apostolic tradition*, for it is only within the primary judgment of the Apostles, the prior judgment upon which the whole historical Church rests, the *ekklesiastikon phronema*, and within the attitude of spirit and worship that belongs to it and is correlative to the mystery of the Incarnation, God manifest in the flesh, that genuine theological activity can take place, and true and faithful theological statements can be made.

Positive theological statement cannot be elaborated apart from tradition, for apart from tradition it would inevitably go astray right from the start. If its *ana-logic* were wrong, if it had no proper reference back to the source of truth and could not be traced back to the truth in its source, it would be quite beside the mark no matter how logically and coherently it was constructed. Regarded in this way, however, tradition does not involve the false idea that the truth of a doctrine is only revealed in the future since the truth of a thing is allegedly what becomes of it in history. Tradition, taken in the Athanasian sense, enables theological activity to test the understanding and formulation of a doctrine in the Church by tracing the actual steps taken in reaching it, and therefore to guide it in the effort to penetrate down to the basic judgments in the apostolic mind through which the objective rationality shines out upon us. It is only as doctrine is formulated under the power of that rationality that it can be said to be rightly related (*orthos* is the Athanasian expression) to its object.

An analogical movement of this kind, when faithfully carried out, calls for another, complementary to it, a movement of logical reconstruction of our previous formulations. As an example of this we may refer to the way in which Athanasius had to recast his treatment of the *paradeigmata* of 'fountain' or 'source' and 'light' as he formulated the basic judgments we must make in bringing to articulation the biblical witness to the Holy Spirit. At first when he was concerned to establish the *homoousion* of the Son he was content to think in terms of Light-Radiance and Fountain-River, but when he had to think it out upon the fuller basis of the biblical witness he had to extend his thought to Light-Radiance-Enlightenment, and Fountain-River-Water in order to speak of the relations of Father, Son and Holy Spirit. So long as we refer only to these *paradeigmata* we are clearly shut up to a doctrine of the procession of the Spirit from the Father, but what happens when we are forced to think out the doctrine of the Spirit on a fuller biblical basis that speaks of the intra-Trinitarian relations in terms of Love? Would this not entail a further step in the logical reconstruction of prior formulations? If it did not lead to the *filioque* at least it would lead to a critical rethinking of the later doctrine of a procession from the Father *only*.

Be that as it may, it remains true that rigorous theological activity is inescapably concerned with tradition because of its analogical reference to the apostolic mind or *phronema*, and in and with that is summoned to logical reconstruction of prior knowledge, in order that the whole body of doctrine may repose more and more squarely upon the foundation once and for all laid in the Apostles, and in order that the understanding of the Church may develop under the power of the objective rationality of the Truth that shines forth upon us from that foundation. That would seem to be the way in which the great Greek theologians of the fourth and fifth centuries particularly went to work, and to be the kind of thinking that took place in the ecumenical councils of the one Catholic Church.

3

The Problem of Theological Statement Today[1]

THIS is a theme as vast as it is important which it would be difficult to treat adequately even in several lectures, but I wish to limit consideration of it by approaching it in three ways, which may also serve to indicate to you the kind of theological reflection in which we are engaged today in Britain.

We shall consider the problem first from the perspective of the history of thought, and this means above all for us in Britain an examination of the question as raised in patristic theology. Then we shall turn to look at the same problem in a distinctively modern way, which we share with all natural science, and inquire into the empirical reference of theological statements. Finally, as scientific rigour demands, we shall allow the subject-matter itself to tell us something about the nature and mode of statements appropriate to it.

I THE PROBLEM OF THEOLOGICAL STATEMENT IN PATRISTIC THOUGHT

We are all aware that today we are in the midst of a great mutation in the forms of thought and speech that are the result of profound changes in our understanding of the universe. This is not something from which theological statement can stand aside, for theology always must make use of the forms of thought and speech that obtain in this world, since it is in this world and not out of it that the task of theology lies. But there are people who insist that the great advances of modern science in the understanding of the universe make it necessary for us to discard the fundamental framework of the Christian faith, as one that is bound up with an obsolete cosmology; even the basic concepts of the classical creeds and doctrines have to be changed, they say, for they are now seen to be the constructs of an objectifying kind of thought that has made

[1] A lecture delivered in the University of Tübingen, May 1963. The German text is in *Theologische Zeitschrift* 19.5, 1963; abbreviated English in *Dialog*. 4, 1965.

use of transitory patterns in man's understanding of the cosmos in order to establish itself. Hence we must dispense with the objective form in which all this is cast, and find new conceptual forms congenial to modern man in which to express our Christian attitude to God and the universe, and so on.

Now to the historian familiar with the history of Christian thought this is by no means new. He will recall at once the vast change in cosmological theory that took place in the sixteenth and seventeenth centuries, with Copernicus, Galileo, Kepler and Newton, but he will also point out that though the formulation of theological statements underwent their due measure of adaptation the essential imagery and the basic conceptuality of Christian doctrine did not change. The Church adjusted itself, and the apostolic and catholic faith continued to be proclaimed without embarrassment. But the historian's mind will go back above all to the first three centuries of the Christian era, when the Gospel was translated out of the world of Hebraic thought with its theological 'cosmology' into the world of Greek thought just at the time when there was taking place the vast change in cosmological outlook initiated by the later Pythagoreans and carried through by the great astronomers of Alexandria, Hipparchus and Ptolemy. There were certainly great struggles with Gnostics and Origenists, with mythologizers and demythologizers, but the Church, fighting for its very life, adjusted itself well, and its basic imagery and conceptuality were strengthened rather than weakened. The apostolic and catholic faith was more than adequate for all that was required of it in the change and advance in understanding of the universe.

It must be noted, however, that it was not change in science or cosmology that constituted the real difficulty for theological statement: it was something much deeper in the culture and thought of the times, the axiomatic assumption of a radical dichotomy between the phenomenal world of the sensible and the real world of the intelligible. That is very apparent in the struggle of the Church with Valentinus, but it was in the struggle with Arianism within the Church that the real core of the problem was brought to light. Theological statements that presuppose that radical dichotomy are quite a different thing from theological statements that reject it. It is above all to the critical and constructive work of Athanasius that I wish to direct attention first of all, for it was through his profound and brilliant analysis of the views of Arius that the true nature of theological statement became clear.

According to Arius the Word of God is not grounded in the eternal

Being of God but is divided or separated from him (*diairetos, choristos*), and therefore mutable or changeable (*treptos, alloioumenos*). This means that the imagery and conceptuality of God mediated to us through the Word or Son of God is correlated to man's own powers of conceiving (*epinoein*), and not to the nature (*physis*) and reality (*aletheia*) of God in himself. We think of the Son or the Father only *kat' epinoian*, i.e. in a purely noetic or putative way. Since in all our thinking of God through the Son we are faced with a dichotomy (*chorismos*), the conceptions we form have no objective truth corresponding to them; they are correlative to the creaturely world and are inevitably changeable, relative, and numberless. They express the view taken by the human mind in its own understanding of divine things.

I have been following Athanasius' analysis of the notions of Arius, but there are three further criticisms of his which we must note.

(i) Athanasius rejects entirely the old hellenistic dichotomy between the *kosmos aisthetos* and the *kosmos noetos* that lies behind Arianism. He found the acceptance of this dichotomy in his own Alexandrian tradition, deriving from Clement and Origen, but he rejected it from the very start, while the philosophical notion of the *logos* which went with it he found more and more impossible as his debate with Arianism proceeded. The assumption of the dichotomy leads to a mythological way of thinking (*mythologein*) to which he contrasted a theological way of thinking (*theologein*) which takes its rise from a centre in God.

(ii) Athanasius rejected the Arian notion of thinking *kat' epinoian*, and the whole notion of a detachable and changeable conceptuality which is related to God only θέσει (by convention) and not φύσει (naturally). Here Athanasius makes use of familiar language from Plato's dialogues in which the Platonic Socrates taught that our words and notions are true when they have a right (*orthos*) relation to the reality of existents (*aletheia ton onton*). In other words *epinoia* is an objectifying and nominalist way of thinking (*thesei*) through conceptions of our own devising (*epinoein epinoias*). Athanasius uses the strongest language of this, calling it a form of madness (*mania*), since it fails to distinguish thinking in accordance with the nature of the realities signified (*kata ten ton semainomenon physin*) from thinking in which men are engrossed with themselves and their own preconceptions, and in which they make a canon of truth out of their own piety or rather impiety.

(iii) The reading of this false way of thinking back into the biblical language, seriously distorts its meaning for it converts the right or proper sense into an oblique or tropical sense, and is therefore unable to follow biblical statements through in accordance with their own *skopos* to the realities they indicate. This is Athanasius' constant complaint of Arian exegesis. In other words, whenever the relation between biblical language and *physis* or *aletheia* is disrupted, then that language is rendered obscure and its difficulty has to be resolved away by a reinterpretation not in accordance with the nature and actions of God but in accordance with what is conceivable and acceptable to the mind of the interpreter. This involves a false method of inquiry, says Athanasius, for it lacks *episteme* or a scientific use of the reason in failing to distinguish appropriate from inappropriate questioning.

We turn from these critical points to note three positive things contributed by Athanasius to the understanding of the nature of biblical and theological statements.

In contrast to the *epinoiai* of the Arians Athanasius insists upon the place of *dianoia* in theological thinking. This is an objective, not an objectifying kind of thought, and is a far more rigorous form of thinking than *epinoia*. *Dianoia* is not the forcing of objective reality into a concept but the letting of the mind assume conceptual forms under the pressure of the objective reality or being of God. There is thus no suggestion in Athanasius that the rejection of thinking *kat' epinoian* is the rejection of conceptual thinking but rather the rejection of the kind of conceptual thinking in which we force reality to conform to our own thoughts, our own piety or preconceptions. *Dianoia* takes place as the objective reality of God comes upon us and presses itself upon our thought in a movement of manifestation (*deloma*) to which we may respond only as we allow our own *epinoiai* to be called in question and to give place to a *dianoia* that is rightly related to the divine reality that calls it forth and establishes it in our minds. This involves a stricter and profounder conceptuality that does not vary with man's many *epinoiai*, since it is rooted objectively in the Word in the eternal Being of God. That is the immense significance claimed by Athanasius for the work of the Fathers at Nicaea as they formulated their understanding of God under the compulsion of his self-revelation in Jesus Christ. In the *homoousion*, therefore, we have a rigorous and accurate theological statement that embodies an objectively derived *dianoia* and not an *epinoia* of man's own devising.

Theological statements of this kind have a twofold character: they are *paradeigmatic* and *economic*.

(*a*) Theological statements are *paradeigmatic* in that they employ

TIR D

images or representations (*paradeigmata*) taken from the visible or
tangible world to point out divine realities that cannot be simply reduced to words. They arise under the activity of divine revelation and
are adapted for its special purpose—that is why we cannot really understand *paradeigmata* apart from the divine condescension or economy,
which we shall consider in a moment. The *paradeigmata*, then, are not
exemplars from which we can draw inferences, or attempts at argument,
for their function is essentially *ostensive*. When images or representations are used in this way they have quite a different sense from that
which they normally have, for their meaning lies not in themselves but
in the divine realities to which they refer. Hence although they are used
to give our minds some hold on the knowledge of God they are to be
interpreted themselves in the light of that to which they point, for they
do not explain the divine reality but are made to reflect it. Of course
when considered in themselves as representations they are very inadequate indications of divine realities, but they are not for that reason
false, for that inadequacy or disparity is part of their paradeigmatic
nature and is necessary for their ostensive function in pointing beyond
themselves.

We cannot pursue this further, but it will be sufficient to remark that
in their paradeigmatic character biblical and theological statements are
discerned to have an essentially objective reference and to have an open
texture determined by the transcendent nature of the independent
reality to which they refer. Thus the *dianoiai* such statements involve
are open concepts, open to the world of the divine Being, and are therefore not concepts that we can cut short or tie down, or resolve into a
this-worldly reference and so manage at will—but they are nonetheless
concepts in the strict sense and are not just some form of symbolic
thinking. Far from any transcending of the subject-object approach,
this is one in which the objectivity is far greater and deeper, and in
which the human subject is really challenged and opened up to genuine
subjecthood precisely through encounter with the transcendent reality
of God who is the free and independent ground of its being.

This emphasis upon the objective and open reference of theological
statements does not imply any neglect of the coherence or sequence
which they must have among themselves if they are to have meaning—
i.e. what Athanasius called their *akolouthia*. But it does mean that it is
not the composition of the statements into coherent patterns that con-
fers on them their content, for the sequence or *akolouthia* in the written
or spoken statements reflects and points and therefore corresponds to

an *akolouthia* in the realities or acts which are signified by the statements. It is upon them that their validity rests, and it is to them that we
must penetrate if we are to interpret the statements in accordance with
their proper reference. That brings us to the other chief character of
theological statements.

   (b) Theological statements are *economic* as well as paradeigmatic, for
the images or representations they employ are not the products of our
own thinking *kat' epinoian*, but are derived from the ordered action of
God, for us and our salvation i.e. from the *oikonomia* which God has
fulfilled in Jesus Christ. Thus the objective reference of the *paradeig-*
mata corresponds to the objective activity of God within our human
existence in space and time. It is within that frame of reference, *kat'*
oikonomian, that biblical and theological statements are validly made.
Hence to interpret these statements by tracing their reference back to
their source in God we have to follow the ordered line of the divine
action that governs it, and not the line of our own notions, *kat' epinoian*.

   We may state this in another way. The *paradeigmata* point osten-
sively to divine realities beyond us, and necessarily fall far short of
them. They are not for that reason false or invalid, provided that they
are economically rooted in God's own acts of self-communication and
condescension and are governed by them. But if we do not take the
divine economy seriously, we are liable to fall into errors on both sides.
On the one hand, we will be tempted to treat these biblical images and
representations as mere names (*onomata*) or conventions which have no
relation to reality, but only the force or significance we put into them
in accordance with our presuppositions or desires. On the other hand,
we will be tempted to push the analogical reference in the images back
beyond their proper limits, in an attempt to break through to God by
the power of our own thinking, but then we only project ourselves upon
God or imagine that through our own treatment of the *paradeigmata*
we are able to bring the mystery of the eternal Being of God within the
compass of our own conceiving and imagining. We make the fatal
mistake of treating the images as pictorial representations or reproductions. Whichever way we take, says Athanasius, we lapse back into
paganism. But the very essence of the Christian faith is in direct
antithesis to both errors, for it is identical with the fact that the eternal
God, without ceasing to be God, has yet become man, and has so
appropriated our human nature as his own in Jesus Christ, that he has
established between us the basis for revelation on his part and true
knowledge on our part. Everything depends on the fact that the essential

images of God which are mediated to us in and through Jesus Christ are the images of One who is consubstantial with the Godhead. It is in and through him who is both the Image and the Reality of God in his own Person and Being that the basic imagery and conceptuality of the Christian faith are objectively and immutably grounded in God.

Several remarks fall to be made about this.

First, for Athanasius the doctrine of the economy is the antithesis of any radical dichotomy between intelligible and sensible worlds. It is the doctrine of the coming of God into our human existence in space and time, and his affirming of its validity in relation to himself as Creator and Redeemer, his activity and self-objectification for us within it. There can be no doubt that it is at this point that the Christian Gospel stands or falls—whether we take seriously (i.e. *kata physin* as opposed to *kata thesin*) the Incarnation of the Word or the *homoousion* of the Incarnate Son. He who conceives of this as an objectifying form of thinking, thereby shows that he is operating with an axiomatic assumption of a radical dichotomy that predetermines the results of his exegesis or dogmatics.

Secondly, if we take the economy seriously, then we have to interpret the objective reference of biblical and theological statements in accordance with it, *kat' oikonomian*, i.e. as an active reference corresponding to the divine activity without our existence. For hermeneutics this means that when we interpret biblical statements by penetrating into their *akolouthia* we cannot rest content with any *akolouthia* which they have among themselves as coherent statements, but with the objective reference of their *akolouthia* to the human economy of God's words and acts. For dogmatic formulation, however, this means that we must develop theological statements with an interior and dynamic logic that enables them to correspond faithfully to and therefore set forth adequately the economic pattern of God's saving acts in Jesus Christ.

Before we go on to draw out the far-reaching importance of this we must look at the same problems from the modern perspective which we theologians share with the scientists if only because we have to think and speak together with them within the same world.

2 THE PROBLEM OF SCIENTIFIC STATEMENT IN THEOLOGY

In modern scientific thought, following a distinction drawn by David Hume in the eighteenth century, we divide statements into two kinds according to their reference—i.e. statements that refer to external facts independent of them, and statements that refer to other statements in a coherent series. We shall speak of them as *existence-statements* and *coherence-statements*. Existence-statements do not have intrinsic but extrinsic meaning, for they are essentially denotative. Their truth lies not in themselves but in the realities to which they point and correspond, and therefore they are not susceptible of theoretic but only of empirical demonstration. Coherence-statements have their meaning in their morphological relations with one another. They are true in themselves in so far as their connections are coherent, and are therefore capable of theoretic demonstration. Very often, of course, we do not operate with different kinds of statement but with a twofold reference in our statements.

This is a distinction that applies to all positive science, that is, to all branches of articulated knowledge. There are, of course, purely theoretic disciplines, such as Euclidean geometry, where we are concerned only with statements that are developed into coherent patterns according to certain fixed roles, but in themselves they tell us nothing about the real world, although these disciplines can play a valuable part, as in formal logic or algebra, in helping us to check the coherence of our existence-statements with one another. In positive science, however, it is the existence-statements that are primary for without them our theoretic constructions are merely a kind of game.

This distinction applies to theology as much as to any other branch of knowledge. There are differences in every positive science, due to the nature of the reality to which existence-statements refer, and that difference applies above all to theology, for it is the nature of God that determines the way in which statements must refer to him and the mode in which they are to be verified. We can know God and speak about him truly only in accordance with his nature. But although theological knowledge is thus different from every other kind of knowledge it still remains true that in theology we are concerned with both existence-statements and coherence-statements. Hence if our theological statements are to be accurate and scientific they must be tested in their twofold reference.

There are several facts about scientific statements and their twofold reference that we must discuss, for they have not a little to say in connection with the problems we encounter today in theological statement.

(*a*) Existence-statements and coherence-statements require one another if they are to be significant. To adapt some famous words of Kant, existence-statements without coherence-statements are blind, and coherence-statements without existence-statements are empty. Or to put the matter quite differently, coherence-statements are properly made, so to speak, at right-angles to existence-statements, and it is in that angle that scientific statements have the hinge of their meaning. Hence it is important to see how they require one another.

In every positive science existence-statements are primary and basic, and yet these are the statements for which we can offer no purely theoretic proof. We can convince others of the truth of our existence-statements if we can get them to see or hear the reality they refer to as we see or hear it—thus the force of existence-statements lies in their persuasiveness, and their acceptance depends on empirical verification. Hence when someone can be induced to engage in the appropriate empirical reference, in accordance with the nature of the referent, then he is in a position to judge the truth or falsity of our existence-statements. That holds of the simplest existence-statement, but when we are engaged in strict scientific activity, we engage in a more complex movement. Here a number of existence-statements are arranged in a coherent series in such a way that the rational pattern of the coherence-statements makes clear and points us to the objective rationality upon which the existence-statements rest and so brings our minds under its power. In that way the existence-statements gain our respect for they command our recognition of the realities they refer to. The coherent patterns of existence-statements are our scientific constructions or theories, which we now speak of as noetic models (i.e. in Greek, *paradeigmata*). These noetic models are by no means to be indentified with ontic laws or structures or blueprints of any kind, but they are the media through which we allow objective reality to impinge upon us and bring us under the command of its inherent rationality. These media are effected in so far as they are transparent or open to the reality they indicate. Hence although we cannot offer any purely theoretic proof of existence-statements, existence-statements compel our assent when their objective reference lays bare an order or rational pattern in things that reaches out far beyond what we can specify at the time, and carries hidden implications which become revealed with the advance of science and convince us of the truth of our original existence-statements because of their fertility in throwing light upon many other aspects of reality. Therein, as Michael Polanyi has so often said, lies the profound truth or objectivity of scientific statements or theories, in the fact that their implications extend far beyond the experience which they were originally meant to control, and therein is lodged their proof.

What are we to say then about theological statements in view of the questions that are inevitably put to us from the side of strict natural science?

Theological statements are basically existence-statements, for they do not have their truth in themselves but in the divine realities to which they refer, but they too would be blind if they did not employ coherence-statements in order to bring to clarity in our understanding the orderly patterns which the objective reference of our existence-statements must take if they reach out to and come under the power of the inherent rationality or *Logos* of God—but here, as scientific rigour compels us, we have to take into account above all the vast difference in the nature of the object of theological knowledge from that of the objects of natural science. The *Logos* with which we are concerned in theology is at once the personal Being and the Word of God in his revealing and saving activity toward us. But when all that is taken into account, or rather just because it is taken into account, it still remains true that theology involves in its own mode and in accordance with its own proper nature the same rigorous scientific method that such a pure science of nature as physics involves.

We cannot pursue that further here, but my concern at the moment is to show that in the pure science of theology, that is, dogmatics, we are engaged in the formulation of dogmatic statements in and through which we inquire after *the* dogma, that is, the inherent rationality of the *Logos*, the *Prima Veritas* of God, by letting him disclose himself to our mind, command our recognition, and order and shape our understanding in basic ways that correspond faithfully to his words and acts. It would be presumptuous and indeed quite false to identify these dogmatic formulations with ontic structures in the Being of God, but it would be equally false for that very reason to discard all objective statements as forms of objectifying thought, substituting *epinoiai* for *dianoiai*. As Athanasius pointed out to Arius, such a procedure would be intolerable in every other branch of rational knowledge. Why should it be tolerated in theology?

I must admit that judged by the rigours of modern scientific method the work of Athanasius stands the test better than that of much modern theology. Indeed as we examine the history of Christian thought we can see that in formulating the *homoousion* the Fathers of Nicaea were engaged in the accurate scientific work of penetrating down to what in our day Einstein has called the *logical economy* of scientific statement which compels our acknowledgment as through its basic simplicity and its indeterminate scope of implication it continues to throw a clarifying light upon many other aspects of theological knowledge, and more and more to bring us in that way under the power of the objective rationality of the dogma after which we inquire. In view of all this what could be more foolish or more unscientific than to denigrate the place of objectivity in biblical and theological statements?

(*b*) Although existence-statements and coherence-statements require one another in rational activity, it is impossible to state in statements how statements are related to existence. Or to use the language of Wittgenstein, it is impossible to picture in a picture how a picture is related to the thing pictured. Nevertheless it shows through. Since this is so we cannot àrgue from our language or our statements to the reality they indicate, but neither may we posit a radical dichotomy between our existence-statements and coherence-statements, for that would open up an abyss of sheer unmeaning. There is a common error here against which positive science is always on its guard, namely, the abstraction of thinking from existence. With that error, either we fall into the naive rationalistic idea that thinking a thing is identical with making actual contact with it, and so discard objective science and kill empirical discovery, or we create a gap between our thinking and existence and then when we find that we cannot cross that gap by our thinking we question the reality of the existents beyond the gap, and lapse into scepticism. Rightly taken, however, the realization that we cannot state in statements how statements are related to objective existence keeps us in a state of humility by reminding us of the discrepancy between our statements and the realities they denote, and keeps us in what Einstein called a state of 'awe', for it tells us that although we cannot account for the rationality or comprehensibility of existence, it nevertheless shows through and keeps commanding our recognition—without that humility and awe there could be no scientific advance in the discovery of new facts.

Now when this error arises in theology the problems it creates are even more pressing, for the object of theological statements is the Lord God, who infinitely transcends us, so that before him we have to acknowledge the infinite discrepancy between our statements and his reality. That does not allow us, however, to posit in theology, any more than in natural science, a radical dichotomy between our coherence-statements and existence-statements. Moreover when posited, it would involve such a complete disjunction of the rational form embedded in our coherence-statements from objective reality, that theological statements would be converted into statements with only this-worldly reference. When that is done no amount of existentialist reinterpretation can preserve the respectability of these statements for they are caught in the vicious circle of the self-understanding, and can be affirmed only in the renunciation of scientific thinking.

A twofold error is involved here.

(i) The first error we may speak of in the mode of Wittgenstein as a radical failure to understand the nature of language as a transparent medium through which we allow the objective realities to show through. Or we may refer to it in a different way, in the mode of Heidegger, as a damaged relation of language to being. Just because the relation of language to being defies description in the forms of language alone, that is no ground for some interpretation of language in detachment from its objective reference, but rather ground for caution lest we allow detached forms to become substitutes for being and so obscure it from us. When Bultmann in his form-critical analysis of the Synoptic Gospels abstracts their literary patterns from the occurrence of certain specific events, and claims to be able to make historical judgments about them in comparison with other relatively fixed forms of literary material likewise abstracted, he falls into fatal error. It is not surprising, therefore, that after detaching the forms from their historical setting, and from their denotative reference to things and events, he is unable to make proper contact again with historical events and concludes that they are for the most part editorial creations. It must be pointed out, however, that forms detached from what they originally stood for are no longer the same, and forms abstracted from existence can be made to argue only to forms. It may be added that even when Bultmann handles formal relations his argumentation is far from scientific. One only needs to transpose his argumentation into algebraic notation, as we learn to do in modern symbolic logic, to see that Bultmann reaches many of his conclusions only by playing tricks with the middle premiss. The lesson we may learn from this is that which Anselm taught us long ago, that the proper way in which to interpret biblical statements is *non secundum formam vocum*, but *secundum rem*.

(ii) The other error we are concerned with here is also a sin against essential scientific procedure, failure to understand or interpret something or to speak about it in the mode required by the subject-matter. In every true science it is the nature of what we know that prescribes for us the mode of rationality in which it is to be investigated and knowledge of it is to be verified. This is particularly important, since to apprehend an object in a way appropriate to its nature and to be con-

vinced of its external reality coincide—therefore, in this respect at
least, the question of truth is inseparable from the question of existence.

All I wish to do at the moment, however, is to single out the problem
of enunciating theological statements in the mode of the *Word* of God
that gives rise to them. Here our difficulty is increased because we lack
adequate linguistic tools. For example, in Latin and English, we have
no word to describe what we hear in the same way in which percept
corresponds to perceive or concept to conceive. Even if we invent a
word like '*audit*' (remembering that faith rises *ex auditu*) we tend out of
habit to translate audits into percepts and concepts, but in so doing we
falsify them. Consequently when we build up our theological statements
out of ideas and images, we naturally find it difficult to trace them back
to their source in God's *Word*. That was one of the problems the fathers
had to face when biblical statements rooted in the *Word* of God became
changed into *eidetic* images, and interpreted under the primacy of *vision*
that dominated all Greek thought. Even in the Western Augustinian
tradition *Word* was always being dissolved into *Light* which made it
easy to accept the dichotomy between the *mundus sensibilis* and the
mundus intelligibilis. Whenever that takes place, as Athanasius found
among Valentinians and Arians, theological statements inevitably come
to be formulated as expressions of *epinoiai* instead of *dianoiai*. In view
of that we can see the immense epistemological import of the *homoousion*
for it asserted that theological statements in Christ are rooted in the
eternal Word in the Being of God.

That is undoubtedly one of the deepest problems underlying the
so-called demythologizing controversy, the failure to discern the objective depth of biblical and theological statements in the consubstan-
tiality of the Incarnate Word in Jesus Christ. *Mutatis mutandis*, this is
the same problem that physicists and mathematicians have to face in
regard to the concept of *number* which transcends the gap between
thought and existence. Hence they often speak of *recognition-statements*,
to describe the kind of statements they *have to* make in objective
reference to an order and rationality in the nature of things. What
corresponds in theology to number is what Anselm called *locutio intima
apud Summam Substantiam*, and what corresponds to the recognition-
statements of mathematical science are the *Hör-Aussagen* of theology.
To reject objectivity in that dimension of depth ultimately reduces all
theological statements to non-sense, just as it reduces our empirical
science to non-sense if we imagine that number is only the projection
of our own ways of thinking into existence without any objective reality

corresponding to it. That is why, when Bultmann operates with a radical dichotomy that does not allow for the objectivity of our *dianoiai* in the eternal Being of God, and so discards the objective framework of biblical and theological statements as merely an objectifying form of thought, his own statements about God are open to devastating critique on the part of the logical empiricists who have little difficulty in showing by the application of the verification principle that those statements have no valid meaning.

(c) Existence-statements and coherence-statements belong to two quite different logical systems. In some respects this can be called the deepest and most intractable problem of modern science—the discovery, the clarifying and testing, of the logic of existence-statements—but it is becoming clearer every day that, when we can disentangle existence-statements from the traditional logic of coherence-statements, very great steps forward in our understanding of the universe can be taken. I point out, for example, the immense importance of four-dimensional geometry, one of the great instruments of modern science, or point to the possibilities that wait upon the discovery of the logic appropriate to existence-statements in nuclear physics. But when we see throughout all this the immense difficulty of relating the language of mathematics to word-language, and the impossibility or futility of their complete detachment, then we may take heart if we find that in serious theological science we have similar problems and difficulties. But let us also learn from the physicists and mathematicians that these difficulties challenge us to hard work, and are not to be solved by recourse to the knife, that is, the shoddy expedient of cutting away the offending data, to which too many biblical scholars are addicted when what is required of them is hard thinking.

I have time to make only three affirmations.

First, it is equally true in theology that existence-statements and coherence-statements belong to two different logical systems. However, in theology the matter is complicated by the fact that the reference of our existence-statements is not only to the eternal Being of God, but also to God within human and historical existence, so that even within our existence-statements we have to do with different strata of logical relation—I cannot but think here of the tiers of logic that von Weizsäcker speaks of in modern physics. This recognition of different logical systems should make us aware of the danger of falling into the error of transposing existence-statements into coherence-statements, or of resolving the logic of the one into that of the other. That was what happened, for example, in the Middle Ages when the objective and empirical reference of theological statements, their analogic, was transposed into mathematical proportions. That is perhaps understandable when the mediaeval theologians had only Euclidean geometry as a guide to scientific statement, but we at least have four-dimensional geometry to challenge us to take space and time seriously in the analogical reference of our existence-statements. That is a challenge we have to direct to the existentialist theologians who erroneously transpose the analogical reference of existence-statements into mythological expressions correlated with the subject.

Secondly, existence-statements by their very nature are open and have an indefinite range because they refer beyond themselves to a reality which by its nature cannot be expressed in the language of abstract forms or symbols. That openness or indefiniteness is part of their adequacy to the object, and belongs to the logic of their reference, and hence it would be most inaccurate or imprecise if it were to be reduced through assimilation to the kind of precision that characterizes the logic of coherence-statements. On the other hand, meaningful coherence-statements cannot be finally detached from existence-statements, for they are never entirely devoid of factual reference. That is why even mathematical statements cannot consistently be treated as tautologies. As Gödel has shown, every arithmetic is incomplete, for in each of the formal systems there are undecidable arithmetical propositions, and in each arithmetic concepts can be found which are not definable within that system. Unless that were so arithmetic would have no applicability to existence—but applicability to existence is the criterion that distinguishes arithmetic as a science from arithmetic as a mere game. In other words, even our coherence-statements must finally involve an open logic. What has this to do with theology? In a word, it shows us that when a theologian like Bultmann understands intramundane connections as a closed continuum of cause and affect, which makes him posit a radical dichotomy between this-worldly and other-worldly relations, and so eliminate the objective framework of biblical and theological statements, he thereby renounces the possibility of scientific thinking either as an interpreter or as a theologian. Instead of facing the difficulties in a scientific way he is playing a game behind the back of science.

Finally, it must be noted that the relation between existence-statements and coherence-statements is not a theoretical but a *practical* one. What we are concerned with here is, so to speak, the logic of action—

but once again we lack the appropriate tools with which to work this out, for we have no logic of verbs. Modern science has had to create for itself new tools, such as the four-dimensional geometry of space and time that I have mentioned, and is still engaged in that kind of arduous task.

Now was this not what Athanasius was after when he insisted that in the interpretation of the Scriptures we have to direct our minds not only to *ta gegrammena* but to *ta genomena*, and that in formulating theological statements we have to think 'economically' (*kat' oikonomian*), that is, according to the order of God's action or the logic of grace? Let me put the matter in a more concrete way: if the connection between the existence-statements and coherence-statements of theology is a practical one, then what we are concerned with here is the *atonement*. In every positive science it is the subject-matter that determines form, content that affects method—and so it is in theology. It is the object of our theological statements that determines the logic of their reference, in accordance with its nature and activity. That object is the Truth of God struggling with us in judgment and mercy, in atoning and reconciling activity. To be truthful theological statements must correspond in form and content to that divine Object, and they must be enunciated in a material mode appropriate to that correspondence. This is the utterly distinctive nature of theological statements, and the reason why they inevitably collide with our other forms of knowing and speaking. And that constitutes the basic problem—the offence of the Cross of Christ.

I cannot now work out the epistemological implications of the atonement for theological statement, and yet strictly speaking this is the point at which to begin rather than to end. But let me add only this, we must beware of the temptation to which we are all subject, to transpose the difficulty in theological statement from the nature of the fact that confronts us in the Being and saving activity of God in Jesus Christ, to the words that are used to speak about it and so to take refuge in mere linguistics, for that is to reject the challenge to take seriously the logic of existence-statements. No sin is worse in theology than that of resolving away the real difficulties and of offering to the world theological statements that are only a form of cheap grace.

4

The Influence of Reformed Theology
on the Development of Scientific Method[1]

MODERN research has shown that already in the mediaeval world there were produced the conditions necessary for the development of western science. I have in mind especially the movement of thought from Grosseteste to Ockham. There we come upon men already trying to relate theory to observation, and struggling with the problems of induction and experimental verification that arose through the application of geometrical demonstration to the world of experience.[2]

Why was it then that modern empirical science had to wait until the beginning of the seventeenth century for its real advance? It is the purpose of this lecture to show that it was the great movement of thought at the Reformation that made this possible, and to discuss the bearing of Reformed theology especially on the development of scientific method.

CHANGE IN THE DOCTRINE OF GOD

During the Reformation there began to take place a change from the Stoic-Latin view of God as *Deus sive natura* to an essentially biblical view of God as the living, active Creator and Redeemer. In mediaeval theology there lay deeply embedded the idea that God is impassible and changeless, and that all created things have existence only as the objects of the eternal knowing and willing of this God, so that creaturely existence is directly grounded in the eternity of God. The implication here of an eternal positing or even co-existence of creaturely being with God's eternal being made it difficult to deny the *aeternitas mundi*, even if it could not be affirmed, or at least made it difficult not to be convinced

---

[1] This lecture was delivered in the Universities of Basel and Berne in May 1962. The German Text is given in *Theologische Zeitschrift* 18.5, 1962. The English text was published in *Dialog*, no. 2, 1963.
[2] Cf. A. C. Crombie, *Robert Grosseteste and the Origins of Experimental Science*, 1953; and *Mediaeval and Early Modern Science*, new edition, 1959.

of the ultimate changelessness of nature. No doubt it is right to argue, as St Thomas did, that from his eternity God sees all temporal things as present to him, for his eternity is present to every moment of time and encloses it, but it is quite another thing to argue that these things in their physical being are eternally present to God and in some sense co-exist with him.

To have given up this view, however, would have implied within the framework of mediaeval theology the ultimate irrationality of creation, and that in turn would have reflected upon its doctrine of God. But so long as this view of the natural world and its changeless and timeless bond to the divine mind prevailed, the rise of empirical science was severely handicapped.

In other words, for mediaeval theology nature was thought of as impregnated with final causes so that not only could an eternal pattern be read off the face of nature (thus giving rise to natural theology), but apart from that understanding of the eternal pattern in God there could be no knowledge of nature. But to interpret nature in the light of final causes left little room for the element of real contingency, to the recognition of which all modern science owes its existence. This had to wait until the period of the Reformation for its beginning when men learned to think differently of God and of his relation to creation as something utterly distinct from him while yet dependent upon his will for its being and ultimate order, and therefore learned to think differently of the nature of nature and of the creaturely nature of its order. Only when nature was liberated from mediaeval rationalism and disenchanted from its secret 'divinity' and only when it was realized that the order of nature—while intelligible to us in principle as a divine creation, precisely because it is a *creaturely* order—can be known only through observation and interpretation of the creaturely processes themselves, could the more or less static science of the ancient and mediaeval world give way to the great movement of modern science.[1]

A new kind of question had to be put to nature, expecting quite a different kind of answer, and calling for the revision of premises that first lay behind the question. The questions of mediaeval thinkers were so philosophically controlled from behind that they were not properly free and open, nor were they put in the mode and idiom of rationality that was congruent with real contingency. They were governed by a fixed notion of nature and were therefore of little use in opening up

[1] Cf. M. B. Foster, *Mystery and Philosophy*, 1957, pp. 53f.; J. Baillie, *Natural Science and the Spiritual Life*, 1951, pp. 18f.

nature, for they excluded from consideration the kind of contingency and the kind of order upon which empirical science is based. For really free questions to arise there had to take place a radical questioning of the whole mediaeval synthesis, and because that synthesis was knotted tight in and through its doctrine of God and nature, it was at the point of the doctrine of God that the real shift in outlook had to take place.

In this respect it is most instructive to study the thought of William of Ockham who seems to have been the first to realize that we cannot understand sequence or succession of events in nature by converting the movement they involve into a logical relationship—yet that is precisely what the mediaeval way of applying geometry and logic to nature involved.

Now Ockham's views have their relevance within the framework of mediaeval scholasticism, but when he sought within that framework to develop a new mode of rationality and explanation appropriate to contingent nature, he could only do that by advocating views that were inevitably regarded as the rejection of rationality and the advocacy of scepticism. The whole mediaeval synthesis had to be questioned, and only a new theology could do that.

That is what happened at the Reformation. The very foundations of mediaeval Roman theology were subjected to searching criticism in an effort to purge it of alien conceptions of deity and nature, and to restore in its fulness the biblical notion of the living God who freely and actively intervenes in history. The result was an immense upheaval which substituted a dynamic and active way of thinking for that of the mediaeval schoolmen, and so made possible the equally great mutation in scientific thinking from static to historical and kinetic questions.[1]

THE DISTINCTION BETWEEN GRACE AND NATURE

Parallel to the distinction between Creator and creature there arose a corresponding distinction between grace and nature. It served to guard the Godness of God on the one hand and the naturalness of nature on the other, by calling in question any blurring of the distinction between God and his creation. Thus it challenged the assumption that there is an inherent relation between the form-structure of the reason and the form-structure of being. The structure of true knowledge does conform to the structure of being, but that does not allow us to posit such a relation between the logical forms of the reason and the nature of the truth that we

---

[1] There took place correspondingly a considerable shift in terminology; see E. A. Burt, *The Metaphysical Foundations of Modern Science*, 1932, p. 26.

can necessarily argue from the forms of our reason to the truth of being.

But this distinction between grace and nature was by no means a dichotomy, for there is a relation of being between the creature and the Creator freely maintained by him and preserved in his love. It is a Creator-creature relation which God established out of pure grace and therefore is not explainable from the side of the creature nor logically definable—and so it is not reversible. Epistemologically this is the obverse of the fact with which we are so familiar in modern critical philosophy, viz., the impossibility of stating in statements how statements are related to being.

In the Augustinian tradition the universe was regarded as a sacramental macrocosm in which the physical and visible were held to be the counterpart in time to eternal and heavenly patterns. As such the world had significance only so far as it reflected or illustrated eternal patterns, but it was not worthy of attention in itself.

With the Reformation, however, there emerged a new outlook involving the primacy of grace as the turning of God toward the world. That gave new significance to the world as the object of divine attention and therefore as the object of human attention in obedience to the divine. Hence the way was opened up for the development of empirical science which was inhibited so long as men looked only away from the world to God to find its meaning in its participation in the divine.

This relation between God and the creature through grace Reformed theology expounded by using the conception of the 'covenant of grace', which embraces not only man but the whole of creation, involving a covenanted correspondence between the creation and the Creator reposing upon the free decision of God.

This way of distinguishing and relating the realm of grace as the way of God and the realm of nature as the course of creation in its distinctness from God bore immense fruit, for it at once disenchanted the world of its alleged divinity and yet claimed the world for God as his creation, thus denying that it was the product of capricious forces. In the realm of grace, grace has dominion and precedence in everything, for man's salvation is due to God alone and even his knowledge of God derives its possibility from God's grace and condescension; but in the realm of nature, man is by grace given dominion and precedence, for all things are under his command. Both in the realm of grace and in the realm of nature man is created and called to be a partner of God, to be a subject in communion with him, to live in dependence upon him, while the dominion he is given over the realm of nature he is to exercise as

TIR E

God's creature and as the recipient of his grace. In theological studies this had the effect of giving man full place as knowing subject over against the object, and rehabilitating theology as a dialogical activity with positive content in God's Word; while in other pursuits it tended to enhance man's sense of dignity and autonomy by acknowledging that God has subjected the whole of nature to him.

The effect of this teaching is nowhere better seen than in Francis Bacon's distinction between the *regnum Dei*, and the *regnum hominis*.[1] Far from leading to a neglect of nature, the distinction between grace and nature directed Bacon to the pursuit of natural science as a religious duty. God has kept the Godward side of nature hidden 'within his own curtain', but whatever is not God he has laid open for man's investigation. It is therefore by keeping within the limits and ends of knowledge which God has set in the creation that man can fulfil his function as an interpreter of nature and build up his kingdom of *scientia*.[2]

This distinction between grace and nature led Bacon to reject the application of final causes to nature. Hence he turned to examine nature as it is in itself, and to devise a new mode of rational investigation of nature in which *activa inquisitio* and *inventio* went hand in hand, in order to let nature declare itself unhindered by patterns which we have already reached by logic.

Bacon was not himself a great scientist by any means, but there can be no doubt that his attempt to give science a new direction by the method of putting the question to nature, and letting nature give its own answers, played a very important role. Our interest in Bacon lies in the fact that this new direction was a product of his understanding of the relation between God and creation. The distinction between grace and nature did not mean for Bacon a dichotomy between faith and reason, but rather that in the realm of grace as in the realm of nature man is summoned to exercise his reason in a way congruent with the given reality and in obedience to it. As in the realm of grace so in the realm of nature man is summoned to activity, but in the realm of nature his task is to regain and exercise the dominion over the world he lost at the fall which belongs to him by the bounty of his Maker. It is at God's command that he must occupy the earth and it is in obedience to that command that he must engage in natural science, the aim of which is to extend the *regnum hominis* over nature. Thus there arose the modern concept of man as *homo faber*.[3]

---

[1] *Novum Organum* I.52   [2] *Valerius Terminus* I.
[3] Cf. F. H. Heinemann, *Neue Wege der Philosophie*, 1929, pp. xii f.

This has had its danger as well as its advantage. In theology, for example, precisely because man is given full place as the human partner in God's covenant of grace, he is constantly tempted to usurp the major role in the realm of grace and to exercise there the dominion he is given by grace only in the realm of nature. From the realm of nature, however, modern man has carried this inordinate sense of his own creativeness into the universe of knowledge until it has become almost axiomatic for him that he only understands what he fashions and shapes and controls with the powers of his active reason.

SCIENTIFIC OBJECTIVITY

It is once again to the Reformation that we must turn for the modern emphasis upon unbiassed and disinterested truth, which arose particularly in the conflict between Reformed theology and Roman tradition. Concentration upon the Word of God and the acknowledgment of its absolute primacy cut the strings of prejudice and prejudgment and determined theological procedure. This was a passion for the truth from the side of the object which indicated a repentant readiness to rethink all preconceptions and presuppositions, to put all traditional ideas to the test face to face with the object, in order to distinguish what is objectively real from our subjective states. It is this masterful objectivity, with its distinction between unwarranted presupposition and proper entailment arising out of the nature of the object, that is one of the great contributions of the Reformation to the modern world, for out of it came the spirit and procedure so characteristic of modern science.

Who can provide us with a better illustration of this than Francis Bacon, particularly in his attack upon the 'fallacious notions' or 'idols of the mind' which we bring with us to the interpretation of nature and with which we distort the understanding of it?[1] Access to the truth requires of us readiness to let our understanding be thoroughly cleansed and freed, and entrance into the kingdom founded on the sciences, he says, is little different from entrance into the kingdom of heaven, into which none may enter except as a little child, *nisi sub persona infantis.* Bacon was not of course advocating a complete *tabula rasa*, but he was advocating a childlike inquiry and a readiness to learn from what is actually given to us in the world of nature.

But this masterful objectivity did not have its way very easily, for it was soon confronted with the notion of the active reason.

In the Roman Church the active reason had come to operate in a

---

[1] *Novum Organum* I xxiiif.; xxxixf.

corporate way in the mind of the developing Church, producing the active tradition out of which are derived the dogmatic definitions of the truth. Here the *intellectus agens*, the power of the mind to form and shape what it knows, is applied to the mind of the historical Church, so that if God, in Roger Bacon's phrase, is the active intellect of all mankind, the Roman Church becomes the active intellect of all theological knowing. From the original deposit of the faith the Roman Church progressively abstracts and elaborates universal forms which are acknowledged to be unalterable structures of the truth, so that all future knowing of the truth is governed by these forms, and all determination of the nature of the faith is controlled by them.

In this way the Roman Church has evolved apparently a new notion of truth. The only reality it acknowledges is that which it finds in the developing structures of its own tradition and continuously makes real for itself through doctrinal formulation; the tradition of a thing is its reality, and truth is that which conforms to this tradition as it is formed and shaped in the consciousness of the Roman Church. Thus the truth of a doctrine is what has become of it in the active tradition, so that in this way the element of objectivity in the tradition is subordinated to a massive subjectivity in the mind of the Church.

In Protestantism, however, the active reason has had a more individualist but equally powerful development, particularly in the notion of the autonomous, self-legislating reason. We need not stop to trace how this Renaissance idea broke through the Reformation into Protestant Pietism, the Enlightenment and Romanticism, and then came to exercise a masterful influence upon Neo-Protestant theology. It is sufficient to point out that the 'God' of this Neo-Protestantism is the 'God' who is correlated with the religious subject and its spiritual potentialities, the 'God' who meets and satisfies the needs and questions of 'modern man'. Truth about 'God' is discerned within the religious subject himself, so that the task of theology is to examine the structures of the religious consciousness, particularly in its historical and universal manifestations. It is not surprising therefore that in this development Christianity even in its origins should have been interpreted as the product of the human spirit, and that the Gospel should be regarded as going back as much to the creative spirituality of the Early Church as to someone called Jesus. This whole conception has been helped on immensely by the application of the concept of evolution, and by the new 'modern' notion of history, stemming from the Romantics and Dilthey, as that which man himself creates and for which he is responsible. Thus the historical truth of the Christian faith is only that which man can envisage for himself, what he can make real for himself, and for which he can make himself responsible through his own decisions. Christian truth is that which has become and continues to become true in and through the history which man himself creates by his existential decisions. The only reality which he can acknowledge is whatever submits to the creativity of his active reason.

There can be no doubt that this development is a first-cousin of that which we have noted in Rome, but of course it is only one line within Protestantism; for there is another line, stemming from the Reformation itself, which maintains within it as one of its chief elements the readiness to submit all tradition to the criticism of the Word of God as heard in the Bible, and therefore to reform its own judgments and think through its theology in obedience to the objective revelation in Jesus Christ. It is this main line of Protestant thinking that is everywhere reasserting itself again with such vigour all over the world, in the recognition that the only real objectivity is that of the object, God himself in his own Being and Act who gives himself to us in his Word and summons us to submit all our traditions, and all our attempts to impose ourselves with our culture upon the Christian faith, to obedient conformity to his Word in Jesus Christ. It is in him that we are confronted with the ultimate and obdurate objectivity of the Word and Truth of God which refuses to be domesticated to our subjectivity, or our active reason, either in its individualist or in its corporate form.

Thus while the history of Protestant theology in the last hundred years is the history of a great struggle between the objective reality of the Word of God and the masterful usurpation of the autonomous reason, it is also the story of how theology has been driven steadily back upon its proper object. Here empirical science, to which the Reformation contributed in its basic doctrines, has in its turn helped theology to refer its thought away from itself to its proper object and to learn again the discipline of genuine objectivity.

THE PLACE OF THE HUMAN SUBJECT IN KNOWLEDGE

Because God brings man into living and personal communion with him, the place of the human subject in the knowledge of God cannot be excluded from the full content of that knowledge. Our knowing of God is part of our knowledge of God—the inclusion of the fact in Reformed doctrine of the grace of God had immense repercussions.

We cannot talk about knowledge of God without taking into account the fact that it is we, human beings, who know him. There is an anthropomorphic element here to which we cannot shut our eyes, and which we cannot do without if we are to have knowledge at all in any sphere. But our concern here is with a profounder fact, to which Calvin particularly gave much attention. He taught that God reveals himself in such a way that man does not need to stretch himself beyond the limits of his humanity in order to know him, and that while there will always remain an element of 'impropriety' in human statements about God, man's knowledge need not for that reason be false.

Two doctrines lie behind this. 1. The doctrine of *accommodation*, i.e. that God condescends to our ignorance, and lets himself down to us in our littleness, adapting himself to our knowing that he may adapt us to himself. Thus God so objectifies himself for us in the incarnation that far from negating he rather posits and fulfils our subjectivity in Christ. But this means that our theological statements arise out of and can only take a form which expresses at once the nature of the object and the mode of our cognition of it. 2. The doctrine of *election* which insists that we do not know God through acting upon him but through being acted upon by him, and therefore we have to distinguish what is objectively real from our own subjective states. Hence election rejects every projection of man and his creaturely forms into the eternal and divine—that is the way of mythology—and teaches instead the incarnation of the eternal purpose among men, the projection, as it were, of the divine into the human in Jesus Christ, and the establishing in him of true relations between God and man and man and God.

These doctrines mean that Reformed theology operates with a truth that upholds both sides of the knowledge relationship, the side of the object over against the human knower, and also the side of the human subject in the form of his knowledge, but they also mean that Reformed theology is seriously critical of any abstract objectivism on the one hand, and that it operates with a severely self-critical and controlled subjectivity on the other hand.

So far we have been thinking mainly of Reformed theology, but there was a parallel line of development in Lutheran thinking that had far-reaching implications, through the peculiar way in which it interpreted the *communicatio idiomatum* to mean a mutual interpenetration of divine and human natures in Christ. In this doctrine divine attributes were ascribed *realiter* to the human nature of Christ. But when we remember that the humanity assumed by the Son of God is that in which we are given to share, how can we stop short at applying those divine attributes to the individual humanity of Jesus and not to humanity in general? Or how can we stop short of a general notion of the conformity of the divine to the human?

That is a problem that lies deeply embedded in German idealism, which infected not only theology but natural science as well, as we see particularly in the aftermath of Kant's 'Copernican revolution'. I have no time to trace this development but let me point out the difficulty created by Kant. He noted rightly that in the pursuit of natural science nature only yields her secrets to us when we compel her to act within limits we impose and according to specifications we bring to her in our coercive questioning, but then Kant went on to convert this into a general principle and to elaborate it in his doctrine of a permanent structure of categories of the understanding. This produced a twofold difficulty: It meant that science operates with a subjective structure of the understanding that inevitably limits the range of its observation and discovery, but it also implied that scientific activity does not so much discover as create reality. If we pass over the scientific theories of the nineteenth century to the more dynamic theories of today, we find natural scientists insisting that science involves an interplay between nature and ourselves, and making use of Kantian notions to make good their claim that reality is neither simply discovered nor merely invented but that it takes shape under the creative efforts of scientific knowledge. Hence many today even insist that the only reality there is is that which changes all the time under our own activity.

Now of course there is a profound element of truth here, for science is creative and productive, but there is also something dangerously misleading. The question Reformed theology must ask these natural scientists is whether they are not projecting their own ontological constructions into nature and identifying them with ontic structures in reality, and whether they do not thus make the fundamental mistake of thinking that they can offer in theoretical statements an account of how their theoretical statements are related to being.

One of the most exciting things of our own day is that the influence seems to be the other way round, for out of empirical science there has developed a new self-criticism which has much to say about method to contemporary theology. I refer to the fundamental notion that real advances in knowledge involve basic changes in the structure of the understanding and of our primary concepts, and that all that empirical science can offer by way of knowledge of the real world beyond us is through the elaboration of working 'models' which may be judged adequate in so far as they are applicable to experience, but which by their very nature must always be regarded as inadequate because the knowledge they involve is limited at its very root by the fact that in empirical science man can never know anything beyond the interplay between himself and nature. Hence the deeper man's knowledge goes, the more he realizes that his knowing cannot transcend the human starting-point without ceasing altogether. The utmost he could do is to push his inquiry to the very brink of his existence where so far as his empirical science is concerned he is confronted only by emptiness or nothing. This is the very point where Reformed theology must ask whether this is not the obverse of its own doctrine of contingency, of creation out of nothing, and whether that is not the point where, as von Weizsäcker has said, we are compelled by emptiness or silence to listen.[1]

THE IMPORTANCE OF KINETIC THINKING

I have already pointed to the immense shift in the mode of thinking that began to take place during the period of the Reformation. One of the first aspects of this to be pursued by natural science relates to *motion*, but right away there was also a change in the notion of time and history, as we can see clearly, for example, when we compare Calvin's discussion of the Lord's Supper with the Roman doctrine of the Mass. The Reformation opened up the historical perspective of understanding and initiated a historical mode of thinking, due as much as anything else to its Old Testament studies. But the Reformation did not have the philosophical or intellectual tools with which to consolidate that insight and elaborate the change in method, and so Protestant theology soon fell back upon the old Aristotelian tools of thought. Consequently the development of historical thinking was severely retarded. When it did finally break out, however, it developed in two ways, each involving a fundamental error at the root, i.e. the historical thinking of the Enlightenment on the one hand and of Romanticism on the other hand. It is this duality that is ultimately responsible for the false problem in which the Dilthey-Troeltsch-Herrmann-Bultmann line of thought is entangled in their distinction between *Historie* and *Geschichte*.

But in the nineteenth century there was a Lutheran thinker who saw into this question more profoundly than all his predecessors and contemporaries. I refer to Sören Kierkegaard, and especially to the mode of thinking he described, very foolishly I think, but as he thought ironically, by 'the leap of faith'. What Kierkegaard was concerned to do was

[1] *The History of Nature*, 1951, p. 178.

to find a mode of knowing appropriate to the fundamental nature of the Truth. The Truth with which we have to do in theology is the Being of God in space and time, the movement of the Eternal in our temporal existence, the Life of God in human history, in the concrete particularity of Jesus Christ. If the reason is to act rationally here, it must allow the nature of this Truth to prescribe for it the mode of thinking and the mode of demonstration appropriate to it. Because the Truth is the Eternal *moving* into time, the reason must *move* along with it in order to know it, and hence must make a break with other habits and structures of rationality which it had to develop in its knowledge of determinate objectivity in the world around. Hence Kierkegaard attacked the static character of the categories which made up the structure of the understanding, and pointed out the basic error they involved in converting temporal movement into logical relation.[1]

Let me indicate the importance of Kierkegaard's contribution to scientific method by a double comparison with the work of Albert Einstein and of Nils Bohr.

We recall how Einstein had to wrestle for some twenty years with Newtonian and Kantian conceptions of space and time before his famous theory of relativity could be formulated. What he had to do was to break through the static structure of the understanding with which classical physics operated, and only when he could abandon a conception of space and time reached from a point of absolute rest could he move into the new perspective that changed everything. Now that is similar to what Kierkegaard had to do. He had to abandon every attempt to contemplate the Truth from a point of absolute rest, and take a step forward in which he allowed his reason to move along with the movement of the Truth in order to acquire the mode of rationality for apprehending Truth that moves and lives and acts upon us in history. That is what I have called *kinetic thinking*.

Thinking of this kind involves a determined act of the reason, for it is the kind of thinking in which, the physicists say, we have to move across a logical gap between knowledge that we already have and knowledge we are yet to acquire, which cannot be inferred logically from what we already know, but which is so rational that it entails a logical reconstruction of what we already know. That is, it entails a fundamental act of repentance, *metanoia*, a radical conversion of our prior understanding. This is where I want to compare Kierkegaard's work with that which

[1] See S. Kierkegaard, *Philosophical Fragments*, especially 'Interlude', and H. Diem, *Kierkegaard's Dialectic of Existence*, 1959, pp. 4-7.

took place about a hundred years later in Copenhagen, when Nils Bohr and his collaborators had to undertake a daring and determined leap forward of the scientific reason in order to apprehend the nature of nuclear activity. It was an act which, from the point of view of classical physics, appeared absurd, but which involved such a logical reconstruction of prior understanding that while showing its limited range of applicability it established classical physics on a surer foundation, and at the same time transcended it, opening up the possibility for a greater range of observation and discovery beyond. But that step could not have been taken without a considerable change in the whole structure of scientific consciousness.

That is what Kierkegaard saw so clearly to be involved in theological thinking that really dares to apprehend the Truth of God in a mode appropriate to its incarnate movement in space and time. But theology has on the whole quailed from the radical extent of the *metanoia* involved. Whereas the physicists have had to invent new geometries, indeed four-dimensional geometries of space and time, in order to develop a system of logic appropriate to what they call 'existence-statements', theologians have so far not responded to the challenge to work out a logic of movement, or if you like, a logic of verbs, in order to acquire appropriate tools for the elaboration of theological statements, which in their own way are also 'existence-statements' like those of modern physics, although of course the *Existent* to which they primarily refer is God himself. Unless the biblical and dogmatic theology of our day is prepared to work hard at forging such tools, perhaps in close conversation with the physicists, it may well be that the evangelical and biblical theology of our generation will be seriously compromised like that of the Reformation in the centuries that followed it, through an uncritical acceptance and employment of ready-made thought-forms from ancient or modern man.

Hence there can be no suggestion that theology should attempt to carry through a new synthesis between faith and some *philosophia perennis* (whether Aristotelianism or Existentialism!), far less seek to 'go further' by bringing its understanding of the Gospel into line with a new modern conceptuality reached apart from the Gospel altogether. By its very nature as a form of thinking with a source and goal beyond itself in God and his Word, theology must break through the frame of every independent form of human thought. As a free science submitting only to the claims of its own subject-matter, and so renouncing all alien dogmatisms, it must lay bare its own basic forms of thought as they arise out of God's objectifying of himself for man in Jesus Christ, and at the same time forge, with every available help, appropriate instruments for its elaboration and faithful exposition. Only if theology is prepared, face to face with God in his revelation, constantly to repent of false habits of mind, and to adopt modes of rationality that actually correspond with the nature of its objectively given reality, can it be established firmly on its own foundations.

5

Knowledge of God and Speech about him according to John Calvin[1]

I T belongs to the great merit of John Calvin that he worked out the difficult transition from the mediaeval mode of thinking in theology to the modern mode, and placed the theology of Reform on a scientific basis in such a way that the logic inherent in the substance of the Faith was brought to light and allowed to assume the mastery in human formulation of it. Calvin has not always been interpreted like this, yet if he has been misunderstood, perhaps it was his own greatness that was to blame. Calvin made such a forward advance in theological thinking that he outstripped his contemporaries by centuries, with the result that they tended to fall back upon an old Aristotelian framework, modified by Renaissance humanism, in order to interpret him. Thus there was produced what history has called 'Calvinism', the rigid strait-jacket within which Calvin's teaching has been presented regularly to succeeding generations.

In modern times, however, Calvin has been given a different interpretation as essentially an Augustinian, and indeed, as Karl Barth has said, the greatest idealist theologian since Augustine. This is a view that has much to say for it, but is not one that I can accept without qualification. Certainly Calvin was greatly indebted to Augustine, as even the vast bulk of his citations from Augustine's writings makes clear. But there is another way to look at this. Augustine was the undisputed master theologian of the Western world. If mediaeval Roman theology was to be overthrown how could it be done better than through appeal to the authority of Augustine? That had been the line taken by Luther, and Calvin followed him, equipping himself with a great armoury of weapons taken from the works of Augustine. That explains why Calvin relied so heavily upon Augustine in his attack upon all forms

[1] Lecture read to the *Colloquy* held in Strasbourg in May 1964, commemorating the death of John Calvin on 27th May, 1564.

of Pelagianism and in his defence of the Reformation against Roman counter-attack, yet in some of the most important aspects of Calvin's thought he was much more indebted to the Greek fathers. Moreover, as far as I can see, Calvin rejected the basic tenets of the Augustinian philosophy.

The examination of Calvin's positive teaching along the line of his indebtedness to patristic theology is one of the most fruitful tasks especially when we relate it to the editions and translations of the fathers that poured out from the publishing houses of Basel, Geneva and Strasbourg. Here, however, I am concerned with another approach, the investigation of Calvin's thought in the light of considerable changes that began to take place in late mediaeval philosophy and theology and in logic and science. What I wish to do is to offer an interpretation of certain epistemological questions with which Calvin struggled in a period of rapid and momentous transition similar to our own. This should serve to throw into clear relief Calvin's thinking as to knowledge of God and speech about him, and at the same time to show its relevance for us today.

Europe has seen two great periods of change in cosmological outlook, the third and fourth centuries, and the sixteenth and seventeenth centuries, and is now in the midst of the third period. In each of them basic epistemological and theological questions have been raised concerned with very similar if not with identically the same issues. Our own involvement in such a situation helps us to appreciate the problems that the Church had to face when it struggled with Gnosticism and Arianism which were, partly at least, by-products of the Ptolemaic revolution in cosmology. When we translate these ancient problems into the setting of the twentieth century we find that they are not so very different from our own. The same applies to the sixteenth century which saw the change from a Ptolemaic to a Copernican outlook upon the universe. Behind it lay the fourteenth and fifteenth centuries in which the mediaeval synthesis began to break up, and ahead of it lay the vast reconstruction of the knowledge of the universe in Newtonian science. That is surely the setting in which Calvin's theology is to be understood, in the midst of a great mutation in the forms of thought and speech. I do not say that this mutation explains Calvin's thought, far from it, but that he took part in it, both in the sense that he took from it many of his intellectual and linguistic tools, and in the sense that he contributed to it through his own theological method.

Let us take as our starting-point the mediaeval background to Calvin's theology.

For more than a thousand years the dominating influence in Western thought had been some form of Augustinianism in which Ptolemaic cosmology, with a powerful ingredient of Neo-platonism, and Christian theology had been blended in a most remarkable way to produce the notion of a sacramental universe in which the visible and physical creation was held to be the counterpart in time to eternal and heavenly patterns. This outlook had taken up into itself the old Hellenic dichotomy between the 'sensible world' and the 'intelligible world', but had sought to span the hiatus between the two by Augustine's theory of illumination and his doctrine of the Church as sacramental organism. But deep in the Middle Ages significant changes began to be made. St Thomas rejected the theory of illumination and turned to Aristotelian philosophy for his tools to effect a new synthesis. Within his own principles he brought about a profound integration between faith and reason, revealed and natural theology, but this in its turn began to break up as a result of Ockham's attack upon the physics and metaphysics embedded in it. The two worlds began to break apart again with a widening disruption between faith and reason, the Church and the world. Meantime Augustinianism began to come under heavy attack at another significant point, in its understanding of creation in relation to eternal patterns or timeless ideas in the Mind of God. This had given rise to the difficult idea of the *aeternitas mundi* with which St Thomas wrestled and imported a sterile changelessness into the conception of nature. Under Duns Scotus, however, and again in Ockhamist thought, creation came to be related to active and creative ideas which God freely and rationally produces along with the created realities themselves. Hence all creation was regarded as contingent upon the freedom of the creative Will of God. In the Augustinian outlook nature was looked at only to be looked *through* toward God and the eternal realities. As such it had no significance in itself but had significance only so far as it reflected heavenly patterns and was moved by an immanent longing for them. In the Thomist modification of this the world of nature was meaningful only as it was understood to be impregnated with final causes, but if it could only be investigated rationally in its changeless and timeless bond to the divine mind the rise of empirical science was severely inhibited. That was the great dilemma of late mediaeval thought, and it was only with the radical change in the doctrine of God that came with the Reformation that the understanding of nature was emancipated from the incubus of a rationalist theology and theology was released from the domination of an alien metaphysics, yet without the disruption of faith and reason feared by the Thomists.

Now in the course of these changes there emerged a very important distinction between *intuitive knowledge* and *abstractive knowledge* and a corresponding distinction between two kinds of statement or two kinds of meaning. Let me expound this in the Ockhamist form, for it is, I believe, in reaction to this that Calvin's own distinctive position in regard to knowledge and speech of God is to be seen.

Intuitive knowledge is the direct knowledge of an actually present object caused naturally by that object and not by another. It is knowledge that is immediately evident, that is, knowledge by virtue of which it can be known whether the object exists or not, knowledge in which the mind cannot fail to attain the truth unless it is obstructed. Intuitive knowledge arises, then, out of direct experience. To this Ockham added a rider: Intuitive perception is sometimes possible of something non-existent or no longer existing (such as a 'dead star'). Moreover God is able to give us intuitive knowledge of something without the actual presence of the object, or knowledge of something without prior intuitive experience of it.

Abstractive knowledge is knowledge in which we apprehend something not as it is in itself, but through abstraction from its existence or through the species abstracted from some other thing. In abstractive knowledge we do not have to do with immediate experience but with ideas detached from experience and related to one another logically through the discursive reason.

This distinction between intuitive and abstractive knowledge reminds us of David Hume's distinction between knowledge of matters of fact and knowledge of the relations of ideas which is so very important for modern science and philosophy. Indeed the late mediaeval form of this distinction is clearly an anticipation of modern thought on the subject.

Now according to Ockhamist thought there is no intuitive evident knowledge of God for man on earth. God is not known experientially. But God is able to give us knowledge of himself that does not repose upon objective experience. This is abstractive knowledge in which we operate with certain revealed truths detached from immediate experience which God has provided for us by his absolute power in the Church. Before we see what this means we must look at Ockham's terminist logic, in which he drew a distinction between two kinds of statement and two kinds of meaning. The statements we make in intuitive knowledge are meaningful because they signify things independently of them—these are statements with 'direct' meaning or 'signification'. The statements we make in abstractive knowledge, on the other hand, are meaningful because of their syntactical and logical relations with one another—these are statements with 'oblique' meaning or 'supposition'. *Signification*, then, is the kind of meaning which terms have in propositions of intuitive knowledge. Strictly speaking it is not a meaning which they have in themselves, but only in their reference to the objects of intuitive experience. *Supposition* is the kind of meaning terms have when they act as substitutes for the things signified. It is the meaning they have only as components of propositions in detachment from the things themselves. This is the kind of meaning we have in abstractive knowledge, but by definition, it involves a deliberate suspension of the significant function of language, for that is replaced by the semantic function of words in their connections with one another, or as Ockham expressed it, in their 'complexes'. Here, therefore, we detach terms from their objective reference and consider them only as linguistic units or logical facts.

Along with this distinction goes another which we must note, the distinction between *first* and *second intentions*.

First intentions are acts of the mind that are made in response to external facts (*ad res ad extra*). These mental acts or intentions have an objective pole, the thing intended or signified, and a subjective pole, the state of the soul intending the external fact. According to Ockham we are more sure of the states of our soul than of the external facts. Now it is the states of the soul that we express in terms, but when we do that the terms themselves become the immediate counters of thought and knowledge. Terms of the first intention, then, signify things.

Second intentions do not signify things—they stand for first intentions. They are not signs of things but signs of signs. The second intention, then, is not a state of the soul but a term, a linguistic or logical fact standing for or employed in the place of a signifying act. The second intention has no meaning outside of a proposition, for since it is the sign of a sign it becomes meaningful only when it is conjoined with other signs through the mind's activity. Terms of the second intention are rationally handled only within grammatical and logical structures, as they are detached from the objective reference of terms of the first intention.

This was a highly ingenious theory. In it Ockham clearly realized that the hinge of meaning is to be sought at the point where we refer our thought and speech both to matters of fact and to the relations of ideas. But the effect of this theory was that Ockham moved away from the empirical to the logical realm, from intuitive to abstractive knowledge, and logic itself became more and more assimilated to language. How far Ockham did go in this direction is evident in his insistence that in the last resort we only know propositions, and that science, real or mental, deals exclusively with propositions as such.

These were the views that were in the ascendency in the Paris of the late fifteenth and early sixteenth centuries. The sharp bifurcation between intuitive and abstractive knowledge served to drive a deep wedge between faith and reason, and that in turn resulted in the domination of an authoritarian and obscurantist fideism. Faith was related to reason only through the highly formalistic sciences of grammar and logic. It was widely held that there is no intuitive evident knowledge of God for man in his pilgrim state, but that God is able to grant abstractive knowledge to man without prior intuitive experience on his part. This means that man is thrown back upon the 'creditive ideas', as Ockham called them, that are lodged in the Scriptures and the Tradition of the Church. It is the task of theology to define and elaborate these ideas in terms and propositions. Once terms are defined we think them directly for they become the immediate objects of our abstractive knowledge, but once theological truths are expressed in this realm of abstractive terms and definitions they fall under the control and manipulation of terminist logic. That is why it was within the tradition of terminism and nominalism that the most reactionary defenders of mediaeval fideism were to be found.

This was the philosophical and theological teaching in which John Calvin was educated in the College of Montaigu in Paris, first under the instruction of Antonio Coronel, a favourite pupil of John Major, and then under Major himself for several years from 1526 to 1528. John Major taught logic through commenting on the works of Peter of Spain and Aristotle, philosophy and theology through commenting on the Sentences of Peter Lombard, and biblical theology through commenting on the Four Gospels with the aid of considerable patristic scholarship. Major himself had been brought up in Ockhamist and terminist logic, and edited the works of several of Ockham's most famous pupils, Buridan, Goddam (or Wodham) and Holkot. Of greater importance was his attachment to Duns Scotus, the most distinguished pupil of his own school in Haddington (as John Knox was later who was also taught by

Major in St Andrews), whose Parisian lectures on the Sentences of Peter Lombard Major edited for the first time, *Reportata Parisiensia*, as they are called. Major considered himself a thinker in the Scottish tradition and sought to reconcile nominalists and realists by using nominalist tools (terminist logic) to establish a position that was basically realist. That is a point of no little importance, for here we see that Major provided Calvin with some of his basic tools, in forms of thought and speech, and showed him that they could be adapted and applied effectively in clarifying and building up quite a different understanding of theological knowledge. The distressing feature about Major was his consuming passion for logical analysis and his multiplication of *distinctiones* to which he might well have applied Ockham's razor, *pluralitas non est ponenda sine necessitate*, as he did with such effect in certain other areas of knowledge. This was an aspect of Major's teaching from which Calvin recoiled and indeed rejected quite vehemently, although he never mentioned him by name in this respect.

Ockhamist nominalism and terminism had deeply infected the Sorbonne since the Rectorate of Buridan, and indeed most of the universities of continental Europe, and gave rise to such arid logistics and such a sterile treatment of language that various attempts were made to deal with the situation by giving the Ockhamist assimilation of logic to language a new direction. Two of these must be mentioned because they were fully considered by Calvin.

The first is the line that was taken by Valla, Agricola, Vives and Nizolius who carried even further the assimilation of logic to language by subordinating dialectic to rhetoric. They were deeply influenced by the study of classical Latin and Stoic logic and reacted against the abstraction and artificiality of mediaeval Aristotelianism. For this line of thinkers language and insight were intimately and naturally connected, so that they pursued the study of language not merely for its literary and cultural values but as an independent science, in the rather naive belief that the investigation of the proprieties of terms, the connections and patterns of linguistic discourse, would lead to the disclosure of the meaning of things. This was an attempt to heal the breach between language and being that resulted from extreme nominalism. Emphases varied, some were more inclined to employ aesthetic categories and others posited a natural propriety between language and things signified but they combined in the view that the independent investigation of language could yield discovery or *inventio*. A further development in the same direction, but in a more formalistic and

Aristotelian way, is found in the work of the notorious Pierre Ramée who took up teaching in the Collège Royal ten years after Major left Paris for St Andrews. Ramist logic became very fashionable in the later sixteenth century and had a really bad effect on 'Calvinism'.

The second line is that taken by the literary humanists, who were more concerned with the relation of language to culture, and most notably by Erasmus who, like Calvin, had been a scholar of Montaigu. Erasmus took up Ockham's doctrine of intention but gave it a more psychological and moral turn. That is to say, he sought to interpret literature by penetrating into the intentions of the authors or into their states of soul. But since Erasmus' interest was primarily in language, this meant for him the primacy of second intentions and the pursuit of oblique meaning. He was content therefore to treat language on the level of suppositional meaning, in detachment from its objective reference, where he did not have to face up to the challenge of direct intuitive knowledge of the Truth. Hence Erasmus was ready on the one hand to rest in an unquestioned fideism, accepting his doctrinal beliefs uncritically from an authoritarian Church, while being ready on the other hand to relate the traditional Scriptures and doctrines to a new moral inwardness interpreted as their final intentions. That is why Erasmus could never bring himself to be greatly concerned for doctrinal questions, nor indeed for their natural or direct signification. All that really mattered is that they should supposit for inward moral experience.

Now it is of great interest to note that during his early life when he was still 'stubbornly addicted' to Roman fideism Calvin pursued a line which combined both these tendencies. That is the way in which I understand his Commentary on Seneca's *De Clementia*, in which the influence of both Valla and Erasmus is very apparent. This was an attempt in a humanist way to heal the breach between language and being and to overcome the frigid sophistry in which he had been brought up, particularly by employing the aesthetic notion of the *propriety* of language. As we know this proved quite futile, for in spite of all his moral earnestness and love of humanist scholarship it left him cold and without conviction. What did remain was his feeling for language clearly registered in his development of Augustan Latin. On the other hand, as soon as Calvin came up against the sheer Majesty of God in his Word he became deeply conscious of *impropriety* in human speech about God, and was forced to think more profoundly of the relation of language to being. At this point John Major helped Calvin once more for it was through Major that Calvin had been introduced to the reflections of Hilary, Athanasius and Basil on this very subject.

As soon as Calvin threw in his lot with the Reformation, he is to be found taking quite a different line from that of Ockham, Valla or Erasmus, namely, that we do have *direct intuitive knowledge of God in his Word*. This involved a rejection both of nominalism and realism, and a decided reorientation in his thinking in which the centre of gravity was shifted from the subjective to the objective pole of intuitive knowledge, but it also involved a new interpretation of language in which it is subordinated to the objective realities it serves. These two elements were supplied by the doctrines of justification by grace or election, and of the mighty living Word of God which sounds through the Scriptures enabling us to hear and apprehend God speaking to us in person.

My concern here is not with the material content of Calvin's re-formed theology, but with the way in which he worked out his view of the knowledge of God over against Ockhamist epistemology, and with the important implications of what he had to say in this respect not only for theological science but for all scientific knowledge.

We shall have to restrict our discussion to three main aspects of Calvin's thought: the intuitive character of theological knowledge, the relation of human speech to the divine Being, and the epistemological implications of the doctrine of the Spirit.

1. In the Christian faith we are concerned with intuitive evident knowledge of God through his Word. We recall that intuitive knowledge was defined as direct knowledge of an actually present object, naturally caused by that object and not by another. This was the kind of knowledge which since Ockham and Buridan was recognized as the knowledge that is gained experimentally. One of the constantly re-peated expressions in Major's lectures was *experientia docet*. After his conversion that was the way in which Calvin regarded knowledge of God, knowledge gained in the immediate experience of his personal presence. Intuitive knowledge of God arises, then, to use the old terminology, under the direct impact or causality of his divine Being. This involved the rejection both of Thomism and Ockhamism. If, as St Thomas taught, our knowledge of God is taken from sense-experi-ence of created realities, it will never be able to rise above created realities and can only construe God in accordance with them. But if, as Ockham taught, abstractive knowledge abstracts from actual existence, then abstractive knowledge prevents us from knowing God in accord-

ance with his own personal mode of Being. We know God, Calvin insisted, through his works or effects, but in his works or effects we meet God speaking to us personally through his Word. This is what Calvin called intuitive knowledge of God, but it is different from our intuitive knowledge of natural objects, for it is a knowledge in accordance with the nature and personal Being of God.

An examination of Calvin's language shows that he was indebted through John Major to Duns Scotus at two points of primary significance.

(*a*) Knowledge of God in accordance with his own essence must be through the willed activity of God in which he manifests himself to us through his effects. There are, according to Duns Scotus, two kinds of objects, a natural object and a voluntary or supernatural object. The natural object is known by the mind of man necessarily through the mode of causality. But God is not given to the human intellect in that way, like a determinate object of nature. The voluntary object, however, is known through its willed activity. That is the way in which we know God, for all knowledge of God is contingent upon his Will. Hence when man knows God a moment of the will is involved, on the part of God manifesting himself, and on the part of man in responsive obedience.

Unlike Scotus, and certainly unlike Ockham, however, Calvin held to the primacy of the intellect over the will, so that he was unable to conceive of this knowledge of God in any arbitrary way, reposing upon the inscrutability of God. Hence within the relationship of knowing set up by the willed activity of God and the willing response of man, the intellect cannot but assent to the truths of God which it apprehends when it encounters the divine Reality in his self-manifestation. This is a point of capital significance. In knowledge of God there is a moment of freedom and yet a moment of compulsion. We do not *have to* know God as we have to know natural objects when we cognize them, but when we do reach knowledge of God we know him only under the compulsion of his *Veritas* upon our minds.

(*b*) The second point that Calvin appears to owe to Duns Scotus and also to Richard of St Victor, arises out of their critique of the Boethian notion of personality, and of their identification of the divine Essence and Existence in the Person (or Persons) of God. God is personal in his own mode of Being involving all his existence and acts. The notion of person here is at once a relational and an ontological notion, for the relationship is not just a determination of our understanding but an inherent and ontic determination of personal existence.

Now knowledge of God, like all true knowledge, is determined by the nature of what is known, and so knowledge of this personal God is determined by his nature as personal Being. Here we have a real and actual relation to God as object, but one that involves in the act of knowing an essentially personal relation. God thus comes to us as One who encounters us in his own incommunicable personal Being, but who wills to reveal himself to us, so that we on our part are placed in a position where obedience is required of us, a movement of the will in which we freely yield our understanding to his Truth and come under the compulsion of his divine Being. As Duns Scotus expressed it, God is *volens et agens* in his relation to us, and that results on our side, as we respond to him, in an *aptitudo obedientiae*. This is the point that Calvin makes when he insists that all true knowledge of God arises out of obedience—freedom, compulsion, personal relation are all involved in our knowledge of God.

These notions, and indeed the language in which they were conveyed, were mediated to Calvin not only through John Major but also through the *devotio moderna* upon which Scotist teaching had left such an impact. It is well known that Calvin's statements are saturated at many points with the language of the *De Imitatione Christi* of Thomas à Kempis, but the distinctive feature of Calvin's use of that is the way in which it is related to his doctrine of intuitive knowledge of God in his personal Being.

Calvin also allows himself to use the language of *evidence* in speaking of this knowledge. In what sense are we to understand that? The evidence of God is not like the evidence we have in our knowledge of natural objects, evidence that arises directly out of natural causality and out of the necessary connections of our thinking and inferring about determinate objects. The kind of evidence we have in regard to God is the evidence of ultimate Reality ($\alpha\dot{\upsilon}\tau o\upsilon\sigma\acute{\iota}\alpha$), which in the nature of the case is self-evidence, the self-authentication of the highest Authority. It would be irrational to ask for some authority for believing in the Highest Authority other than the Highest Authority or higher than It. So with the kind of evidence we have in the knowledge of God, which derives immediately from the impact of his Being as he gives himself to us to be known. This is bound up with Calvin's doctrine of the Spirit and of the kind of recognition created in us by the power of the Spirit, to which we shall turn shortly. Meantime we note that for Calvin intuitive knowledge is one in which we are thrown upon the objective reality of God himself, beyond us, independent of ourselves. We know the truth out of the Truth himself, and in accordance with God's own witness to himself—hence our grounds for statements about the truth of God are grounds that the Truth itself provides. We know God only on his own ground. And if he is God, then as God he comes absolutely first. That is the epistemological aspect of Calvin's doctrine of election which we also find in John Major. The absolute priority and objectivity of God is the ground for all genuine knowledge of him.

Now what is so distinctive in Calvin's doctrine of our intuitive knowledge of God is that it is in and through his *Word*. In the language of John Major, it is *intuitiva auditio*, intuitive *auditive* knowledge of God. Major himself failed to think this out to the end, for in the last analysis he tended to lapse back into the Augustinian notion of vision through the lack of the biblical doctrine of the Word that gripped the Reformers.

There are two important elements in Calvin's notion of intuitive auditive knowledge of God that I should like to note.

First, knowledge of God is reached primarily by hearing rather than by seeing. This was of course one of the most characteristic aspects of Luther's teaching—we recall his contrast between *regnum audibile* and *regnum visibile*, and how he used to urge his congregation to stick their eyes in their ears! The same teaching is found earlier in John Reuchlin who derived it from the study of the Hebrew Scriptures and insisted that knowledge of God arises *ex auditu* or *ab auditu*. It was known also to John Major who was one of the commission appointed from the Sorbonne to examine the works of Reuchlin. Even Major insisted on thinking through the problems of perception in our natural knowledge in terms of hearing as well as seeing—this means, as Calvin must have realized through Major's teaching, that the place of vision in our knowledge has but a limited range and that perceptibility cannot be taken as the final criterion of intuitive evident knowledge. There is no point, of course, in rejecting the proper place of vision in theological knowledge, but it cannot be allowed to dissolve away the auditive element which is basic and essential. Even Major rejected the view that the saints in the presence of God have beatific vision apart from his Word. Certainly knowledge of God for man in his pilgrim state, the *viator*, derives from the Word and rests upon the Word. Hence biblical and theological statements are basically *heard-statements* (in German, *Höraussagen*). It is one of the handicaps of Latin that it has no expression for this, so that Calvin had to employ periphrastic ways in which to state it.

The second point about Calvin's doctrine of auditive knowledge I wish to note is his understanding of the ultimate objectivity of the

Word as such in the eternal Being of God. At this point, as Calvin shows himself aware, we are up against an ancient problem that the Church had to face in the Arian controversy and which it answered in the doctrine of the *homoousion*. Is the Word only an immanent cosmological principle, or a determination of the understanding? Is it but a fleeting emanation from God that serves its purpose and then vanishes away into the eternal Light of God? Or is the Word really something that reaches us from the other side of creaturely being, that proceeds out of the very essence of God? Calvin is very clear about the epistemological import of the *homoousion*—the Word is eternal reality and resides as Word in the eternal Being of God himself and proceeds from him without being less God. The Word is in fact God himself speaking to us personally, for he personally resides in his Word even when he communicates it to us.

The radical dichotomy between the *mundus intelligibilis* and the *mundus sensibilis* and the doctrine of the ultimacy of vision in the Augustinian tradition had made the doctrine of the Word problematic. The difficulty was clearly seen by Anselm when he insisted that in the eternal Being of God there remains a *dicere* that cannot be understood by resolving it away simply into *intelligere*. The extent of the mediaeval aberration from the teaching of the Early Church becomes clear when we find Thomas Aquinas criticizing Anselm at this very point, and speaking of the Word in the last resort as a metaphorical expression for the divine understanding. This was a point that both Major and Reuchlin in their different ways attacked in St Thomas. Calvin was not unaware of what was at stake even in his pre-reformation days, but as soon as he wrote the *Institute* we find that he had already returned very decidedly to the teaching of Athanasius and Hilary, and departed from the Origenist and Augustinian notion of the *Logos*. The Word of God which we hear in the Holy Scriptures derives from and reposes on the inner Being of the One God; and that is the objective ground, deep in the eternal Being of God, upon which our knowledge of God rests. In his own eternal Essence God is not mute or dumb, but Word communicating or speaking himself. That is the Word which we hear in the Holy Scriptures, which works or effects in us through the Spirit intuitive, auditive, evident knowledge of God.

What about man's response to this? How are we to think of the relation of human language to the divine Being? That takes us to the second aspect of Calvin's epistemology I have selected for discussion.

2. In theological knowledge we are not engaged in pictorial thinking

of God; i.e. theological language is not descriptive of God. Here we are concerned with the problem of the relationship of thought and language to being, and above all to the divine Being.

In many ways mediaeval realism and nominalism were both attempts to explain how language is related to being. But the more logic was assimilated to language, the more there developed the so-called *logica sermocinalis,* and the more acute this problem became. Hence we find at the close of the Middle Ages and early in the Renaissance, and indeed in the Reformation, renewed study of Plato's dialogues, the *Cratylus* and *Sophistes.* That is apparent in the writings of Reuchlin and Erasmus, Major and Calvin, all of whom were aware that the same problems engaged the attention of many of the fathers. In late mediaeval language, this was the problem of the *propriety of terms* which we have already noted. According to Plato words are images of the realities of things. They are not of course exact reproductions; if they were we would be unable to distinguish between images and the things imaged. The difference between words in different languages is of course due to convention, yet basically, according to Plato, there is a natural, not a conventional relation between speech and the things signified. But Plato hastened to add that the relationship is such that we cannot argue from language to things, even though the relation that subsists between them is mimetic; nevertheless language points to things in such a way that they *show through.* This all-important modification tended to be forgotten in the Middle Ages, but it was not forgotten by the great patristic thinkers, like Athanasius and Hilary, who used it in their rejection of the view that theological language is essentially descriptive. There is a place for images in biblical and theological statements but only as pointers to what cannot be reproduced and is known only through the Word. It was to this patristic teaching that Calvin returned, but he was deeply influenced from two other sources.

(*a*) Through John Major Calvin learned of Ockham's rejection of the doctrine of representative perception and seems like Major to have been deeply influenced by it. In his doctrine of intuitive perception Ockham denied that the mind operates with *media* between it and objects that are somehow copies of those objects. We apprehend objective realities directly not by means of some sensible or intelligible *species in medio.* This view was modified to a certain extent by Major who recognized more than Ockham some place for *species in medio,* but where they do arise, he insisted, our thought does not terminate at the image but at the reality itself which we perceive through and beyond the image.

The language that Calvin uses again and again indicates that he had this in mind when rejecting the notion that we think of God by means of images or pictorial representations of God, but Calvin is more substantially indebted to something else.

(b) This is the biblical teaching which condemns the fabrication of images of God, images of the imagination as well as images of clay or metal. It is at this point that we see how sharply Calvin's thought contrasts with that of Roman and indeed of Lutheran theology, for both Romans and Lutherans rejected the applicability to Christians of the second Commandment on the ground that it was meant only for the Jews. In view of that it is quite startling to find right away in the *Institutio* of 1536 the restoration of the second Commandment with its prohibition of images, together with its epistemological implications fully worked out. The two main points that Calvin is concerned to advocate are the following.

(i) God is not imaginable. All the images we invent are idols of the mind, the products of our own imagination, for God ever remains like himself and is not a spectre or phantasm to be transformed according to our own desires or dreams. It is a fact, however, that the mind of fallen man is a perpetual factory of idols and false conceptions of God, so that he is always projecting his own inventions upon God. This is to say, man is constantly tempted to corrupt the knowledge of the truth through the creations of his own brain. True knowledge of God is objectively derived and cuts against the speculations of the human mind. To employ an interesting and helpful distinction of Major's, true knowledge of God is active (*cognitio activa*), but not factive (*cognitio factiva*). That is to say, while knowledge is certainly a human activity, we do not cognize the Truth of God through our own artificial fabrications, that is through images of our own forming, but only through modes of knowing imposed on us from the nature of God and from his own self-manifestation through the Word.

This does not import the abolition of images in our thought and speech of God, but it does mean that our use of them must be sober and critical, and must be kept within the bounds prescribed by the Word through which God reveals himself to us. Even so, however, the images are not copies or pictorial representations or replicas, but are rather ways of pointing beyond to what is unimaginable though knowable. They are ways adapted by God to our human modes of thought and speech, but not for that reason false, for while they do not represent truth in themselves they allow it to be exhibited as the reality given to us from beyond ourselves. That is to say, images in our thought and speech of God do not have a mimetic but only a signitive relation to divine Truth, and that somehow (*quodammodo*) as they direct us to look at God or rather to listen to him, we allow the divine Truth to break through to us apart from the images. Their function is *ostensive* and *persuasive*, not descriptive.

(ii) Calvin directs a similar argument to ideas as well as images, and so rejects a doctrine of representative apprehension as well as a doctrine of representative perception. It will be remembered that Ockham rejected the notion of intermediary images in intuitive perception, for we perceive objective realities directly under the impact of their causality, and that this was modified by Major who insisted that we look through images at the realities they indicate. But whereas Ockham denied that we have intuitive knowledge of God and so had to fall back upon the abstractive knowledge of communicated ideas, Calvin applied the same rigorous critique to communicated ideas, for abstractive ideas are just as much speculative constructs of our own as the images we produce in our brains. Moreover, we do not think ideas, nor do we think propositions that intervene between our cognizing and the realities we cognize. We think realities and things although we employ ideas and propositions in thought and speech of them. Thus by claiming that we do have intuitive knowledge of God Calvin laid the axe to the whole conception of theology as the systematic correlation of representative ideas, i.e. as a science of abstractive knowledge. We do not operate in Christian theology with 'ideas in the middle', so to speak—abstractive ideas that intervene between us and the divine Reality, and from which we infer knowledge of God or deduce truths about him. While the divine revelation does certainly involve the communication of truths and ideas and propositions, in and through these God speaks to us personally and confronts us with the majesty and dignity of his own Truth. The function of ideas and statements in biblical or dogmatic theology is not to convey creditive ideas detached from the divine existence but to direct us beyond ourselves to the divine Existence and to bring our minds under his Reality. Thus their function is *ostensive* and *persuasive*, not demonstrative.

Two corollaries are to be drawn from all this which are of great significance for our understanding of Calvin's thought.

(*a*) Knowledge of God calls in question and dethrones all idols of the mind. We only know God truly as we allow our own inventions and fictitious presuppositions to be unmasked before the direct disclosure of the Truth of God. Right from the start of Calvin's theological writing, this reference of our knowledge back to God himself, which he called the *analogy of faith*, with its critical questioning of our own prior notions, was seen to be the basic principle of all true knowledge. This is the principle of objectivity in which we allow ourselves to be detached from all preconceptions and prejudgments, that came to exercise such a forceful role in all scientific knowledge immediately after the Reformation.

(b) It is impossible to say in language how language is related to being. Belief that this can or ought to be done was one of the root errors of mediaeval epistemology and hermeneutics, but it is only in intuitive knowledge of God that it really becomes clear that we cannot through language relate language to being, or through thought relate thought to reality—in the nature of the case we cannot pass from ideas to being, or by ideas from what we already know to some unknown reality. All knowledge presupposes the given and operates within the relation set up between the given reality and our knowing of it. This was the point that emerged so clearly from Calvin's insistence that in knowing God we are cast wholly upon his own prior and given *activity* in presenting himself to us, but that snaps any possible argument from our own speculative notions to God himself. This had immense implications for hermeneutics, for it meant, as Calvin learned also from Hilary, that we can never subordinate the *res* to the *sermo* but must always subordinate the *sermo* to the *res* which it serves through its signification of it. This represents, then, a radical rejection of nominalism, and a return to the Anselmic doctrine that faithful interpretation is *secundum rem* and not just *secundum formam vocum*.

It is not difficult to see the relevance of this critique for much contemporary theology which has become obsessed with myths and images and has become entangled in the pseudo-problems that arise from the theory that theological language is essentially descriptive. But here too we can see how close Calvin's way of thinking in theology is to that now being forced upon modern science when it understands its own scientific theories and statements, to use the latest expressions (I. T. Ramsey), as *disclosure models* and not *picturing models*. Of course it cannot be claimed that Calvin originated this way of thinking, for as he himself knew, something very akin to it is to be found in some of the most important writings of the fathers.

3. The third main aspect of Calvin's thought that we are to discuss in relation to our knowledge and speech of God is his doctrine of the

Spirit, the living action and personal presence of God himself among men.

Let us approach it from the same line of thought that we found to lie behind his doctrine of the intuitive knowledge of God, and return to the question of the relation of language to being. How language is related to being cannot be stated in language, yet it does take place, for they are related in *action*. Now the relation of language to being takes on a different form in accordance with the nature of being we are concerned with, creaturely being or the Creator source of all being. In this regard the Spirit of God is to be understood as the living action of the Creator upon which we rely for the effective actualization of the relation between language and the divine Being. That is the epistemological relevance of the doctrine of the Spirit for Calvin's theology. No work of ours can establish a bridge between our understanding and the Truth of God. Knowledge of God is in accordance with his nature as Spirit, and takes its rise from his living personal action upon us. The relation between our statements about God and God himself in his own Truth is not one that we can create or describe in statements, but one that we can only allow to happen to us and which we accept in yielding our minds and speech obediently and gratefully to his revealing and saving acts. Christian theology is therefore ultimately a *scientia practica*. Full place for that divine *action* must be given in any true account of theological knowledge.

The action of God is the action of his Holy Spirit, the unique causality of his Being as he presents himself to us as the object of our knowledge—but it is a unique causality determined by the nature of God as Creator Spirit and as grace. This action takes the form of Word and of personal communion—Word establishing the relation between our language and God's Being, and personalizing presence establishing man as a person whom God takes into communion with himself. It is through the Word and the Spirit that God sets up the relation of knowledge between man and God which we speak of as involving subject-object, yet I-Thou relation. There are several elements in this way of regarding our knowledge of God and our speech about him that require to be drawn out further.

(i) It is the Spirit who provides *transparence* in our knowledge and language of God. In all acts of knowledge we employ forms, cognitive forms, mental forms, language forms, linguistic and eidetic images, etc., and these forms are naturally taken from our structured relations with the creaturely world around us, the world of perception and cognition and the world of immediate and personal experience. In themselves these forms are opaque for we cannot argue from the forms themselves to the realities we cognize through them. That is even more the case in our relations to God, for creaturely forms have in themselves only creaturely reference and are particularly opaque when used for knowledge and speech of God even when they are stretched to the breaking-point or as Calvin would say to the point of impropriety beyond their natural usage. Now the Holy Spirit is the living divine action through which these forms when appropriated for the operation of his Word, are made transparent, the action in which the reality we seek shines through, or as Calvin prefers to express it, in which the Word *sounds through* (*per-sonare*) to us.

Consider the Holy Scripture. Apart from the Spirit its cognitive and linguistic forms are quite opaque, but through the Spirit they are made to direct us away from them to God himself. Apart from this action of the Spirit the Truth of God does not break through to us and we do not break through the linguistic forms employed in the Scriptures to experience or feel or sense (Calvin uses all these terms) the living God himself. This action of the Spirit in making the Scriptures transparent for us results in what he called the *perspicuity* of the Scripture. It is not a quality inherent in the Scripture itself, but what happens to interpretation of them under the action of the Spirit. Neglect of the Spirit, therefore, leads to the suppression or evasion of the Reality of God and the transmutation of knowledge into our own constructs and so the translation of all theological problems into psychological or linguistic problems. It would involve the fatal mistake of confounding in theology language with being or imagining that we can state in language the relation of language to being—that is, the Being of God. The presence of the Holy Spirit disrupts that, for he makes the content of what is revealed burst through the forms employed so that our acts of cognition are formed from beyond us by the reality disclosed in the very act of disclosure.

This takes us to our second point.

(ii) The doctrine of the Spirit does not mean that theological knowledge is basically non-conceptual and requires to be converted into concepts if it is to be rational, as, for example, Paul Tillich teaches. On the contrary the Spirit means that our knowledge derives from and reposes upon an objective rationality inherent in the given Reality known. The Spirit inheres in the Truth, as Calvin puts it. Hence through the Spirit we are given to participate in God's own rationality, in his own self-knowledge or self-witness. The Word we hear through the Spirit is really a Word that resides in the eternal Being of God, and is not just something that necessarily arises as we seek to put into cognitive form what we experience intuitively and directly. As I understand it this is Calvin's doctrine of the *testimonium internum Spiritus Sancti*. By the word *internum* Calvin does not refer primarily to what is internal to us but to what is internal to God himself, to what Anselm called the *locutio intima apud Summam Substantiam*, but because it is God's self-witness inherent in his own Truth it is a witness which he causes to echo within us also as we hear his Word.

In order to make clear what Calvin means let us consider the analogy of *number* and its place in physics. Is number something that we men invent or is it something that we find? Of course all scientific knowledge is a compromise between thought and being. We do not find ready-made equations in nature. We have to form these ourselves, but we do so not by imposing patterns of our own invention on nature but by acting in obedience to the rationality inherent in nature itself. Number thus represents, surely, the most implacably objective element in all natural science. So it is with the *Logos* or Word of God in theology.

Now the kind of statements we make in mathematics in which we echo the inherent rationality of the universe, are called by mathematicians themselves *recognition-statements*. Recognition-statements are not basically human constructs, for they derive from beyond ourselves and arise out of an obedient relation to the pattern and order of objective reality. *Mutatis mutandis*, that is the nature of our basic theological statements: they arise by way of recognition or acknowledgment; that is, the kind of knowing in which our minds fall under the compulsive impact of what they seek to know and are obedient to what is known in accordance with its own inherent witness and order. This is what John Major meant when he spoke of theological knowledge as *active* but not *factive*, but whereas Major deliberately rejected the term *agnitio* as appropriate here Calvin just as deliberately accepted it and made it central. There is of course a great difference between the Reality we recognize in theological knowledge and that which we recognize in natural knowledge, for the object of theological knowledge is not a *dumb idol*, it is not a mute but an eloquent Reality, God speaking in person, so that here the expression *recognition-statements* is even more appropriate than it is in mathematics.

It is through the Spirit that this takes place, in his testifying of God and in his action upon us. Hence in forming our acts of cognition we

have to do with the Spirit of Truth who resists the forms we bring to
him and by the sheer impact of the objective truth of God upon us, our
forms of thought and speech are opened up and reshaped from an
objective ground in God. That is what takes place in the Holy Scripture
and what continually takes place as we yield our minds to the action of
the Spirit of Truth in interpreting them. It is in and through this action
of the Spirit of God, therefore, that we learn to distinguish the objective
Reality of God himself from our own subjective states and conditions,
and the truths of God from our own mental constructs or speculative
concepts, precisely because through the Spirit we are carried beyond
the cognitive forms we employ, and so easily manipulate as we will,
into the inexhaustible nature of the truth of God and are really opened
up for him.

Here there takes place in a unique way something that is characteristic
of all knowledge, for in all relation of thought and language to being we
are up against something that is inexhaustible, that is, something that
remains transcendent and resistant so far as our knowledge is concerned,
and something that can never be subdued to our statements. This is
what is forced upon us in the severe limitation which modern science
puts upon 'picturing models' in favour of 'disclosure models': all forms
of description are finite and limited and are incapable of carrying our
thought into anything like an adequate relation of thought to being. It
is for this reason that scientific constructs or theories have to be kept
indefinitely open if they are to serve advance in knowledge. This is the
aspect that comes out so strongly, of course with all the difference that
knowledge of God involves, in the way in which Calvin relates the
Spirit of God to our cognitive forms, for through the Spirit we are cast
upon the inexhaustible Reality of God in an infinite depth of objectivity.
Here we could easily get lost and swallowed up as in a labyrinth, he says,
unless we follow the 'line' or 'thread' of the Word, but here also we find
a depth of knowledge with an indefinite range of enlightenment in all
things relating to God and ourselves.

Calvin's doctrine of the Spirit, and especially the *testimonium internum
Spiritus Sancti*, met with considerable misunderstanding and distortion
after the Reformation, when humanist, pietist and Cartesian thought
gained the ascendency. Then the Spirit was interpreted in a subjective
way, whereas in Calvin's thought the Spirit stands for the ultimate
majesty of God, the ultimate objectivity in which we are carried over
from ourselves to knowledge of God out of God, and not out of ourselves. The testimony of the Spirit is essentially that which inheres in

the objective truth of God, and when it echoes in our hearts it directs them away from themselves to God in his own eternal Being.

(iii) The Holy Spirit is God's creative personal presence among men. In him we come up against the truth in the form of personal Being, God speaking to us in Person, who is himself in his own personal nature the Word he speaks to us.

It is at this point that we see, in some respects, the transition from mediaeval to modern thought most clearly, that is, the transition from a dialectical to a dialogical mode of thinking, and from thinking of the relations of ideas to thinking of personal objectivity or transcendence. Because the Spirit of God is God's personal presence and is yet God's living creative action, his impact upon us creates personal relations, posits us as subjects over against the divine Subject, and at the same time gives us God as the Object of our knowing in such a way that God remains in control by presiding in all our judgments about him. Therein lies his implacable objectivity even when we are personally and intimately related to him through the Communion of the Spirit.

Now knowledge of God in this personal relation involves the impingement of will upon will (as we have already noted), and so there arise questions of reconciliation, freedom and obedience. The need for reconciliation between man and the Truth of God is doubtless a distinctive characteristic of theological knowledge. It is therefore quite appropriate that in the Apostles' Creed the forgiveness of sins should come in the articles of belief in the Spirit. The problem of freedom is really the problem of self-will. Of course we are free in our wills—all men have and exercise *voluntas*, as Calvin says, but the free-will of man is his *self-will* and man is not free to escape from his self-will. If we are really to know God truly we must be emancipated from self-will for self-will determines *de profundis* all our own ways of knowing and thinking. We need a truth that will set us free from ourselves, otherwise we ourselves with all our preconceptions, prejudgments and inventions, will distort knowledge of God and from the very start convert it into untruth. It is here again that Calvin sees the action of the Spirit upon us, for through the Spirit we are involved in a reconstruction of our prior understanding and of ourselves as we inhere in our prior understanding. This is the point at which Calvin begins his *Institute*, both in the preface to Francis I and in the opening sections where he writes of the relation between the knowledge of God and the knowledge of ourselves. How very modern Calvin sounds here, for he gives the human person its full place in theology and yet in the midst of this vivid personalism, and the mutuality between God and man that it involves, the stress is emphatically and clearly upon the majesty and truth of God. In our personal relations with God and in the very act of faith we engage in a movement of the mind in which we presume everything of God and nothing of ourselves, so that from beginning to end it involves us in a reshaping of the self and a reconstructing of our prior understanding. Thus one of the outstanding marks of Calvin's theology is that he is able to hold *objectivity* and *personalism* closely together, whereas in much modern theology they tend to fall apart with disastrous consequences. As Calvin saw it, it is only when we allow the Truth of God to retain his own majesty in all our knowledge of him, and when we allow God himself to preside in all our judgments about him, that we may be truly personal ourselves and have personal relations with one another, whereas he who ceases in this way to speak with God unlearns even the art of speaking with his neighbour.

6

The Word of God and the Nature of Man[1]

Qui Deum vere colit atque honorat, in hominem contumeliosus esse verebitur.

AT no point is theology more relevant today than in the issues it raises about our knowledge of man. This essay is an attempt to set forth some of these issues, particularly as raised by John Calvin and brought to bear upon the thought of our own day by Karl Barth, against what they both believe to be an unbiblical view of man.

Calvin laid it down from the very start that there can be no true knowledge of man except within our knowledge of God. For this reason, Reformed theology has always been shy about erecting an anthropology, not because it lacked a view of man, but because such a view cannot be enunciated as an independent article of faith as if it could of itself condition or contribute to our knowledge of God. On the other hand, it has always insisted that, unless our knowledge of God strikes home to us in such a way that we come to a true knowledge of ourselves, our knowing of God is not real. 'Therefore it is evident that man never attains to a true self-knowledge until he has previously contemplated the Face of God, and come down after such contemplation to look into himself.'[2] These words 'come down' are important, for they indicate the essential direction and motion of all Christian thought. *In lumine tuo videmus lumen.*[3] They are also important, however, because it is upon this downward motion of God's grace that the very being of man is grounded. Therefore, while a Christian doctrine of man, like every other article of faith, is grounded upon the acknowledgment of a revelation, in this instance the knowledge involved is essentially reflexive, both of a Word of God about himself, and of the creative activity of his love. Thus, what Calvin would have us note at the outset of a doctrine of man

---

[1] Reprinted from *Reformation Old and New*, ed. F. W. Camfield (*Festschrift* for Karl Barth) Lutterworth Press, 1947.
[2] *Inst.* I.1.2.   [3] Ps. 36.9; cf. Calvin, *ad loc.*

is that the direction and motion of our knowing must correspond with the essential direction and motion of grace, for that is the ground of man's existence as a being made to know God. Therefore we must try to formulate a doctrine of man not by an activity which inverts the motion of grace but by an activity which responds to it. Inasmuch as 'man is only an image in regard to God',[1] though to image the glory and grace of God belongs to his true nature as an intelligent being, we may know man truly only in his 'existential' answer to the Word of grace.

Calvin was fond of basing a discussion of the nature of man on the statement of St Paul that as men 'we live and move and have our being' in God.[2] Those words, he said, expressed the three gradations of human existence. We have being in God in the same sense as all other created being; and we have motion or animation in the same sense as other living creatures; but we have a higher life in God proper to us as men, in which life is peculiarly matched to grace.[3] At this point Calvin laid great stress upon the words of St John's Gospel: 'In him was life, and the life was the light of men.'[4] Therefore, in describing the biblical account of creation, Calvin pointed out that man was created in such a way as to be given a special relation to the Word of God upon the communication of which he lives. All things were indeed created by the Word, and maintained in being by the Word, but man's true life consists in an intelligent motion in answer to the action and Word of God's grace. That is man's peculiar dignity, that, being under deeper obligation, he might use his special endowments in thankful acknowledgment of God's gracious self-communication, and that he might devote himself entirely to knowing God, and meditating upon his perfections.[5] In that responsive motion alone does man find his true life and destiny. Calvin has given a particularly clear account of his views here when speaking about the tree of life which was planted in the Garden of Eden. It was the intention of God that 'as often as man tasted of the fruit of that tree, he should remember whence he received his life, in order that he might acknowledge that he lives not by his own power, but by the kindness of God alone; and that life is not (as they commonly say) an intrinsic good, but proceeds from God. . . . The life of all things was included in the Word, but especially the life of men, which is con-

---

[1] Pierre Maury, in *The Christian Understanding of Man* (Oxford Conference series, *The Church, Community, and State*, 1937, pt. II), 1938, p. 252.
[2] Acts 17.28; and Calvin's *Comm. ad loc.*
[3] Calvin, *Serm. on Job* 10.7f.
[4] John 1.4. See Calvin, *ad loc.* and *Serm. on Job* 35.8f.
[5] *Inst.* I.5.9; I.14.21; *Comm. on Acts* 17.27.

joined with reason and intelligence. . . . Wherefore by this sign, Adam was admonished that he could claim nothing for himself as if it were his own, in order that he might depend wholly on the Son of God, and might not seek life anywhere but in him. . . . He possessed life only as deposited in the Word of God, and could not otherwise retain it, than by acknowledging that it was received from him.'[1]

This means that, unlike the other creatures of the world, man lives truly as man only in conscious and thankful relation to the grace of God, and in the consciousness of his own creaturehood. It is here that we see the important part played by self-knowledge in Reformed theology, for it is only when a man knows himself to be a creature utterly dependent on the grace of God that he is able in his knowledge of God so to live in a thankful fashion corresponding with the motion of grace that he reflects in the mirror of his intelligent life the glory of God. That is man's chief end and true felicity. We may state this in other words by saying that man has been created an intelligent being in order to know God in such a way that in the act of knowing man is brought to re-live consciously, and in a qualitatively different fashion, the very movement of grace in which he is created and maintained in being, so as to be carried beyond himself in responsible union with God in whom he finds his true life and felicity.

Of supreme importance here is the interwovenness of the knowledge of God and the knowledge of self, for therein consists man's life. Man is made to know God, so that he is not truly man unless he knows God. His whole manhood depends not only upon the grace of God in creation, but upon such a communication of his Word of grace that the image of God becomes engraved, as Calvin said, on his person.[2] But we do not know God truly unless we know that our knowing is due to God alone; we must be able to trace the light back to its source in God, realizing that in so doing we are brought into immediate relation to the very fountain of Life. Otherwise the light shines in the darkness, and the darkness comprehends it not; but no man can be said to *live*, in the proper sense of the word, in that condition. True knowledge involves in the very act of knowing an acknowledgment that the Known is the Master of our life and that we depend entirely upon his grace in our being and knowing, and, as such, it carries with it a profound knowledge of self. It is not that the knowledge of self is in any sense a precondition of the knowledge of God, but that the knowledge of God has not really come home to us unless it has brought to us, in the realization of our

---

[1] *Comm. on Gen.* 2.9.   [2] *Comm. on Gen.*, Introd. Argument.

utter dependence on the grace of God, a true knowledge of our own creaturehood. Therefore, we may say, man has been made in such a way that he is not truly man except in the realization of his creaturely dependence on the grace of God, and that he cannot retain his life except in a motion of thankful acknowledgment of the sheer grace of God as Creator and Father in whose Word man's life is deposited, and in the continuous communication of which alone may life be possessed. Nothing is more characteristic of historic Reformed theology, and especially of John Calvin, than this overwhelming sense of the grace of God, and the note of unbounded thanksgiving as the true life-answer of created man to the Father. The whole of the Reformed doctrine of man is set forth in this context of grace and thanksgiving.

It is in its teaching about the *imago dei* that Reformed theology sets forth its doctrine of the creaturehood of man and his relation to God; but that, in the nature of the case, can be done only from the standpoint of the man renewed in Jesus Christ. If man does not truly know himself until he knows God truly, and until in that knowledge he becomes a true man, then it is only from the standpoint of renewed man, face to face with God in Christ, that we may understand the significance of the fact that man is made in the image of God. Moreover, the coming of God in Christ, and his self-communication to man, have taken such a form in the Incarnation, that it is there only that we may see human nature set forth in its truth as creature made to be the child of the heavenly Father. Thus there can be no question of trying to understand man out of himself, or from his relation to the world. He must be understood primarily from the Word made flesh. It is as we behold the Word made flesh to be the glory of the only-begotten of the Father, full of grace and truth, that we know not only that we are called to be the sons of God, but that our relation as sons to the Father rests, not on the will of man, but in faith on the will and power of God alone. The *imago dei* interpreted in this light carries the Reformed view of man.

Man is a creature in total dependence of being, and motion, and life, upon the gracious will of God. He is created out of nothing, and has neither origin nor being in himself, but is given being, and maintained in being, by the grace of God. In relation to God, therefore, man is only an image. That is to say, his life is absolutely reflexive of the action of God, and can be lived only in a motion of continued reflection. This is a very important point in the Reformed doctrine of man, for it is just here that a decisive break is made with the Aristotelian man of scholastic theology, in which the living, dynamic relation of man to God is translated into a substantival and logical relation. Calvin was so firm upon this point that he would have nothing to do with secondary causation in theology, and inveighed against the tendency, becoming rampant in his own day, of speaking of *Nature* instead of *God*, thus *falsely transferring to nature what belongs to grace*.[1] Calvin's view of creation, and of the fallen world, was deeply biblical and Hebraic in his insistence that everything created and worldly had to be related to the direct action of the gracious will of God. It was only after his day, when the mighty genius of Thomas Aquinas began to be felt, that the Reformed doctrine of man became hardened, and lost its essentially Reformed character. Then there came into being that strange amalgamation of Thomist logic and the Reformation view of man which came, unfortunately, to be known as 'Calvinism'. It is Karl Barth who has called Reformed theology back to its true position by insisting once again that we view man exclusively in the context of grace and the will of God in the sense of the Bible.

It is a mistake to think that Calvin believed in the primacy of the will, for he expressly repudiated the idea. On the other hand, he did not regard the will as an intellectual fiction, as it was apt to be regarded in the Aristotelian tradition. He gave it a significant place in his theology, and nowhere more so than in his doctrine of man. The creation was not just the utterance of a rational fiat upon the part of God, which then left created being with an existence in itself, even if it was a derived existence. He thought of creation as continuous and as continually depending on the communication of the divine Word, in such a way that it was maintained in being, and governed by immediate relation to the will of God. Man is a created being, in body and soul, utterly dependent from moment to moment, though not in any atomistic fashion, upon the gracious will of God to create him, which refuses to allow God's original intention to be set aside even by the contradiction of sin. So closely did Calvin think of man's being as bound up with the will of God, that he said man would simply cease to exist if God were in any sense to withdraw his Spirit from him. Man depends from moment to moment on the grace of God as willing his existence. In this sense, Calvin used to think of man as being consumed and renewed every instant of his existence, for he was continuously being called out of nonbeing into being and life by the Word and will of the Creator, the Lord

[1] *Inst.* I.5.1; I.16.6; II.2.1, 27; *The True Method of Giving Peace and of Reforming the Church*—Calvin's *Tracts and Treatises* (Oliver and Boyd, 1958), vol. 3, p. 243.

of life and death. Thus, the Spirit of God must be regarded as present to all existing things, maintaining them in existence, even in the case of the wicked and the reprobate. All creaturely endowments, such as wisdom, and craftsmanship, come directly as gifts from God, whether in the instance of unbelievers or of believers. All being and motion and life, wherever found, are due to the immediate action of the Spirit of God. Karl Barth has expressed this continual relation of the creature to the Creator very memorably in his teaching about the Holy Spirit. 'The Holy Spirit is God Himself in so far as He is able, in an inconceivably real way, without being less God, to be present to the creature, and in virtue of this presence of His to realize the relation of the creature towards Himself, and in virtue of this relation to vouchsafe life to the creature. The creature requires the Creator in order to live. He thus requires relation to Him. But this relation he cannot create. God creates it through His presence to the creature, i.e. in the form of a relation of Himself to Himself. The Spirit of God is God Himself in His freedom to be present to the creature, and so to create this relation, and thereby to be the life of the creature.'[1]

That can be said of any living creature, but the distinctive thing about man is that he was created in order to enjoy this relation in a conscious and intelligent fashion. And so, according to Calvin, man gets no profit from the presence of the Spirit except through the Word;[2] but he was created to that very end, with a special duty to give ear to the Word in which his life was deposited,[3] and in the hearing and acknowledgment of which he finds his true life as man, which is a life qualitatively different from that of mere creaturehood. He is thus a creature in the image of God, who knows that he is but a creature with no life in himself, and who also knows that God has not only called him into being, but has set his love upon him in order to assume him into the divine fellowship as a child of the heavenly Father. Since we may only worship God willingly, man can retain his life in the Word only by a continuous thankful acknowledgment of this gracious calling of God which carries with it the confession of his creaturehood. Thus he can presume upon nothing in himself, and arrogate nothing of life or endowment to himself as if it were his own, and not the pure gift of God.[4] That is the meaning of *imago dei* in Reformed theology. It is not a doctrine about man's being in himself, but rather an acknowledgment that he depends en-

---

[1] *Church Dogmatics* I/1, pp. 515f.
[2] *Inst.* I.9.2f.
[3] *Inst.* I.6.2; I.15.6.
[4] *Inst.* II.2.1; II.2.10; *Comm. on Gen.* 2.9; 3.6; *Serm. on Job* 28.10f.

tirely upon the will of Another, whose grace and truth he images in a knowledgeable and obedient relation to the Word of grace. The *imago dei*, according to Calvin, consists essentially in the objective act of grace by which God sets his love upon man, and communicates to him, created with intelligence, his Word accommodated to his creaturely capacity.[1] Thus the *imago dei* is grounded in the divine will to create man in fellowship with himself, and that original intention remains, no matter what happens.[2] Were it not to remain, man would simply pass out of existence as man.

The objective basis of the *imago dei* lies, therefore, in the grace of God, but man was made an intelligent being for fellowship with God in order that he might conform to the will and Word of God. This conformity of man is the imprinting of the *imago dei* on his person, as the Holy Spirit 'with a wondrous and special energy forms the ear to hear, and the mind to understand' God.[3] And so the *imago dei* is the conscious but creaturely reflection in man of the Word and grace of God—that is, the *imago dei*, in its subjective sense, is regarded as man's witness to the grace of God, and such a witness that the power and substance of it lie in the object witnessed to, and not in the witness itself. The strength of the *imago dei* and its continued maintenance in the believer lie in the Word of grace, and not in the soul. The *imago* has to do with man's being renewed in the spirit of his mind when it becomes formed to the Word by the *testimonium internum Spiritus Sancti*. In other words, it is lodged in man's thankful acknowledgment of God's grace in setting his fatherly favour upon him and choosing him to be a child of his love. But, as such, it is essentially a supernatural gift grounded in grace and possessed only in faith. It is not that which God has put into us by nature, but that which he has put into us by grace.[4] It has not first to do with our imaging God, but with God's beholding the work of his grace in us, and our consequent response to his beholding or his knowing of us, in thankfulness. Only thus can we image the glory of God, and only thus can we be men in the image of God.

This means that Reformed theology decisively repudiated the idea of St Augustine that 'in the mind itself, even before it is a partaker of God, his image is found'.[5] In calling this Augustinian doctrine the discovery of antichrist, Karl Barth is closely following in the steps of John Calvin and the Reformers who asserted that the attempt by man to take advan-

---

[1] *Comm. on Ex.* 33.19f.; *on John* 5.37; *on Rom.* 1.19; *on I Peter* 1.21; *Inst.* II.6.4.
[2] *Comm. on Gen.* 9.6.   [3] *Inst.* II.2.20f.
[4] *Serm. on Job* 10.7f., concluding prayer.   [5] *De Trin.* XIV.8.

tage of his imago-dependence on God, arrogating the image of God to himself as if it were a natural possession of his own being, was the very root motion of original sin suggested by the whisper of the serpent to our first parents. Ever since, said Calvin, this has continued to be the irrepressible source of all idolatry, for whatever man's reason conceives of God in this way is mere falsehood.[1] Once again this has become a living issue. What is at stake is the biblical view of grace, and the biblical account of the dynamic relation between man and God.

The next point to be discussed in any doctrine of man is the question of depravity. Here, again, Reformed theology starts from the fact of grace, and forms its judgment upon man's present depravity only as a corollary of the doctrine of grace. The revelation of the grace of God in Christ, which results in a new creation, carries with it a total judgment upon the natural man, including his mind and will. The fact that man must receive in faith his salvation, his true life, his righteousness, and wisdom, from outside of himself in Christ alone, carries with it the inference that, in himself, man has been utterly deprived of the *imago dei* wherein his life consists. That is the great Reformed inference from grace which forms the basis of the doctrine of sin. And it is just because faith must speak of salvation and forgiveness in total terms that it must also speak of sin and depravity in total terms. But it is only within the context of grace, and on the ground of grace, that we have any right to make such a total judgment upon man as he is—that is, it is only in the event of the new creation that we set aside the old man and all that pertains to him as having come under the total judgment of the Cross. It is important that this should be emphasized today, because the Reformed judgment on man's total depravity has been much misunderstood. Calvin himself often issued warnings against this sort of misunderstanding when he insisted that: 'God does not delight in the degradation of man.'[2] Apart from the judgment of grace there can be only an unhealthy knowledge of human depravity which is not only misanthropic but an insult to the Creator.[3] When grace is taken seriously it must be maintained that even the sinner who contradicts the grace of God is maintained in being by the same grace, while all his endowments and virtues are themselves directly due to the Spirit of God. The total judgment of grace, therefore, does not indicate a judgment upon these, in themselves, but means that they have been wholly polluted in the

---

[1] *Comm. on Ex.* 32.1.
[2] *Comm. on Gen.* 1.26; cf. *on I Cor.* 1.31; *Inst.* II.2.15; III.2.25.
[3] No one has spoken more forcibly on this view than Karl Barth: *Credo*, 1936, pp. 43f.; *Church Dogmatics* I/1, p. 466.

active perversity by which the sinner is mastered. Grace indicates that the whole relation between man and God, called the *imago dei*, has been perverted into its opposite, so that the truth of God is turned into a lie, and the glory of God into dishonour.[1]

This is a total judgment in the sense of the dynamic relation which Reformed theology thinks of as between man and God; but such a total judgment would be utterly impossible on the scholastic view of man, and of evil defined as negation, and as involving necessarily privation of being. Total depravity does not entail on the Reformed view any ontological break in man's relation with God, but it does mean that the essential relation in which true human nature is grounded has been utterly perverted and turned into its opposite. Thus, it views 'sin as properly of the mind',[2] and thinks of it as an active perversity which drags the whole man into pollution and inverts the whole order of creation. Sin in such a total affair that it suborns the good gifts of God, and indeed the whole man, who is maintained in being by the very grace of God, and directs man into an active relation of enmity to God. That is the astonishing revelation of sin which is given in the Gospel. By refusing to let man go, and therefore fall back into nonbeing, the grace of God, in an event of inconceivable kindness, by holding on to its original intention for man, and by holding on to man himself, actually maintains him in the impossible existence of a sinner, in order at last to save him by the total judgment and forgiveness of God enacted in Christ Jesus and inserted into his life by the Cross.

This impossible situation of the sinner in active perversity against the will of God, and yet maintained in being by the mercy of God, is set forth in the doctrine of the Law. The Law indicates that God's original intention for man, which is the law of his being, is not dropped, but it is maintained in spite of the Fall of man. Now that he has fallen, however, it becomes man's judgment. That means that the *imago dei* was not dragged down by the Fall and made a prisoner of man's fallen nature, so that it might be manipulated by human thought or action within the abstraction of the world fallen from God; but it continues to hang over man as a destiny which he can realize no longer, and as a judgment upon his actual state of perversity. Wherefore, inasmuch as the *imago dei*, in the words of Calvin, is comprehended in the Law,[3] for God will not forgo his original intention any more than he will contradict his own

[1] Calvin's expression is that the *imago Dei est tournée en son opprobre*, *Serm. on Job* 33.1f.
[2] *Comm. on Rom.* 2.1; cf. *Serm on Eph.* 2.1f.; 4.17-26.
[3] *Inst.* III.6.1.

glory for which he created man, we must treat our fellow men as made in the image of God, even though we see nothing in them but perversity. That we must do if we continue to acknowledge God's grace and creative intention toward man.

The very essence of sin, according to Calvin, is ingratitude. That is to say, instead of a thankful acknowledgment of God's grace, and of his creaturely dependence on it, wherein consists the *imago dei*, man has ungratefully presumed upon his relation to God, as made in God's image, and arrogated it to his own being. Sin, as the motion contradictory to grace, perverts man's relation to God into the exact contrary to the *imago dei*. Regarding the matter thus, Reformed theology cannot but talk in terms of total depravity or perversity, and, to be consistent, cannot talk about there remaining in fallen man, as such, any portion of the *imago dei*. If the *imago dei* is a dynamic *imago* corresponding to grace, then sin which is active perversity, blots out the *imago dei* in man, though it cannot alter in one iota God's gracious intention by which man is still grasped in the hand of God. Fallen man is utterly corrupt inasmuch as he is mastered by the contradiction of sin, which, just because it opposes the grace of God, means the obliteration of the *imago dei* in man. No doubt he has been formed in God's image (*ad imaginem Dei*), but, now that he is fallen, this is not something that lies behind him and which can be passed on by human effort or by ancestral inheritance; rather does it lie in front of him as a destiny which he cannot achieve.[1] In other words, the fall of man means that the *imago dei* can be interpreted only in eschatological terms; certainly not in terms of natural inheritance, as if the grace of God could be bound to the perverted order of nature.[2] Thus, although God refuses to let go his original intention of grace enshrined in the conception of the *imago dei*, yet he 'complains that the order appointed by him has been so greatly disturbed that his own image has been transformed into flesh. . . . God gives the name of flesh as a mark of ignominy to men, whom he, nevertheless, had formed in his own image. . . . Indeed, the whole man is naturally flesh until by the grace of regeneration he begins to be spiritual.'[3] 'It was a sad and horrible spectacle that he in whom recently the glory of the divine image was shining, should lie hidden under fetid skins to cover his own disgrace, and that there should be more comeliness in a dead animal than in a living man!'[4]

Nevertheless, fallen man continues in his original sin—making more

[1] *Comm. on Rom.* 5.12; on *I Cor.* 15.45; *Serm. on Job* 14.1f.; 33.1f.; 39.8f.
[2] *Comm. on Gen.* 48.17.   [3] *Comm. on Gen.* 6.3.   [4] *Comm. on Gen.* 3.22.

out of the *imago dei* than he ought. He continues to sin against the Word and Law of God in trying to lay hold upon the *imago dei* as comprehended in the Law and arrogating it to himself, thus turning himself into a thorough hypocrite by pretending that the Law of God is his own higher nature. This hypocrisy on the part of the carnal man, itself the very motion of sin, is devastatingly exposed at the Cross, where man finds that all efforts at self-justification are in enmity to God, and where justification by grace alone declares in no uncertain terms that fallen man is utterly destitute of *justitia originalis* or *imago dei*. It must be imputed by free grace. 'Have we it through our own effort? Have we it by inheritance from our ancestors? No—but we have it by God's free gift through his own mere goodness.'[1] Thus, the original intention of God becomes event in man's existence only by the Word, and the *imago* is possessed only in faith and hope until we see Christ as he is and become like him. In Christ, therefore, we see the *Imago Dei* to be the ground of our existence beyond our existence, but which becomes sacramental event here and now in the hearing of faith, as we are sealed with the Holy Spirit until the redemption of the purchased possession.

We come now to the problem of natural theology, and here, too, it must be emphasized, Reformed theology takes its stand only within the inference from grace. When we come to know God in the Face of Jesus Christ, we know that we have not seen that Face elsewhere, and could not see it elsehow. Christ is the Way, the Truth, and the Life, and there is no door, nor way leading to the Father but by him. And so the natural wisdom of the world about God is made foolishness at the Cross, and our natural knowledge is completely set aside by the new creation. Christ was not given to us, said Calvin, in order 'to fill up or eke out our wisdom', but that 'the accomplishment of the whole might be assigned exclusively to him'.[2] But that is known only in the actual event of grace, whereby man is made a new creature in Christ, old things are made to pass away, and all things become new.

Calvin laid great stress in discussing this question on the active perversity of the mind and the will, which he called *concupiscentia*. The very citadel of the mind, he said, had been seized by a sinful motion of pride and self-will, which was nothing else but ingratitude and hostility to grace. Therefore every effort by the natural man to know God, even over against the evident tokens of God's grace manifested in the creation of the world, inevitably led him astray; so that, from the very first step, he was off the course, and, indeed, fighting against God.

[1] *Serm. on Job* 33.1f.   [2] *Comm. on I Cor.* 1.30; cf. *on Col.* 2.3.

Thus natural theology can do nothing but move in a direction directly away from God, for, by every step it takes, it turns the truth of God into a lie.

In such a dynamic conception of man's relation to God as the Reformers envisaged, there are only two directions attributable to human existence: toward God, or away from him; that is, in a direction corresponding to the motion of grace, or in a direction hostile to it. But grace reveals that the natural man in the very motion of his mind is enmity to God. He is unable to know God, not only because he himself perverts the truth when it confronts him, but because God, who cannot be known against his will, that is, against his gracious self-revelation, will not reveal himself to human self-will and perversity. God does allow, said Calvin, enough light to reach man in his self-will to render him quite inexcusable (for even in disobedience there is an acknowledgment of God), but such that when, in a self-willed motion which refuses to surrender in thankfulness to grace, he attempts to make use of this to his own advantage, God 'blinds' him and delivers him over to a reprobate mind. Reformed theology is quite clear upon the fact that no self-willed or self-propelled motion by unrepentant man can make the slightest progress toward knowing God. In fact, God has laid a 'curse' upon natural knowledge, lest men should know him and still remain in their perversity, so that now natural theology is in reality a bottomless pit in which a man is engulfed more and more in blindness and darkness. 'If the light that is in thee be darkness, how great is that darkness.' 'The light of nature is stifled sooner than take the first step into this deadly abyss',[1] and so 'the natural reason will never direct men to Christ.'[2]

The position of Reformed theology in regard to man's epistemological relation to God is exactly parallel to its position in regard to man's ontological relation to God. We noted above that Calvin, for example, thought of fallen man as maintained in being and maintained in being as a sinner, by the continuous creation of grace, else he would lapse back into sheer nothingness. Hence, we must think of all his natural endowments, reason, skill, etc., as maintained in being by the giving of grace. That means that grace reveals the sinner to have an inconceivable existence in grace itself, though that existence is over against the Law which becomes the challenge of grace accosting man in his sin and laying claim to him in his antagonism for God.

We must think of the natural man's cognitive relation to God in the same way, as maintained in an impossible existence by the same action

---

[1] *Inst.* I.2.24; cf. I.4.1; *Comm. on I Peter* 1.21.   [2] *Comm. on John* 1.5.

of grace, and yet as coming under the total judgment of grace in the event of the Cross and the new creation in Christ. And so Calvin called natural religion a 'shadow religion' over against the manifestation of God,[1] and Karl Barth, who has championed the Reformed rejection of natural theology today, has called it 'the shadow-side' of the Revelation of God.[2] Barth has been seriously misunderstood here, but, in his essential position, he is not different from Calvin. He warns us, for example, that we have no right to deprive the natural man of his natural theology, for it is his only consolation in life and death, and that our rejection of natural theology must not be any kind of metaphysical denial; rather must it be grounded only upon the actual event of grace as setting it completely aside for faith.[3] There is no room whatever for it in a Christian theology, precisely because a Christian theology has to do with a new creation. But, in the event of this revelation, which is our new creation in Christ, we discover that even in our disobedience there was involved an acknowledgment of God, for it was only by God's Word that we were maintained in being as sinners against God. But, in the nature of the case, there is absolutely no road that way to God. There is only one road, by the Cross and the Resurrection of Jesus Christ whereby we are slain and made alive, but slain only in that we are made alive in Christ. The relevance of natural theology lies in the fact that God suspended his righteous judgment on man, and in that merciful suspension of his judgment kept man in being over against his Word, though in such a way that man could not realize his destiny of himself. But when God at last delivered his final judgment against sin and sinful existence, in the death of Christ, the apparent ground for a natural theology was destroyed, for the whole of natural man comes under the total judgment of the Cross. It was in the mercy of God, said St Paul, that God suspended his total judgment until he prepared his new creation; but just because that is the event by which the natural man with all his goodness and knowledge is slain, we have no right whatsoever to take up an attitude toward natural theology except within that event of grace. But within that event the Christian Church must stand by its own position in Christ, and refuse to build upon any other foundation than that which was laid in Christ Jesus, the self-revelation of God.

That alone is the ground for the Reformed polemic against the incursion of natural theology. It was on that ground, for example, that Karl Barth broke with Gogarten, in 1933, when the latter adopted a

---

[1] *Inst.* I.4.4.   [2] *Church Dogmatics* II/1, p. 119.
[3] *Op. cit.*, p. 169; cf. pp. 128ff.

conception of the natural man in which his 'nature' was not thought of as coming under the total action of Christ on the Cross, in judgment and new creation. It was then that Karl Barth became convinced that the vitality of natural theology is the vitality of the natural man, and that the whole question of natural theology is at stake in the Cross. Gogarten's position he held to be a betrayal of the Gospel, for it involved a reversal of the action of God in the death of Jesus Christ.[1] Gogarten wanted to base Christian theology upon the essential motion of the natural man, such that the Christian revelation perfects it and completes it. But that, said Barth, was the very motion of self-assertion and self-justification; in fact, the very motion which the grace of God in Christ contradicted on the Cross, and completely inverted. Therefore, now that the Cross has happened, we must forget the things which are behind, and begin again, laying no other foundation than that which has been laid in Christ Jesus. That is not to deny natural theology, as such, for that would mean a denial of the natural man in his actual existence, but it does mean that a Christian theology cannot be built upon a carnal foundation: to do that would be to open the flood-gates of naturalism and to inundate the Church with paganism. That that actually happened in Germany, in spite of Barth's warning, is evidence enough that the Christian Church is faced with a battle for its very existence in the issue of natural theology. To go back to the language of John Calvin: if the essential motion of sin is an unthankful and self-willed perversion of the gifts of God, then the divinely given 'light of nature', and the 'divinely deposited seed of religion' in man, can be nothing else in the activity of the natural man than the very 'fountainhead of all superstition and idolatry'; and so we must regard natural religion as an 'irreligious affectation of religion'.[2] Once again the Church is faced with this pagan challenge mounted upon the irreligious affectation of religion whose roots go down to the light in the darkness of nature. The danger is, not that this should raise its head without the Church, but within it; and that, said Calvin long ago, can only be a 'deadly abyss that swallows up all our thoughts'.[3] The Reformer's point was that unless we regulate our knowledge carefully by the way in which God has willed that we shall know him, then the perverted motion of our minds will only lead us into terrible darkness and confusion.

This perverted motion of man's mind Calvin described as the un-

---

[1] See the last number of *Zwischen den Zeiten*, and *Church Dog.* II/1, pp. 165f.
[2] *Comm. on John* 3.6; cf. *on Ps.* 97.7; *on Gen.* 8.21; *Inst.* I.5.4, etc.
[3] *Comm. on I Peter* 1.21.

grateful attempt to turn the *imago dei* into something of man's own possession by the manipulation of which he could conceive a likeness of God. But, inasmuch as man possesses the *imago dei* only in a grateful response to the Word of grace, it is impossible for him to retain it in a motion of hostility to or alienation from the Word of grace. What man actually does in this perverted motion of the mind is to manipulate a wicked imagination, thus conceiving a dishonourable image of God which is a lie and not the truth. It is certainly true, said Calvin: that God cannot reveal himself to us in any other way than by a comparison with things which we know. In his revelation God accommodates *himself* in his Word to the capacity of our understanding, and in such a way that he not only makes himself little, as it were, that we may grasp him, but forms our ear to hear and shapes our minds to understand. Apart from that self-accommodating motion of God's grace, we have no predisposition or faculty to know him. Therefore, any attempt of theology which builds up a knowledge of God upon its own self-willed attempts to know God, not regulating its knowledge by the very activity of God's Word in and by which he fashions the only way in which we may know him truly, can only invert the basic principles of Christian knowledge, and build up a false theology. 'In order to know God, therefore, we must not frame a likeness of him according to our own fancy, but we must betake ourselves to the Word, in which his lively image is exhibited to us. Satisfied with that communication, let us not attempt anything else of our own. . . . How ridiculous is the blindness of men when they claim anything for themselves; for they gain by their boastings just as much as if some small creatures, such as locusts, would elevate themselves by leaping; but they must immediately fall back upon the earth.'[1] 'It is hence evident', said Calvin again, 'that men in vain weary themselves in serving God, except they observe the right way, and that all religions are not only vain, but also pernicious, *with which the true and certain knowledge of God is not connected.*'[2]

Once again, this position has been championed by Karl Barth, particularly in his discussion of the question of analogy by which he has worked out the Reformed teaching into a clear consistency. Barth makes no denial of analogy, as many English-speaking theologians imagine.[3] Indeed it might be argued that the whole of his theological position is based on a vigorous affirmation of analogy, but it is an analogy of grace, not an analogy of being; therein, Barth maintains, is the great difference

---

[1] *Comm. on Isa.* 40.19f.   [2] *Comm. on Heb.* 11.6; cf. *on I Cor.* 2.12.
[3] E.g. R. Niebuhr, *The Nature and Destiny of Man*, II, 1945, p. 69.

between the theology of the Reformers and that of the Schoolmen. There can be no doubt that all our knowledge of God is analogical, for we cannot know God except as human beings, and therefore only in analogical proportion to our human minds. Two things must be said, however, if this is to be understood aright.

(*a*) We must think of this analogy as dynamic and not static. That falls into line with the whole Reformed conception of man and his relation with God. In other words, Reformed theology has reinstated in the doctrine of analogy that essential moment of the will which had been left out, for example, in the doctrine of Thomas Aquinas. But the emphasis is first on the will of God, for it is God himself who accommodates his word to our understanding, and so it is God himself who must preside in all our judgments about him and about ourselves. This is what Barth has called the *analogia gratiae*, which is grounded essentially on the Incarnation, for it is there that God in definitive fashion accommodates his Word to our knowing. If therefore there is a true analogy of proportionality, as the Thomists aver, it must be one grounded, not on any abstractly conceived ontological continuity between man and God, but on the *unio hypostatica* in which we have the union of God and man as God himself has set it forth in Christ, and in which we may be united to God by partaking of that union in faith. We cannot, therefore, set forth a doctrine of the image of God or of analogy already lodged in the being of man, as Augustine taught, before men are partakers of God. Thus, the true analogy of proportionality grounded upon the Word and grace of God will be set forth in this fashion; man and God are related in the mutual relation of faith and grace *proportionaliter* to the relation of Man and God in hypostatic union in Christ Jesus. That means that a Christian doctrine of the Word of God and human decision, of election and human faith, of the Divine Presence and the worldly element in the sacrament, etc., will be grounded entirely upon the hypostatic union as its true and only valid analogy; that is, upon the central relation and union of God and Man of which every other relation must partake.

The fundamental mistake in a doctrine of analogy is to turn the dynamic analogy into a static analogy of being. That may be done by converting the dynamic relation into a logical (ontic-noetic) relation, or/and by a view of grace as a transferable quality infused into and adhering in finite being, raising it to a different gradation where it can grasp God by a connatural proportion of being. Both these activities are repudiated by Reformed theology as unbiblical and quite untrue.

Reformed theology goes a step farther, and points out that the desire to stabilize the analogy, or to transubstantiate it into an analogy of being, so that it can be humanly manipulated at will, belongs to the very essence of sin and human pride by which our first parents fell. It is the desire by man to possess likeness to God in the continuity of space and time secure at every moment in his own hand and being, instead of being ready to live in the acknowledgment that his life is deposited only in the Word of God, and may be retained only by acknowledgment that it is not his own but belongs to God, and is only his by continual communication through the Word of grace.

(*b*) From man's side, the analogy must correspond with the essential motion of grace. That is to say, the analogy cannot be possessed by man or used except in a motion that is correlative to the motion of pure grace. No analogy grounded upon the self-asserting or self-explanation of man, or partaking of self-will, will pass the required test and correspond with the downward movement of grace. In Calvin's view, a true motion corresponding with this analogy of grace is the self-emptying of faith, and the acknowledgment of thankfulness which carries man out beyond himself to depend entirely upon the movement of grace. To grasp the grace of God in such a way as to do justice to grace, man must stretch out an empty hand. Thus, the motion corresponding to grace entails on the part of man a downward or a humble movement; not a movement of self-assertion, as if by an *analogia entis* he would or could add one cubit to his stature. The true movement of grace, Reformed theology holds, is impugned by a doctrine of *analogia entis*. By the entry of sin, the true analogy of grace has been inverted; and that perverted or inverted activity, said Calvin, never ceases, so long as we are unredeemed. But all our natural theology is built upon this inverted analogy of grace, so that we indulge in a 'wicked exercise of the understanding that always contrives in what way it may rob God of the praise which is his due'.[1] It is that active perversity, or the inversion of grace, that constitutes the difficulty for theology, for, whenever the Word of grace confronts us in Christ, the inverted analogy must be re-inverted, and restored to its truth in the motion of grace.

The Incarnation, as culminating in the Cross and the Resurrection, is the great act of God in which he entered our perverted order of nature, and wrought the basic soteriological inversion by which we are reconciled to God. But that basic soteriological inversion must be pushed through the whole region of the mind, inasmuch as we are alienated

[1] *Comm. on Isa.* 48.5.

from God, as Calvin said, 'in the whole of our mental system'.[1] Therefore 'let this mind be in you, which was also in Christ Jesus. . . .' That
takes place in the Christian *metanoia*, when the believer, transformed by
the renewing of his mind, knows that he has not chosen Christ, but that
Christ has chosen him; that his knowing of God is grounded on his
being known of God; and that every analogy of men, such as fatherhood,
is grounded reflexively upon the action and love of the heavenly Father,
after whom every fatherhood in heaven and earth is named. Unless
theological activity is grounded upon, and made to conform to, this
motion of grace, then every step of theology can only be from alienation to alienation in the continued assertion of self-will; instead of from
faith to faith, in the continued receiving of grace for grace, in which the
true life of man consists. The Christian revelation discovers to us that
our existence is grace through and through, but also grace in a special
sense: that we have been so made, as intelligent beings, that we must
give an intelligent life-answer to grace in such a way that our existence
is ours only as we re-live our grace-existence in a thankful and knowledgeable motion in answer to the Word of grace. Therefore, there can
be no true *ordo cognoscendi* (order of knowing) which is not based upon
an *ordo essendi* (order of being) conceived entirely as grace, and the *ordo
essendi* reaches its true destiny in the *ordo cognoscendi*. This is the problem of analogy as Reformed theology sees it today. The *analogia entis*
is entirely grounded upon the *analogia gratiae*, and only in an *analogia
fidei* corresponding to the *analogia gratiae* does the *analogia entis* have
any truth or reality.[2] Outside of that, the truth of God is inevitably
turned into a lie.

For this reason, Reformed theology is grounded upon the 'mutual
relation of faith and grace' through the Word.[3] It is the Word, the lively
and essential Image of God, which is the *analogia analogans*, so that
only over against its activity does man have an *analogia analogata*: that
is to say, an *analogia fidei* corresponding with an *analogia gratiae*,[4] that
we may know God truly, and, in that knowledge, truly be what God
meant us to be, men in the image of God.

---

[1] *Comm. on Col.* 1.21; cf. *on I Cor.* 1.21; *Inst.* II.15.9.

[2] It is interesting to find Franciscan theology attempting to make a similar
movement today. Thus Gottlieb Söhngen insists that the *analogia entis* must be
subordinated to the *analogia fidei*, on the principle that *esse sequitur operari*, and
not *vice versa*: *Catholica*, 1934, vol. 4, pp. 97f.; cf. vol. 3, pp. 10f.; and also
Wissenschaft u. Weisheit 2. Jahrg., pp. 97f.

[3] *Comm. on Acts* 15.9.

[4] Cf. *Church Dog.* II/1, pp. 79ff., 237ff.

7

Questioning in Christ

ONE of the most impressive features of the evangelical narratives is the way in which they bring out the fact that wherever Jesus went and in whatever situation he was to be found he became the centre of tense and bewildered questioning in which the lives and thoughts of men were torn wide open. The Gospels themselves clearly fall within the orbit of this upheaval for they are not offered to the world as the reports of disinterested observers but as material that is referred to Jesus Christ himself as its creative source and as reports that are so deeply implicated in the upheaval that they are media through which Jesus continues to be the centre of volcanic disturbance among men, if only through the very questions which he forces them to ask about him. Yet what is most disturbing is the way in which the questioning of men is handled through the counter-questioning of Jesus. He elicits questions and answers them by making them his own, for by asking them out of the depth of his own existence among men he opens them up to questioning far beyond what they are capable of in themselves, and opens up the way for answers far beyond anything they can ever anticipate.

Nowhere is this more evident than in the very last question Jesus asked before he died: *Eli, Eli, lema sabachthani?* 'My God, my God, why hast thou forsaken me?' (Mark 15.34). These are not primarily the words of Jesus; they are the words of the Twenty-Second Psalm which Jesus made his own on the Cross. They are the desperate question which man directs to God out of the depths of his God-forsakenness and despair. By taking them on his lips Jesus revealed that he had put himself in man's place, made man's questions his own, in order both to ask them in truth and in truth to receive the answers. He was no doubt reciting the Psalms, as other utterances on the Cross seem to indicate, but when he gave out this fearful cry of dereliction, he was surely not just reciting, but descending into the hell of our darkness and godlessness. He was asking the ultimate question from the point of identification with man in his ultimate need.

In doing that Jesus not only determined for us in himself the true mode of religious and theological questioning but constituted himself as the very centre of reference for our questions about God. If we are to understand this adequately we must consider what happened in his incarnation and life and death and examine the interplay of question and counter-question between Jesus and those who came up against him, and then note how in reaction to him there took place the decisive discrimination between those who were of the Truth and those who retreated from it into their own predeterminations and prior decisions. It was in the midst of that tension that the nature and activity of the Truth became manifest, and it was out of resistance to it that the crucifixion finally took place. Our immediate concern is to draw out the significance of this for theological inquiry in a world that is subject as much as ever to the pressures of scepticism and godlessness.

Jesus Christ was the Son of God become flesh, God himself among men as man, confronting men with himself. He was the ultimate Truth of God but his coming into the world put the supreme question-mark to man, and forced men to ask questions about him. How did they react? In answer to that question the Evangelists provide us with a twofold account of the relations of Jesus to his own disciples and to the Jewish authorities with whom he came into conflict.

The disciples were chosen by Jesus to be his companions, called to be with him and to learn through association with him, walking in the Light as he was in the Light. Very early, however, they began to find out how uncomfortable it was to live with Jesus. His presence searched them through and through, and forced them to ask questions about him just because they found themselves called into question before him down to the very bottom of their being. To be with him like that was to be called to give an account of themselves to God, and to learn that they had no answer to give but their shame. They found themselves recoiling from him. 'Depart from me, O Lord, for I am a sinful man.' And yet they were compellingly drawn to him. What manner of man was this?

All through that period of training Jesus did not tell the disciples who he was, but with gentle and holy majesty he kept the pressure of his presence upon them which forced on them the question as to his being and person. And then when the time was ripe he drew them aside to a quiet place and voiced the question he knew to be in their minds, 'Who do you say that I am?' And there came from Peter the answer that stood for them all, 'Thou art the Christ, the Son of the living God.' At once Jesus pointed out that this was not an answer that could be given from the side of man, but from the side of God. It was from God himself that this revelation had come to them, for the Reality of God is not to be discerned through natural insight.

Then Jesus began to initiate the disciples into the mystery of the Cross, but immediately he met with resistance. The answer to the first question forced upon the disciples another, whether they were ready to cast in their lot with Jesus unreservedly, even to the point of denying themselves and taking up the cross. The disciples had come to the point where they had to let themselves be displaced by Jesus as the centre of all their being and knowing and doing if they were to go forward into the Kingdom, or where they could only fall back into darkness, darkness that would be greater than ever for they had learned that before God they were altogether questionable creatures.

Jesus had confronted them as the Truth of God who required of the disciples to relate themselves to him absolutely; to relate themselves to him only relatively would be a refusal to keep faith with him and to turn their relationship with him into untruth, for it would mean a retreat into their own selves as the centre from which they could control relation to Jesus and protect themselves from the pressure of his divine Lordship. 'If any man will come after me, let him deny himself and take up his cross and follow me.' And so Jesus set his face like a flint to go toward Jerusalem and the Cross, for God's questioning of man had to plumb to the depths of human existence and only *de profundis* could the answer be given.

Meantime the religious authorities also had been forced to ask questions about Jesus, for in his presence they were searched and questioned down to the foundations of their faith and the very roots of their existence, until their innermost secrets and hostilities were laid bare—and they resented it. Again and again they challenged Jesus' authority. Where is the seal of your teaching? What sign can you give us from God that will justify you? And so right to the end they sought for a compelling demonstration of his actions, an empirical verification for his message, within the conditions they prescribed and on the level of their desires. And then in the final clash a few days before the crucifixion they questioned Jesus outright for the source of his authority. 'By what authority do you do these things? Who gave you this authority?' 'And Jesus answered and said unto them, I will also ask you one thing, which if you tell me, I will also tell you by what authority I do these things.

The baptism of John, whence was it, from heaven or of men?' (Mark
11.28f.).

In answer to the question about his ultimate authority Jesus asked a
searching question on his part which was designed to force the Jews
back to the great unanswered question God had already put to them in
the preaching of John the Baptist, the question as to sin and repentance,
as to cleansing and obedience to God's will. In other words, the only
place to answer the question as to ultimate authority is at the point of our
guilt where we are questioned by God himself, and are at the bar of his
holy Word. At that point, as a Psalmist had once said, doubts are a
frivolity. Only a morally irresponsible man can then ask, 'Where is
God?' Now it is worth noting how the religious authorities met the
question of Jesus: by a dialectic that balanced alternatives over against
each other; and so they avoided interrogation. Therefore no answer
could be given. An answer in truth can be given to us only when we are
ready really to make the question our own, and to ask it truthfully and
receptively. A direct answer meeting the condition of the question as it
had been asked could only have been false, and therefore the question
itself had to be questioned.

In any case, an answer in word only would not have been true to the
nature of the authority of Jesus which was bound up with his person and
being as the Son of God and Saviour of the world. Hence it could be
answered properly only by his life and his action.

That is surely why all the way through his ministry Jesus refused to
disclose the truth about himself in word only, for speech about him in
abstraction from the work he had come to do could not be truly given
or received. That is why he kept his messianic secret to the very end,
unfolding it only as his action advanced to the completion of his mission
from the Father. Had Jesus spoken openly about himself, for example,
as very God and very Man, there is no doubt that he would have been
severely misunderstood and his teaching could not have been heard
aright, far less transmitted aright. He taught them, therefore, only as
they were able to hear, through parables, but what he communicated
to them was in a form that immediately took on a deeper dimension of
meaning when his mighty acts were completed and his person confronted them from the side of the resurrection.

Hence at this point too Jesus could only tell a parable in which he
communicated the truth clearly if as yet indirectly. It was a parable
about the tenants of a vineyard who resisted the claims of the owner and
even killed his son and heir in order to usurp ownership and authority

over the vineyard. The hearers did not discern, immediately at any rate, the fact that Jesus was pointing once again to the Cross as the answer to the question of supreme authority, but they did discern that he told the parable to lay bare their resolve to kill him, so uncovering their self-deception and revealing that the bitterness of their hostility concealed a wilful blindness to the truth.

A further point must be noted, however. There is no authority for believing in Jesus outside of Jesus himself. The Jewish rulers wanted some other authority outside of Christ and higher than him for believing in him, so that they would not have to submit to him, but could control relation to him from a superior position. What Jesus revealed to them, on the other hand, is that any question about the ultimate authority is irresponsible and self-contradictory, for it is an attempt to find some authority above the highest authority. We cannot ask questions like that about the Ultimate for they are not genuine, but we may address our questions *to* the Ultimate. When we do that we are answered by a question directed back to us which we can answer not by seeking a place above ultimate Authority but by respecting it and letting ourselves be questioned and directed by it.

Genuine questioning here leads to the disclosure and recognition of the Truth in its objective reality, in its own majesty and sanctity and authority, which cannot be dragged down within our dividing and compounding dialectic in order to be controlled by us. It is the prerogative of the ultimate Truth, the Truth of God, that it reigns and is not at our disposal, that it *is*, and cannot be established by us, Truth that is ultimate in its identity with the Being and Activity of God and cannot be dominated by man, Truth that is known only by pure grace on God's part and in thankful acknowledgment on our part. In the last resort it is we who are questioned by the Truth, and it is only as we allow ourselves to be questioned by it that it stands forth before us for our recognition and acknowledgment.

And so Jesus confronts us as the centre of reference for our questions, from which alone our questions can be directed properly and effectively toward God. By Word and Person Christ directs his supreme question to us: 'Who do you **say** that I am?' That is the point to which the inquiry of faith is always finally driven back, for the truth with which we are concerned in Jesus is not just an objective reality but one that presses upon us the question of the truth, the question of our acknowledgment of the truth, of our readiness to be open to it and to be directed by it. That is the truth which we cannot tell to ourselves. We can only let it question us and press itself upon us in its majesty and ultimateness for our recognition and worship. That is what takes place still when we are face to face with the Truth of God as it is in Jesus, for through its questioning of us in answer to our questions, it does not hold itself aloof from us, so throwing us back on ourselves for the verification and answer we need, but associates us with its own activity in which it attests itself and so provides the answer to the question of its truth at the same time as it exposes our untruth.

That was the interplay of question and counter-question that lay behind the Cross. Indeed it was precisely the interaction between the questioner and the questioned in which the Truth of God in Jesus penetrated more and more deeply into the inner secrets of men that led directly to the crucifixion; for by the life he lived in their midst Jesus questioned his contemporaries down to the roots of their being, and forced them to the boundaries of their existence where they had either to take refuge in their own preconceptions and crucify him in self-protection, or give themselves up wholly to the scrutiny of God that both slays and makes alive.

In that interplay of question and counter-question Jesus remained in complete control, for he came not just to rouse the questions of men in their estrangement and despair or in their antagonism to God, but to make those questions his very own by penetrating into the existence of the questioners, even to the point of their ultimate rejection of God, and by penetrating into their existence in such a way as to reconstruct their questions from below, to ask them in such a way that they would yield the fruit of inquiry and bring light into darkness. And so Jesus came in the form of a servant, the form of a man called in question, called in question not only by the misunderstanding and hatred of men but by the searching judgments of God, in order to step into our place where we are questioned by the Truth and are found wanting, and to let himself be questioned in our name. He came in order to embody in himself both our questions to God and God's answers to us, as well as God's questions to us and true answers from us to God.

That is the way the God of Truth deals with us. He turns to us where we have closed ourselves to him and are imprisoned in our self-will and blindness; he penetrates into our existence and life as one of us in order to open us up from below to the Truth of God and to bring us to acquiesce in the Truth of God. That is Jesus—who stood in our place, the prisoner at the bar interrogated by man and by God, he who plumbed the deepest depth of our questioning of God in order to take it upon himself and receive the counter-questioning of God. Therefore that Man on the Cross, questioned down to the bottom of hell, for our sakes, is the ultimate question that God puts to us.

Unless we recognize that we too are called in question by the Cross, we can neither put our questions to God in truth nor truly hear the answer he provides. Jesus Christ stood in our place: that is God's answer to us. For Jesus stood in our place not only to be questioned, but to ask the question in truth as we are unable to, and to give a true and faithful answer to God. He stood in our place and made our ultimate question his own, 'My God, my God, why hast thou forsaken me?' But in taking that question on his lips, he asked it as we cannot, for he altered it from the depths into the cry, 'Father, into thy hands I commend my spirit.'

What, then, is the nature of true questioning?

A genuine question is one properly open to the object of inquiry, but a question cannot be open to the object of inquiry if it is foreclosed from behind. Hence to be genuine, a question must allow itself to be called in question; it must be ready for reconstruction in the light of what the inquiry reveals. True questioning involves a backward movement of critical revision of its premisses and a forward movement of reformulation of its questions. The further questioning is pushed, the more radically preconceptions are called into question, until real listening becomes possible and judgments are formed under the compulsive power of the objective reality. Genuine questioning is a strenuous form of repentance.

Moreover, behind the questions stands the questioner himself. Every question that is raised has behind it the being of the questioner, and it reacts upon him. Really to ask, we have to put ourselves into our questions. If so, then really to ask, we must allow ourselves to be called into question. The questioner must allow his questions to react critically upon himself, if he is to ask them relentlessly and scientifically.

There is all the world of difference between doubting and questioning. The questions of the doubter are poised upon himself, upon the self-certainty and proud autonomy of the doubter. *Cogito, ergo sum. Dubito, ergo sum.* By their very nature they will not allow the doubting self to be called into question. Scientific questions are of another kind, for they are poised not upon the subject of the thinker but upon the object of inquiry, and react critically upon the self. It is attachment to the object that detaches the questioner from his presuppositions, and by liberating him from prejudgments rooted in the self makes him free for knowledge of the object. Hence in proportion as a person wills to put his whole existence into his question, he wills to let himself be questioned down to the roots of his existence, in order that he may be really free from prejudice and really open to the truth. But the more ultimate the object of his inquiry is, the further he must push his questions, right to the very frontiers of his being, in order that he may allow the ultimate reality and objectivity to disclose itself to him, unhindered and unobscured as far as possible by his own deceptions and unrealities. Thus the more ultimate his questioning is, the more completely he lets himself and all his prior understanding be called in question. Ultimate questioning involves for the questioner the ultimate judgment of the self.

Who can question like this? Who is there who can press his questioning to the outermost boundaries of his existence where he is altogether called in question, and can only listen? Who can carry his inquiry to the utmost limit where he can go no further, to the very horizon of being itself where it presses upon nothing, and project his questions beyond? How is it possible to pose a question except on the same level as the questioner himself? And if perchance his questioning is a leap beyond into the nothing, how can that be anything but an empty movement of thought, a movement in the void? Yet unless our questioning is projected beyond the horizon of our being, how can our questioning open up the source of our being in an ultimate ground beyond? How can we pose the ultimate question in such an ultimate way that it leaves us the questioners behind, as it must do if it is to get really beyond us? How is it possible for the questioner to pose a question which by its reaction upon him brings the ultimate judgment upon himself and his questioning? And if he cannot pose the ultimate question, in which his own self is called in question, how can he be emancipated from his own deceptions and ever know the truth that makes him free? How can man raise the ultimate question that is to carry him beyond himself, if the questioner still remains the man who questions himself? If it is into death or into nothing that he leaps, as Heidegger would have it, there is then no Other to question him, so that to the end he is left alone with himself. How then can man raise the ultimate question without distorting it into atheism, that is, without either identifying God with nothing or death, or retreating at last into his own preconceptions and confounding God with himself?

It is just at this point that we come up against the essence of the Gospel. What man cannot do of himself, God has done for him, in the

Man on the Cross. 'My God, my God, why hast thou forsaken me?'

Theological inquiry cannot hurry past that terrible cry of God-for-sakenness of the Man on the Cross, for it is there that we are carried to the extreme edges of our existence, to the very brink of the abysmal chasm that separates us from God. It is there that we see the end of all *our* theologizing, in sheer God-forsakenness, in the desolate waste where God is hidden from us by our sin and self-will and self-inflicted blindness and where, as it were, God has 'died out on us', and is nowhere to be found by man. Search the universe as relentlessly as we may, all we find at last is the utterly unbearable silence or the despairing and frightening cries of dereliction, for the questions we direct come bouncing inexorably back upon us to reveal that they are but empty and deceptive movements of inquiry. And so the world is forced into atheism, not the atheism of the sophisticated which is only a cloak for ulterior ends, but the unwilling atheism of those who have come to an end, to the frontier of the pure void, and find nothing more authentic than to choose the silence of emptiness or nothing, or the defiant atheism of those whose guilty enmity against God is provoked by the pressure of the Truth as it is in Jesus into anti-Christianity. The Christian Church has contributed immensely to the agnosticism and atheism of the modern world, by natural theology, that is, by seeking to interpret to man the Truth of God within the framework of what he has claimed to know without God. Yet there is hope for man—*in atheism*, if atheism means that his questioning has carried him to the very boundary of creaturely existence, to silence and emptiness and God-forsakenness, to the pure void where man has nothing to say but can only cease and listen. Then it may be that a genuine theology can interpret to him the terrible question of Jesus as the descent of God himself into the dereliction of man in order to take man's atheistical questioning upon his lips, to ask it as we never can in pure truthfulness, and by laying hold of us in our blind hostile questioning in the dark to change it into something that brings light and truth.

We recall that behind our questions there lies our existence, for every form of thought has behind it the being of the thinker. Hence it is we who misshape and distort our questions as to God, at their very source, so that even in raising the question we direct it past God into the void, and then cry out in God-forsakenness. But God himself has penetrated into our existence in Jesus, down into the very roots where we are alienated and antagonistic, down into the pit of our darkness and despair, in order to lay hold of us and our questions from the very bottom, to reconstruct our existence from within and recast our questions from their very source, so that they may be asked aright and directed straight to the Father. In penetrating into our existence like that, in both life and death, and in taking our questions on himself, the Son of God has put *his* whole being into his questioning, so that though they are our questions, they are yet questions from a centre in God, capable of answers from a centre in God—that is, questions that are so shaped by the object of their inquiry, the divine Nature, that they are fruitful questions, yielding the results of their inquiry, in the true knowledge of God the Father.

The New Testament has another way of putting this, in speaking of the relation between the incarnate Son to the heavenly Father. In Jesus Christ the Son of God entered into our rebellious humanity, laid hold of the human nature which we had alienated from the Father in disobedience and sin, and by living out from within it the life of the perfectly obedient Son he bent our human nature in himself back into obedience to the Father. Standing in our place, in life and in death, not only to be questioned but to give a faithful and true answer, he answered for us to God; even in his terrible descent into our God-forsakenness in which he plumbed the deepest depths of our estrangement and antagonism, he reconstructed and altered the existence of man, by yielding himself in perfect love and trust to the Father. 'Father into thy hands I commend my spirit.' 'Father'—that had been the answer of his whole life on earth, the answer of the obedient Son, for through the whole course of his obedience from birth to death he bent our human nature back into a perfectly filial relation of faith and truth toward the Father. 'Not my will, but thine be done.'

And the Father answered the cry of his Son from the depths, answered not in word only but in deed, answered by resurrecting Jesus from the dead as his own Son with whom he kept faith and truth even in the midst of judgment and death. 'Thou art my beloved Son.' But that is the answer that God directs to us all in the Gospel for Jesus' sake, that through Jesus the Son of God become our Brother, we may be restored to faith and trust in the heavenly Father. Through sharing brotherhood with the incarnate Son of God, we share with him also one and the same Father Almighty. Hence the first word which Jesus sent to his disciples after his resurrection ran: 'Go unto my *brethren* and say to them, I ascend to *my* Father and *your* Father, to *my* God and *your* God' (John 20.17). Then at last the prayer which Jesus had taught them, when he put his own words into their mouth, could really be their prayer and their true answer to God. 'Our Father who art in heaven, hallowed be thy name. Thy kingdom come. Thy will be done on earth as it is in heaven.'

True theological questioning is possible only through Jesus, because only in Jesus do we know the truth that makes us free from ourselves and reconciles us to the Father, because only in Jesus can human questions be directed to God from a ground where they are not distorted in their source and from which they are not deflected past God into nothingness, and because only in Jesus who acts for us from the side of God toward man and from the side of man toward God is a questioning possible which carries us beyond the limitations of our creaturely human being into God himself. Jesus Christ in whom alone there is perfect communication between God and man and man and God is constituted the centre of reference for all our inquiry of God, for he is the Way, the Truth, and the Life, and there is no road to the Father except through him.

8

The Place of Christology in Biblical and Dogmatic Theology[1]

CHRISTIAN knowledge of God arises out of the self-revelation of God in and through Jesus Christ, for in him the Word of God has become man in the midst of man's estrangement from God, committing himself to human understanding and creating communion between man and God. Biblical and dogmatic theology is the careful unfolding and orderly articulation of this knowledge within the sphere of communion with God, i.e. the sphere of reconciliation into which we are drawn by the activity of his Word, and of the obedience of faith in which all our thinking and speaking is brought into conformity to the self-communication of his Word. The way which God has taken in Jesus Christ to reveal himself and to reconcile us to himself is the way which we have to make our own in all true understanding and thinking and speaking of him. Theology, therefore, involves a knowledge which is determined and controlled in its content by what is given in Jesus Christ, and operates with a mode of rational activity which corresponds to the nature of the object of this knowledge in Jesus Christ. It is the incarnation of the Word which prescribes to dogmatic theology both its matter and its method, so that whether in its activity as a whole or in the formulation of a doctrine in any part, it is the Christological pattern that will be made to appear. That does not mean that all theology can be reduced to Christology, but because there is only one Mediator between God and man, the Man Christ Jesus, in the orderly presentation of the doctrines of the Christian faith, every doctrine will be expressed in its inner coherence with Christology at the centre, and in its correspondence to the

[1] In writing this article in honour of Karl Barth I wish to acknowledge my indebtedness throughout it to the second half-volume of his prolegomena to the *Kirchliche Dogmatik*, which I have been helping to see through the press in an English edition at the time of writing.

[Reprinted from *Essays in Christology for Karl Barth*, ed. T. H. L. Parker (Lutterworth Press), 1956.]

objective reality of God's revelation in Jesus Christ who is true God and true Man.

In the nature of the case, we are not concerned in dogmatic theology with working out into a logical system our understanding of God and creation, grace and human nature, in terms of the divine Being and creaturely effect after the fashion of scholastic theology in philosophical *Summae*. Nor are we concerned with the religious consciousness and with working it out into a systematic form according to its own immanent laws and the knowledge obtainable from our understanding of these laws, after the fashion of Schleiermacher, even if that is conditioned and determined by the historical consciousness of the Church as in so much post-Tridentine Roman theology. In contrast, dogmatic theology is concerned above all with the Word of God made flesh in Jesus Christ, with the revelation of the Word fulfilled in the apostolic testimony and tradition, and with the obedient conformity to the Word on the part of the Church in its listening to it and its teaching about it. The task of dogmatics is therefore to unfold and present in an integrated and ordered form the content of the Word of God in the sphere of its effective operation in the Church; not only to give consistent expression to the response of the Church in faith and understanding to the Word, but to bring the mind of the Church to ever-renewed conformity to the work and activity of God in his Word, and so to serve the Church in its attainment unto the unity of the faith and of the knowledge of the Son of God, and in its growing up in all things into Christ who is the Head of the Church.

The significance of this should become clearer if it is presented in the three stages that correspond to the activity of the Word: in the incarnation of the Word, in the apostolic foundation of the Church, in the disciplined articulation of the Church's understanding of the Word.

I THE INCARNATION OF THE WORD OF GOD

We begin with faith in Jesus Christ as truly God and truly Man, and seek to unfold our understanding of the double fact that in Jesus Christ the Word of God has become man, has assumed a human form, in order as such to be God's language to man, and that in Jesus Christ there is gathered up and embodied, in obedient response to God, man's true word to God and his true speech about God. Jesus Christ is at once the complete revelation of God to man and the correspondence on man's part to that revelation required by it for the fulfilment of its own revealing movement. As the obedient answer to God's revelation Jesus

TIR I

yields from the side of man the fulfilled reception and faithful embodiment which belong to the content of God's complete revelation of himself to man. In the Hebrew idiom, revelation is not only the uncovering
of God but the uncovering of the ear and eye of man for God. It is revelation which achieves its end in man and does not return void to God.

Several facts require emphasis here.

(a) The incarnation shows us quite unmistakably that there is an
essential bi-polarity in God's revelation of himself to man. God is God
and not man, and yet in the incarnation God has become man, this
particular Man, Jesus Christ, without ceasing to be God. In him divine
nature and human nature are united, really and eternally united, in one
Person. In him the eternal Word of God has assumed human nature
and existence into oneness with himself in order thus, as truly divine
and truly human, to become the final Word of God to man and the one
Mediator between God and man. In other words, the incarnation shows
us that God reveals himself (God) in terms of what is not-God (man),
that revelation is given to us only in terms of what it is not, in the
humanity of those to whom it is given, so that from first to last we have
to reckon with an essential bi-polarity. In the nature of the case we cannot get behind the 'what he is not' to the 'what he is in himself', any
more than we can get behind the back of Jesus to the eternal Son of God.
We cannot divide between the so-called form and content, between the
human word of revelation and revelation itself, any more than we can
divide asunder the human and the divine natures which are united in
the one Person of Jesus Christ. The *inconfuse, immutabiliter, indivise,
inseparabiliter* of Chalcedonian Christology apply equally to our understanding of revelation. Revelation is not only act from the side of God
but also from the side of man, in the form of the Humanity of Christ
which is of the very substance of revelation. The divine form and the
human form of revelation must neither be confounded nor be separated.
The incarnation means that now revelation is determined and shaped by
the Humanity of Christ, that we know of no revelation of the Word of
God except that which is given through Christ and in the form of Christ.
Jesus Christ is the Truth, Truth as God is Truth, and that same Truth
in the form of Man, Truth answering itself, Truth assuming its own
true form from the side of man and from within man. As such he is not
only the Truth of God in man, but the Truth for man and in man, and
therefore the Truth of man.

(b) The Incarnation shows us that revelation is not only act of God
in man and from the side of man, but real act of man achieved through

human obedience to the Word of God. The Incarnation was wholly act of God but it was no less true human life truly lived in our actual humanity. Jesus Christ is not only Word of God to man, but Believer. In his obedient life he yielded the perfect response of man to the divine revelation which is that revelation in human form. Here the doctrine of *anhypostasia* and *enhypostasia* applied to the incarnation applies equally to our understanding of revelation.[1] Revelation is entirely God's action but within it, it is the concrete action of Jesus Christ that mediates revelation and is revelation. Revelation is supremely God's act but that act is incarnated in our humanity, giving the human full place within the divine action issuing forth out of man's life. The human obedience of Jesus does not only play an instrumental but an integral and essential part in the divine revelation.

Revelation involves, then, the freedom of God to be present to man and to open up man for God and to realize from the side of man his understanding of revelation and his obedient response to it, to effect in man real meeting with God in revelation and to give him capacity for revelation. This capacity for revelation is not to be judged in terms of the receiver, as if he could achieve it on his own, but in terms of the Giver, the Father in Heaven, who acts by his Spirit upon man, from beneath and from within man, but who effects from the side of man and issuing out of man's life a really human understanding of revelation and a really human obedience to it. In other words, in revelation we have the divine assumption of our human word into union with God's own Word, effecting it as the human expression of the divine Word, and giving it, as such, real and full place as human word in obedience to the divine.

In revelation, therefore, we are not concerned simply with *anhypostatic* revelation and with human response, but with *anhypostatic* revelation and true human response *enhypostatic* in the Word of revelation. We are not concerned simply with a divine revelation which demands from us all a human response, but with a divine revelation which already includes a true and appropriate and fully human response as part of its achievement for us and to us and in us. Thus the Incarnation shows

---

[1] 'By *anhypostasia* classical Christology asserted that in the *assumptio carnis* the human nature of Christ had no independent *per se* subsistence apart from the event of the incarnation, apart from the hypostatic union. By *enhypostasia*, however, it asserted that in the *assumptio carnis* the human nature of Christ was given a real and concrete subsistence within the hypostatic union—it was *enhypostatic* in the Word. *Anhypostasia* and *enhypostasia* are inseparable. In the incarnation the eternal Son assumed human nature into oneness with Himself, but in that assumption Jesus Christ is not only real man but a man (*Scottish Journal of Theology* 7.3, pp. 249f.).

us that the revelation of God fulfilled in Jesus Christ provides us with a truly human but divinely prepared response: and that is at once the divinely given objective reality of our knowledge and response, and the divinely appointed norm and pattern of our knowledge and response.

In the Humanity of Jesus Christ, in his mind and in his life, in the whole obedience of his incarnate being and knowing, we are given not only the revealed knowledge of God but the embodiment of that knowledge in our humanity. Jesus Christ the Word made flesh is not only the object of our theological knowledge but he is the Lord of it: as the Word become man, he is the criterion of our knowing and as the man assumed into oneness with the Word he is the pattern of our knowing. He is not only the content of our theological knowledge but he provides for us in himself the way which our theological knowledge must take. 'I am the Way, the Truth, and the Life. No man cometh unto the Father but by me.'

(*c*) The incarnation shows us that revelation and reconciliation are inseparable, for revelation does not achieve its end in humanity apart from reconciliation. Obedient as he was throughout the whole course of his life, Jesus had yet to *learn* obedience. Though conceived by the Holy Spirit and born of the Virgin Mary, Jesus was yet born in the womb of a sinner, within the compass of our sinful flesh. As the Son of Adam he was born into our alienation, our God-forsakenness and darkness, and grew up within our bondage and ignorance, so that he had to beat his way forward by blows, as St Luke puts it, growing in wisdom and growing in grace, before God as well as before man. He learned obedience by the things which he suffered, for that obedience from within our alienated humanity was a struggle with our sin and temptation; it had to be fought out with strong crying and tears and achieved in desperate anguish and weakness under the crushing load of the world's sin and the divine judgment. Throughout the whole course of his life he bent the will of man in perfect submission to the will of God, bowing under the divine judgment against our unrighteousness, and offered a perfect obedience to the Father, that we might be redeemed and reconciled to him.

That is the way which the Word of God made flesh takes in the midst of our sinful humanity, the way of vicarious suffering and judgment and atonement. Revelation does not achieve its end as revelation apart from reconciliation, for only through reconciliation can revelation complete its own movement within man, bringing out of our humanity the obedient reception of revelation which is an essential part of its very substance. Revelation involves a communion through the reconciliation of the estranged parties, a reconciliation of the will and mind of man with the will and mind of God. Revelation entails the entry of the Mind of God into our darkness and estrangement in order to redeem our understanding and to achieve its reconciliation to the Mind of God. Revelation is unthinkable, therefore, apart from the whole movement of divine humiliation from the cradle to the Cross, apart from the grace of the Lord Jesus Christ which means that the Word which was rich with the Wisdom of God for our sakes became poor, making our poverty his own, that we through his poverty might be made rich with the wisdom of God. It is only through that atoning exchange that God's revelation achieves its end as revelation to and within a sinful world.

Once again, the way which God has taken in his revelation and re-conciliation, the way of the Son of Man, the way of humiliation, is the way which we must make our own, adopting it as the way of our think-ing and speaking and of all our theological discipline. As God and yet as Man, Jesus Christ penetrated into the midst of our humanity in order to overcome our estrangement and to reconcile us to the Father. He who is God and Man in one Person acts from the side of God in the faith-fulness of divine truth and love, and acts from the side of man in the faithfulness of a life wholly obedient to the Father. In that unity of the divine-human faithfulness the Word of God is spoken and the truth of God is actualized in our humanity, in and through the whole assent of Jesus to the will of God as it confronts the will of man: 'Not my will but thine be done.' That is the way in which revelation comes to us, in which the Word of God confronts us, so that we have no option but to follow it. Therefore to all discipleship, including all theological *discip-lina*, Jesus Christ says, 'If any man will come after me, let him deny him-self and take up the cross and follow me.'

The significance of the incarnation for dogmatic theology lies here: not only, though supremely, in providing our theological knowledge with its unique content, but in providing it with its normative pattern in the obedient humanity of Jesus Christ. In the incarnation we have a divine-human Word in the unity of the divine and the human natures in Christ, so that we are unable to separate out the human word from the divine, for the Word of God to us is precisely this one divine-human Word in the mutual involution of revelation and reconciliation. It is for that reason that the Humanity of Jesus Christ is of inescapable and essential importance for dogmatic procedure and method; for it sets before us the actual Way which the divine Word has taken and takes in our human communion with it and our human knowing of it. The Humanity of Christ provides us not simply with an externally imposed norm for theological understanding and articulation, but the actual medium in and through which God acts upon our thinking and speaking, giving them an inner obedience to his Word through our participation in the holy communion of Father, Son, and Holy Spirit.

For too long in Protestant, as well as in Roman, theology the full place of the Humanity of Christ has been neglected. The thinking together of divine revelation and human response, with inadequate attention to the *tertium datur* in the Humanity of Christ, in Roman theology has meant the subordination of revelation to the natural forms of man's rationality and piety, and in Protestant theology has meant the transmutation of revelation into the subjectivity of the religious consciousness or Christian experience or faith. Against both tendencies we have to insist again that in the incarnation we are given not only the objective Word of God but the objective Word subjectively realized in complete and final form in the Humanity of our Lord. For Roman theology that will mean the rediscovery of the Lordship of Christ and the radical inversion of all its thought-forms and patterns of piety, and their critical renewal in thorough and consistent conformity to Jesus Christ. For Protestant theology that will mean the rediscovery of the ontological and objective ground of faith, not only in the act of God for us in Christ but in the subjective embodiment of that act in the Humanity of Christ, and therefore it will mean the critical reorientation of faith in a repentant self-denial of its own subjectivity and a renewed subjection of itself to the reality of its object, Jesus Christ as true God and true Man. The crucial issue for Catholic and Evangelical theology is the disciplined grounding of it upon Jesus Christ as himself the Truth: Truth as God is Truth, and that same Truth in the form of Man, Truth answering itself, Truth assuming its own true form from the side of man and from within man. The subjective reality of this Truth can never be made a separate theme for theology any more than the Humanity of Jesus in abstraction from the Incarnation. That Humanity as the subjective reality of the Truth is already enclosed in the objective reality of the Truth: that is precisely the significance of the Humanity of Christ for the procedure of dogmatics. From end to end, therefore, dogmatic theology must be determined and shaped by the Humanity of the Son of God.

2 THE APOSTOLIC FOUNDATION OF THE CHURCH

The Incarnation shows us that the Word of divine self-revelation is objectively and subjectively fulfilled and complete in Jesus Christ: but as such it is objective to the Church and requires subjective realization within the mind of the Church. The Word of revelation declared to mankind achieves its end in that it is heard and understood, received and obeyed, in the Church, which is therefore given to share in the election and assumption of our humanity in Christ and which is assimilated to that Humanity in its own human life and thought. The Incarnation shows us that the divine revelation is given not apart from reconciliation but is mediated within an atoning life and death offered on our behalf: but as such it is objective to the Church and requires subjective realization within the life of the Church. The Word of divine reconciliation proclaimed to mankind achieves its end in that it is accepted by sinners who allow themselves to be drawn into the sphere of its effective operation in the Church which is given through the communion of the Spirit to share in the union of the Father and the Son. The subjective actualization of revelation and reconciliation is wrought out in the institution of the Apostolate, the foundation upon which the whole Church is built.[1]

In Jesus Christ the Word of God entered into the midst of our flesh of sin and worked out in our existence the perfect obedience of man to God. In him alone we have the holy and perfect Word of God not only from the side of God to man but from the side of man to God. From beginning to end he is that Word in representative and vicarious action in our midst. But this pure and holy Word of God gathers round him the apostles to be the inner nucleus of his Church, to be in a special way one body with him, the Word made flesh, and to be the receiving end within our sinful history of the complete incarnate revelation. Here revelation assumes certain men and incorporates them in revelation from their own side not as co-revealers nor as co-redeemers, but as recipients of revelation and as ambassadors of reconciliation. They are the specially chosen witnesses, the specially appointed vessels bearing the treasure of revelation and reconciliation. They are the apostles of revelation and reconciliation, put in trust with the Word of reconciliation. But they are sinners, they are Christians saved by grace, who come under the judgment of God and the cleansing of the Blood of Christ. And it is as such, redeemed sinners, not as redeemers, that they are given apostolic function with regard to the incarnational revelation.

As such the Apostles stand over against Christ in entire contrast to him. Jesus Christ was not a Christian. A Christian is a sinner saved by

[1] See *Royal Priesthood* (*S.J.T.* Occasional Papers, 3), 1955, pp. 26f.

Christ, saved through Christ, for a Christian's relation to God is entirely through the mediation of Christ in revelation and reconciliation. Christ is Redeemer, Mediator. He is not a Christian, not a sinner saved by God, but the Saviour himself. He is both the author and the content of revelation and reconciliation, but as such he has instituted the Apostolate as the means whereby he passes his revelation and reconciliation into the world of sinners, so that in that world his revelation may achieve its end as revelation subjectively realized in the mind of sinners, and his reconciliation may achieve its end as reconciliation subjectively actualized in the life of sinners. The Apostolate is elected and instituted as the specific point among sinners where revelation and reconciliation are, so to speak, earthed. Corresponding, therefore, to the particularity of the Incarnation, there is in the Apostolate a particularity of fulfilled revelation and reconciliation within our sinful minds and our sinful lives. As such the Apostolate stands with sinners among sinners, and belongs to the sphere where salvation is bestowed. But within that sphere, within the perspective of redeemed sinners, the Apostles provide us with the divinely appointed, the divinely prepared, and therefore the normative realization and actualization of revelation and reconciliation. It is as such that the Apostles are given to sit upon twelve thrones sharing with Christ his authority and judgment over the Church. In other words, it is the point of view of the Apostles which is the point of view which Christ means us to have of him. Their point of view is the point of view of those who have been forgiven and reconciled by Christ, the specifically Christian point of view. And as such it is the divinely guided and inspired point of view from within the perspective of redeemed sinners, providing us with the definite and normative pattern of response to revelation and reconciliation which God himself has willed and constituted in the Church.

This doctrine of the Apostolate belongs also to the doctrine of the Holy Spirit. As long as Jesus was with his disciples in the flesh he formed them round him as his Body and taught them as they were able to hear. He had yet many things to say to them but they were unable to understand them then. He promised, however, that the Father would send the Spirit in his name, the Spirit of Truth, who would teach them all things, remind them of what Christ had already taught them and interpret it to them, leading them into all Truth. He would not speak of himself but speak of Christ and show him to the disciples. In fact, Jesus promised that in the sending of the Spirit he himself would return to the disciples and his Word would abide in them. And that happened after the incarnational revelation was complete, after the reconciliation of man to God had been carried out in the death and resurrection of Christ. God poured out his Spirit upon the Apostles and the apostolic Church, and the risen Lord returned to them clothed in the power of his Spirit and gave himself to them to be known and appropriated in his own Spirit, in his own Light, and in his own Truth. Clothed with the historical facts of the Gospel Jesus Christ now returns to shine with the light of his glory within the apostolic mind and to fulfil in them his own interpretation of himself and his work. This is not any new revelation, nor any new interpretation externally put by the apostles upon the historical facts, but the actual unfolding of the mind of the risen Lord within the apostolic Church. The revelation of God objectively given and subjectively realized in the Person and Work of Christ now through the Spirit subjectively takes shape in the mind of the apostolic Church in final form.

We have to think of this also in terms of reconciliation, for that which was atoningly wrought out in Jesus Christ on our behalf is now through the Spirit subjectively actualized in the apostolic foundation of the Church. In the Apostles the mind of the Church is so reconciled and joined to the Mind of Christ that the Mind of Christ is not to be separated out from the mind of the Apostolate, or the *kerygma* of the Apostles to be distinguished from the Word of the Lord (except, of course, in those rare instances where the Apostle himself may do so). The Lord reconciled the Apostles to himself and breathing upon them his Spirit wrought out that reconciliation in the inner obedience of their witness, and was pleased to control and assume that witness into oneness with his own Word, so that the apostolic word is Word of Christ. Thus the apostolic witness is incorporated by Christ into his own Word, so that through the apostolic *kerygma* it is Christ himself who is at work testifying to the mighty acts whereby he has redeemed the world and offering himself to men as their Saviour and Lord. This is the apostolic revelation of the Gospel in which the whole witness of the New Testament is delivered to the Church, and in which the Gospels as well as the Epistles are written as the Word of the Lord to the Church.

This doctrine of the Apostolate, therefore, belongs also to the doctrine of Holy Scripture. As bearers of the incarnational revelation, the Apostles are the hinges where that revelation is folded out horizontally into history, but as such they are hinges in two senses: as disciples, in which they are the hinges between the Old Israel and the New Israel; and as apostles, in which the foundation of the Church is once and for all laid, and from which the Church is sent out into history. The revelation of God which selected Israel as the sphere of its prophetic operation in the world and the means of its translation appropriately into our human speech was fully and finally consummated in Jesus Christ in the midst of Israel. That entire revelation which was gathered up, transcended and fulfilled in Christ was once and for all bestowed upon the Church in the Apostles. Thus in and through the medium of the Apostles the Old Testament revelation belonging to Israel, made to shine out in its divine revelation as through the Spirit the glory of the crucified and risen Lord is shed over it, is subsumed under the New Testament revelation to form together, as the one apostolic-prophetic revelation of God in the language of our human flesh, the perpetual foundation of the Church as the Israel of God. The Scriptures of the Old Testament are therefore annexed to the Scriptures of the New Testament as the divinely appointed means in which there is folded out and delivered in written form to the Church the joining of the revelation of God with the corresponding reception which it requires from within the community of the redeemed, and therefore as the divinely instituted norm and pattern for the obedience of the Church to Jesus Christ from age to age.

That is the basic fact in the doctrine of Holy Scripture: that God has willed and constituted in the apostolic foundation of the Church a creaturely correspondence to his own Word, assuming it into union with his Word and effecting it as the human expression of his Word. As such the Holy Scripture, like the Apostolate, stands with sinners and among sinners, and belongs to the sphere where salvation is bestowed. That gives us the peculiar problem of Holy Scripture and its peculiar place. Holy Scripture is assumed by Christ to be his instrument in conveying revelation and reconciliation, and yet Holy Scripture belongs to the sphere where redemption is necessary. The Bible stands above the Church, speaking to the Church the very Word of God, but the Bible also belongs to history which comes under the judgment and the redemption of the Cross. That double place of Holy Scripture must always be fully acknowledged, else we confound the word of man with the Word of God, and substitute the Apostles in the place of Christ.

On the one hand, then, we have to insist that the creaturely correspondence of the Holy Scriptures to God's Word is a correspondence which is actualized from within the perspective of redeemed sinners, but because it is a human expression corresponding to the Humanity of Jesus Christ, we have to understand it according to him who as Word of God in our midst learned obedience to the Father. We can no more speak of dictation in the doctrine of the Scripture than we can speak of the life of Christ as dictated by the Father. Just as we speak of his life in terms of obedience, so we must speak of the Bible as obedience to the Divine self-revelation, in which the human word of Holy Scripture bows under the divine judgment just because it is part of his redemptive and reconciling work. In the Bible, therefore, the Word of God is not given to us ready-made. We see it growing in wisdom and grace before God and before man. We see it in the midst of our God-forsakenness and darkness, struggling with our temptations and our rebellious will. The Word of God comes to us in the midst of our sin and darkness at once revealing and reconciling, but it comes with strong crying and tears, pressing its way through the speech of our fallen flesh, graciously assuming it in spite of all its inadequacy and faultiness and imperfection, and giving it a holy perfection in the Word of God. The doctrine of verbal inspiration does not, therefore, mean the inerrancy and infallibility of the biblical word in its linguistic and historical and other characteristics as human word. It means that the errant and fallible human word is, as such, used by God and has to be received and heard in spite of its human weakness and imperfection. The Bible has to be heard, therefore, as Word of God within the bi-polarity of revelation and reconciliation, in which we acknowledge that in itself, in its human expression, the Bible is word of man with all the limitations and imperfections of human flesh, in order to allow the human expression to point us beyond itself, to what it is not in itself, but to what God marvellously makes it to be in the adoption of his grace.

On the other hand, we have to insist that the creaturely correspondence of Holy Scripture to God's Word is so miraculously assumed and used by the divine revelation that even within the perspective of redeemed sinners it is adapted by the Spirit not only to mediate the Holy Word of God but to be the holy expression of that Word in human form. The word of God has wrought so effectively in and with the human language of the Bible that it has achieved from within it a true obedience to God. The Word has so imprinted its own image upon the human word as to make it a faithful reflection of its own revelation. Through the power of the Spirit the perfect obedience of Christ is so actualized within the humanity of the Bible that it is given to manifest the normative Humanity of Christ.

Although we cannot speak of a direct identity between the human word of Scripture and the Word that was made flesh in Jesus Christ resting in the essence either of the divine Word or the human word, we must speak of an identity between the word of man and the Word of God in the Bible which rests upon the gracious decision of God to unite it with his own Word, and so to give it a divine perfection in spite of its human imperfection. Therefore the Bible has to be heard as the very Word of God in which we acknowledge that, although in itself, in its human expression, it is involved in the limitation and imperfection of human flesh under judgment, it is so inseparably conjoined with the divine Word as to be the written Word of God to man, and is brought into such a faithful correspondence with the divine revelation that it mediates to us in and through itself the exemplary obedience of Christ as the authoritative pattern and norm for the obedience of the Church in all its thinking and speaking. It is because the humanity of the apostolic Scriptures is already incorporated in the revelation and already enclosed within the reconciliation of Christ that these Scriptures are both the organ through which Jesus Christ from age to age conveys his Word to men with saving power and the canon by which he rules his Church, shaping its mind and forming it to be his Body.

3 THE FUNCTION OF BIBLICAL AND DOGMATIC THEOLOGY

The Church that is built upon the apostles and prophets continues to be the Church as it continues in the apostolic tradition of obedience to Jesus Christ, that is, as it continues to be a follower of the Apostles as the Apostles were followers of Christ. But to be a follower of the Apostles is to be bound to the apostolic Scriptures of the Old and New Testaments and through them to be schooled and moulded and incorporated into the apostolic foundation, for it is through those Scriptures that Jesus Christ the Word made flesh begets the Church from age to age as his own Body and forms it ever anew into his own Image. It is by listening to the Word of God speaking to us through the Holy Scriptures delivered to the Church by the apostles, by being drawn into, and by continuing in, the sphere of the apostolic community in which the risen and ascended Lord fulfils his own revelation and reconciliation among men, by submitting in the obedience of faith to the same revelation and reconciliation, that the Church continues to be ever the same, *semper eadem*, identical with itself in its sole foundation in Christ, living throughout all the changes of history and all temporal succession in such a way as not to be conformed to this world but to be transformed by the renewing of its mind and so to be conformed to Christ. It is within that whole movement of growth and change, continuity and identity, that we are to understand the significance of biblical and dogmatic theology as the edification of the Church in hearing and appropriating the Word of God, and as the discipline of the Church in assimilating all its thinking and speaking to the Mind of Christ, that it may continue to become what it is, the One Body of the One Lord.

It is the perpetual duty of the Church to listen to the Word of God speaking in Holy Scripture, to accept and appropriate it through a true interpretation, that it may become the Church's own word in preaching and teaching. But the Word of God comes to us in Holy Scripture in human words which as such are always ambiguous and need faithful interpretation. That interpretation is faithful when we explain it according to the objective reality in the Word of divine Revelation to which they point us. 'Why do ye not understand my speech (*lalia*)?' asked Jesus of the Jews. 'Even because ye cannot hear my word (*logos*).' The *lalia* of Jesus, his human speech, is ambiguous, and is not to be understood except in terms of the *logos* that utters it and stands behind it, but on the other hand there is no revelation of the *logos* apart from the human *lalia*. It is the work of the *logos* to explain the *lalia* which it adopts and the work of the *lalia* to reveal the *logos* which it serves. Thus the Word of God which speaks to us through Holy Scripture in human words is to be understood and appropriated as we interpret the human word (*lalia*) faithfully in accordance with the objective Word (*logos*) which adopted and moulded it as its instrument of communication, and which still uses it to communicate to us the divine revelation.

That confronts us immediately with several important considerations.

(*a*) We are not concerned here with the Word of God *in abstracto*, i.e. in abstraction from the *lalia*, but we are concerned with the Word of God *in concreto*, in the actual human situations in which the Word has addressed itself to men in the Old Testament and in the New Testament, in and through the actual humanity with which the Word has wrestled, achieving within it, in spite of its recalcitrance and intractability, an obedient instrument for its revealing purpose. If we are to listen to that Word and appropriate it today we must allow ourselves to be drawn into the effective and creative operation of the Word in its original sphere, in the witnesses of the Old and New Testaments, and in that original sphere subject ourselves to the manifestation and sanctification of the Word and Truth of God. This means of course that we have to give the most rigorous attention to the actual text of the Scriptures and to their actual setting in history, that we may stand in the place of the original witnesses and go along with them in all that they suffer under the impact of the Word of the Lord. Arduous exegetical study is the foundation for all theological discipline in the Church.

(*b*) We are not concerned here, however, with the human speech of the Bible as an independent theme of study, that is, with the humanity of the original witnesses in themselves, all of whom without exception point away from themselves to the Word of the Lord which has laid hold upon them and drawn them within its saving operation. That is to say, true hearing of the Word of God coming to us through the human words of the Bible which is faithful to those words can take place effectively only within the sphere of reconciliation to God. Only then can we stand in the place of the original witnesses and go along with them in all that they suffered under the impact of the Word. It is as we allow ourselves to be drawn into the community of the reconciled that the Word of revelation speaks to us effectively by adapting us to its hearing, judging our sin and darkness and restoring us into union and communion with God's Word. In other words, we have to be drawn into the place before God where our enmity to him is exposed and judged, where our opposition to his revelation is overcome, where the lines of communication between God and man disrupted and damaged by sin are healed, where there is real reconciliation so that there can be real communication. Just as the doctrine of Scripture cannot be divorced from the doctrine of Atonement, so biblical interpretation cannot be genuinely undertaken apart from reconciliation to God.

(*c*) All this means that to hear and interpret and appropriate the Word of God speaking to us in the Holy Scriptures we have to subordinate our own presuppositions and conceptions and indeed the whole of our own humanity to the critical and creative activity of that Word effectively at work in the humanity of the Bible. We find ourselves at the bar of the divine judgment where we are summoned to repentance and are forced into ruthless self-criticism. Our great problem is that we are unable really to listen to the Word of God speaking in the Bible, for our listening is a strange mixture of listening and our own speaking, and it is our own speaking which is usually uppermost. The Word of God summons us to listen to it not as though we know already what it has to say, not as though it only confirms what we have already said to ourselves, but to listen in such a way that we are lifted outside of ourselves and hear what only God can say to us. How can we do that except in repentance? To listen and deny ourselves, to listen and to repent of what we want to make the Bible say, to listen in such a way as to let the Bible speak against ourselves, that is to listen indeed to the Word of God.

(*d*) We are confronted now with the problem of theology in relation to biblical exegesis, which arises when the coherent pattern of our own conceptions and presuppositions conflicts with the coherent pattern of obedience to the Word of God revealed in the Bible. We all have our own schemes of thought which we inevitably bring to the interpretation of the Holy Scriptures. Doubtless it would be wrong for us not to have them, and certainly wrong for us not to realize that we have them, for then they would have supreme power over us as unconscious canons of interpretation imperceptibly determining and damaging our exegesis. But we have to face the fact that in faithful listening to the Word of God, we allow ourselves to be drawn into a sphere where human thought-forms are already shaped and knit together in a pattern of obedience to the Word of God, while faithful interpretation and appropriation of the Word of God mean that we allow ourselves to be schooled into this obedience, in order that we may yield to the Word of God the mode of rational activity which it requires of those to whom it gives itself to be known.

This is where the Old Testament has an incalculable importance for Christian theology. All through the history of Israel as a people brought into covenant relation with God, the Word was wrestling with our stubborn and rebellious humanity and dealing faithfully with it in judgment and mercy and truth to achieve a coherent pattern of obedience, a sphere in human understanding and human speech, with appropriate forms of thought and language, which could be used as the instrument of divine revelation to all men and at last as the sphere of actual revelation and reconciliation for all men. The Word of God comes to us in the Scriptures of the New Testament only through that schooling in the Old Testament, and we need that schooling too, not only to hear the Word of God in the Old Testament, but even to hear it in the New. We cannot do without the Old Testament if we are to acquire the obedient orientation of mind with which faithfully to apprehend the Word as it gives itself to us to be known.

Here then in the school of the biblical world of communication we learn to yield to the Word of God that mode of rational activity which it is the responsible thing to do, if we are really to behave according to the nature of the Word of God in revelation and reconciliation. We have to allow the Word in its obedient humanity to impose itself upon us, and allow ourselves to go along with it, to be led and guided and corrected in all our thinking and speaking, so that it becomes our own. It is this activity which gives rise to biblical theology which seeks to unfold the content of the Word of God as it has taken human form in the witnesses of the Old and New Testaments, and therefore to unfold the pattern of inner obedience to it which the Word requires of us. The Word of God comes to us in the Bible in such a way that the appropriate obedience to it from within our humanity is already enclosed within it, in such a way that the objective revelation already includes its subjective realization in the humanity of the Bible. We are not concerned therefore in biblical theology simply with revelation and response, or with listening to the Word of God simply in the presentation of exegetical results, but with revelation and a divinely schooled, prepared and coherent response revealed not only in the thought-forms of the biblical revelation but in the essential unity of their correspondence to the Word of God.

It is important, however, to insist that the biblical thought-forms cannot be abstracted from their context in revelation and be interpreted and used as universally valid principles. They have their meaning and importance only within the concrete situations where the Word of God uses them, and in inseparable relation to the objective revelation which has given them shape. They belong to a coherent pattern of revelation and actualized response which is gathered up, transcended and fulfilled in the incarnation. It is Jesus Christ, the Word made flesh in the midst of Israel, in his exemplary obedience to the divine will, who provides us with the criterion for our interpretation of the thought- and language-forms of the Bible. They have their authority and significance not in themselves as such but as they point to him and as they are ultimately made to cohere in him.

There is a significant difference, however, between the theology of the Old Testament and that of the New Testament, for the theology of the New Testament gives rise to dogmatics as the theology of the Old Testament does not, except in so far as it is subsumed under the New Testament. The Old Testament thought- and language-forms receive their fulfilment in the Incarnation where they are given critical reinterpretation, so that we can no longer stand with the witnesses of the Old Testament in precisely the same way that they stood under the impact of the revelation, for the revelation has moved on beyond that concrete human situation into the Incarnation and the concrete human situation bound up with it in the apostolic Church. But when we stand within the pattern of human obedience actualized in the incarnational revelation, we are able to stand in the place of the witnesses of the Old Testament in a profounder sense; for we are able to give an interpretation of their forms of thought and language in terms of their fulfilment in Jesus

Christ, which is entirely faithful to the concrete human situation in which they were schooled in Israel.

All through the history of Israel in the Old Testament the Word of God which had bound Israel into covenant-union with itself insisted on being translated into the flesh of Israel so as to adapt Israel to its purpose, to fashion within it a womb for the incarnation of the Word and a matrix of appropriate thought- and language-forms for the reception of the incarnational revelation. But in the nature of the case, although the Word of God and the existence of Israel are bound up inextricably together, the concrete form of Israel in the Old Testament is revealed by the Incarnation to be a passing form which exhibits the judgment of our stubborn and rebellious humanity in its restoration to union with the Word of God, although the pattern of obedience already apparent in Israel, in the Servant of the Lord above all, points through judgment and death into resurrection, to the recreation out of Israel of a new humanity which, in the finality of the Incarnation and the new concrete human situation begotten by it in the Church, exhibits the permanent form of the Israel of God, which will not pass away but will endure throughout all the changes of history into the glory of eternal consummation.

Here, however, within the sphere of the incarnational revelation and the new concrete human situation where everything reposes upon the finality of the Incarnation and the foundation once and for all laid in the apostolic Church, we are concerned with a pattern of obedience which is completely coherent and of final authority, but we are concerned with more than a pattern, namely, with an actual *structure* of obedience inserted with its appropriate forms of thought and language into the midst of our humanity in the Church as the Body of Christ. As biblical theology lays bare the inner coherence and structure of the Word of God as it has taken human form in obedient correspondence to it, biblical theology passes over into dogmatic theology, which is concerned with an integrated and orderly unfolding of the content of the Word of God according to its own essential norms as they operate effectively and creatively within the mind of the historical Church, bringing it into conformity with Jesus Christ and into unity within its own understanding and appropriation of his Word.

Biblical theology passes over into dogmatic theology where two significant things happen: (*a*) Where our hearing and receiving of the Word of God is not in isolation either from our fellows in the contemporary situation or from our fathers in the context and continuity of

TIR K

history, that is where it is a conjoint hearing with all saints in the life and
growth of the Church in accordance with its apostolic foundation;
(*b*) where we have to assimilate all our thinking and speaking and acting
in the Church to the biblical revelation so that it may be assimilated
truly and faithfully into all our thinking and speaking and acting from
age to age. That gives us two primary characteristics of dogmatic
theology.

(*a*) Dogmatic theology acknowledges that all our hearing and thinking
of the Word of God is conditioned by our place in the Church. Our
hearing is determined by previous hearing of the Word in the Church,
and our thinking is conditioned by the thought-forms which we have
inherited in the traditional teaching of the Church. That is to say,
dogmatic theology seeks to unfold and present the content of the Word
of God within the limits of the Church prescribed for it by the Incarnation and the apostolic foundation, and to articulate that content today
through an examination of the doctrinal decisions in the past which have
shaped and moulded the listening of the Church in the present. Dogmatic theology operates not only within the sphere of the Church as the
sphere of revelation and reconciliation, but within the historical continuity of the Church in its learning obedience to the Word of God, and
in its growing up into the full stature of the Humanity of Christ. It is
undertaken in reliance upon the promise of Christ to send his Spirit
upon the Church to lead it into all truth concerning himself, and is
undertaken in the constant prayer that faithful expression of the Mind
of Christ may be given in and through the mind of the Church. In all
this, dogmatics is the instrument whereby the Church inquires whether
its traditional teaching is in conformity with Christ, and is the means
whereby as far as possible it is emancipated from the *Zeitgeist* which
always threatens the thinking and teaching of the Church with historical
relativity, and is the discipline whereby the Church is prevented from
imprisoning the truth in definitive dogmatic formulations of any age.
Thus the Church is kept ever open to the renewed understanding of
Christ the Truth who alone can renew the mind of the Church from
age to age.

(*b*) Along with all this belongs the duty of dogmatic theology to bring
the thought- and language-forms used by the Church in its preaching
and teaching under the review and judgment of the Word of God, that
they may be so assimilated to the obedient Humanity of Christ as to
become proper and adequate instruments for the proclamation of the
Gospel and for the instruction of the Church. The constant task of

dogmatic theology is thus to test the mind of the Church in accordance with the biblical revelation, to protect the Church from becoming independent and self-willed (i.e. heretical) in its teaching, to protect the preachers of the Church from preaching themselves and their own preconceptions or merely private interpretations of the Gospel, and so to direct the Church back to the self-unfolding of the divine Truth within the Body of Christ and to help the preachers of the Church to point away from themselves to Jesus Christ, the Way, the Truth and the Life.

Dogmatic theology is able to undertake this critical task only if behind it all it engages in a great positive attempt to expound and set before the Church the whole movement of obedience to God's Word in the Incarnation, in the apostolic foundation, and in the history of the Church, and in the light of that to articulate afresh in the thought- and speech-forms of the present a coherent account of all the doctrines of the Christian Faith. In undertaking this task, dogmatic theology will show the Church not only where our forms of thought and language conflict with the Word of God and the Humanity it assumed in Jesus Christ, but how these forms can, and must, be bent to meet the needs of theological articulation. Dogmatics is not primarily interested in the forms of thought and language which the Church must use from age to age to proclaim the Gospel. It is primarily concerned to unfold the objective content of revelation and is only interested in the forms of thought and language as the expressions of that content. Dogmatics must show the Church, therefore, how the objective content of the Word of God transcends the forms of our thought and language from age to age and from nation to nation, but also how it can make abundant use of them, adapting them to its purpose, while preserving its own freedom and sovereignty over them. But dogmatics can do this only as it expounds the objective content of the Word of God in and through the subjective form which it has already taken in the Humanity of Christ and assumed into its own objectivity. The objective reality of the Word and the subjective actualization of it in the obedient Humanity of Christ together, in their inseparable union, form the objective content of revelation which is delivered to the Church for its understanding and appropriation. The task of dogmatic theology, therefore, is above all to expound the doctrine of Jesus Christ as true God and true Man, but also to show how in obedient conformity to him a Christological pattern is made to appear in the forms of thought and language which we are bound to use of him.

It is thus that there emerges a twofold criterion of theological pro-

cedure prescribed to us by the very nature of the Word and the control
which it exercises over our knowing and articulation of it. Not only
must the content of our theological knowledge be determined and controlled throughout by its object, the Word made flesh in Jesus Christ,
but the modes and forms of our dogmatic activity must exhibit an inner
structural coherence reflecting the nature of the object. This twofold
criterion or norm can be described as *correspondence* to the Word of God
speaking to us through the Holy Scriptures in the midst of the Church,
and the *coherence* of our doctrinal forms in an essentially Christological
structure. Though these may be distinguished they are not to be regarded as two norms, for they cannot be separated from one another.
They work together as one norm in the inseparable relation of *kerygma*
and *dogma*, of biblical theology and dogmatic theology.

We have already seen how biblical theology lays bare and operates
with a pattern of obedience to the Word of God revealed in the humanity of the Holy Scriptures, and as it seeks to articulate that in the understanding of the Church it passes over into dogmatic theology. Dogmatic
theology, on the other hand, lays bare and operates with a pattern of
doctrine prescribed to it, in its unfolding of the whole content of the
Word, by obedience to Jesus Christ as true God and true Man; but in
the nature of the case this pattern of doctrine cannot be abstracted from
the self-disclosure of Jesus Christ through the biblical revelation and be
erected into an independent norm with its own inherent authority. In
itself it is only a formal pattern, but it derives from, and reposes upon,
the actual structure of the Incarnation. This pattern of doctrine, therefore, can be used as a dogmatic norm only in conjunction with correspondence to the biblical revelation and in subjection to it. Within that
subjection, however, and within the subordination of all our thought-
and language-forms to the critical and creative activity of the Word of
God, dogmatic theology must proceed to lay bare the essential inter-
relation of all the doctrines of the faith, and their integration within the
one Body of Christ, within the whole structure of obedience to Christ.
This is the *interior logic* of dogmatic theology which is in the object of
our knowledge before it is in our thinking, but which imposes itself
upon our thinking as our minds seek to behave in terms of the nature of
the object, that is, to be conformed to Jesus Christ.

In other words, dogmatic inquiry discovers that there is a structural
and essentially Christological pattern running throughout the whole
body of our theological knowledge, which can be studied and used as a
norm or criterion for helping to shape the true form of each doctrine,

for testing and proving the different doctrines to see whether they really fit into the essential structure of the whole. This cannot be undertaken in any arbitrary and authoritarian fashion but only in the form of a humble inquiry, for the thought-forms used in the expression of the structural pattern are subject throughout to the review and judgment of the Word of Revelation. Thus, for example, when we take the doctrines of the *hypostatic union* and of *anhypostasia and enhypostasia* which arise out of the Church's articulation of the doctrine of Christ, and use them as dogmatic norms, we have to remember that these doctrinal forms have no inherent authority and are themselves subject all the time to modification by our hearing of the Word of God in the Holy Scriptures. They can be used only in humble obedience to that Word and in coherence with the whole body of biblical theology; but within that coherence and along with correspondence to the Word of God speaking to us in the Holy Scriptures they may be used legitimately, and can be used with the greatest gain in understanding and clarification of our theological knowledge. As such, this is a specific but important illustration of the dogmatic procedure in which we adopt and make our own, in our thinking and understanding, the way which the Word of God has taken in human form in Jesus Christ.

9

Justification:
Its Radical Nature and Place in Reformed Doctrine and Life[1]

I THE TEACHING OF JOHN KNOX

IN his debate with the Jesuit, James Tyrie, John Knox claimed that the controversy of the Reformers with the Roman Church was the same as that of St Paul with the Judaizers of Galatia, in which the Gospel of grace was at stake, 'for it concerneth the chief head of justification', as Knox expressed it.[2] On the other hand, when we examine the writings of Knox we do not find that 'justification', as a term at any rate, plays a prominent part, while the expression 'justification by faith' is hardly ever found—for when he did speak of justification he preferred to be more concrete and to use an expression like 'justification through the blood of Christ'.

This calls for two observations. 1. The whole question of the Reformation is at stake in the doctrine of justification. 2. Justification is not a principle in itself: it directs us at once to Jesus Christ and his mighty acts.

When we turn to the *Scots Confession* of 1560, and ask what place justification occupies in it, we find ample confirmation for the two observations we have just made. There are, in fact, three important facts about justification in the Confession that we must note.

1. There is no separate article on justification. It has no place of its own; rather does justification belong to the inner texture of the Gospel and becomes evident as its cutting edge. That is to say, justification

[1] Presidential address delivered to the Scottish Church Theology Society, 18th January, 1960. Reprinted from *Scottish Journal of Theology* 13.3, 1960, and from *Christianity Divided* (Sheed & Ward), 1961; French text in *Catholiques et Protestants* (Ed. du Seuil), 1963.
[2] *The Works of John Knox*, ed. Laing, VI, p. 499.

makes decisively clear the very essence of the Gospel of salvation by grace.

2. What is absolutely central is Jesus Christ. Man's salvation is exclusively the work of God in Christ, God in union with Man, and therefore Man in union with God. It is an outstanding characteristic of all the documents of the Scottish Reformation that a place of centrality is given to the union of God and Man in Christ, and therefore of our 'blessed conjunction' or 'society' or 'fraternity' with Christ. That union with Christ lies at the heart of our righteousness in him, for it is through that union that we actually participate in his holy life. Knox laid immense stress upon the saving Humanity of Christ, that is, upon his positive obedience and filial life in our flesh. Consider, for example, this sentence that comes from the *Form of Confession* in the *Book of Common Order*: 'We must always have our refuge to the free justice which procedeth of the obedience which Jesus Christe hath prayed for us.'[1] What Knox refers to there is the fact that the prayer of Jesus was part of his atoning obedience and oblation to God—it was the worship of God the Father with his Life. In that Life of the worshipping and obedient Son we are made to share and are well-pleasing to the Father as through that participation we are clothed with the Name and holy life of Christ. In his unity with man the Son of God lived out a perfect Life on earth in obedience, love and worship, and as such died and rose again. Therefore it is in and through our union with him, that all that is his becomes ours. It is only as such, that is in the Name of Christ, that we appear before God, and as such that he regards us—in Christ.

3. The accent lies very strongly here on the positive side of salvation. Thus justification is expressly linked with the resurrection of Christ,[2] to which a whole chapter is given in the Confession of 1560, while a further chapter is devoted to the Ascension of Christ.[3] Now that is one of the great characteristics of Knoxian theology—Resurrection and Ascension are part of the Atonement—indeed, 'the Resurrection' is often called 'the chief article of our faith'. What is the significance of this emphasis? In the Resurrection and Ascension we have the affirmation of man by God, and his exaltation to be a partaker of a new humanity, a new righteousness, and a new freedom as a child of God, as a brother of Christ, as a joint-heir with him, as one who together with him has the same Father. Justification is not only the forgiveness of sins, but the

---

[1] *Works*, VI, p. 364.
[2] Rom. 4.35—a favourite verse with Knox, as with Calvin.
[3] *Scots Confession*, Articles X and XI.

bestowal of a positive righteousness that derives from beyond us, and which we have through union with Christ. Justification is not the beginning of a new self-righteousness, but the perpetual end of it, for it is a perpetual living in Christ, from a centre and source beyond us. To be justified is to be lifted up above and beyond ourselves to live out of the risen and ascended Christ, and not out of ourselves.

Justification is interwoven with Incarnation—the union of God and Man in Christ, and with the fulfilment of that union in Reconciliation and Mediation between God and man which was wrought out in the life, death, resurrection and ascension of Christ—although the final execution of it so far as we are concerned awaits the coming again of Jesus Christ. Justification is rooted in the Incarnation and therefore it reaches out to the final Advent of Jesus as the Incarnate Son—it is both Christological and eschatological. In none of the Reformers was the stress upon incarnational union so strong as in Knox; and in none of them was the place given to the *Parousia* so powerful; while it is Knox's highly distinctive doctrine of the Ascension that links those two together, or rather reveals the relation of the Incarnation to the *Parousia*. It is in the Ascension that we have *the fruit* of the Incarnation (including the Death and Resurrection) of Christ, and it is in the *Parousia* that we have the full *fruit* of the Ascension.

Now the reality of all this is what Knox called *Veritie*, that is, the truth and reality of our justification and renewal in Jesus Christ. But the *Veritie* is in Christ and *is* Christ, and it is in us through the operation of the Spirit, and through faith. The *Veritie* of God is in us only as by faith we seek it, not in ourselves, but in Christ alone, for it is through the Spirit that we partake of the blessed conjunction between Christ and ourselves and are presented before the Father in the Body of the Son as those who share in his life and righteousness, and are one with him.

If it is through the Spirit that this Verity is in us, it is through the two Sacraments as instruments of the Holy Spirit's operation that we are *exercised*, as Knox expressed it, in that Verity or blessed conjunction, unity, society, or fraternity with Christ. In Baptism we are ingrafted into Christ to be made partakers of his justice by which our sins are covered and remitted, and in the Supper we are continually nourished through that union with Christ.[1] Both sacraments tell us that we live not out of ourselves, but that we find our life and righteousness outside of ourselves, in Christ alone, through union and communion with him. Therefore, we are required, as Knox and his colleagues put it in the

---

[1] *Scots Confession*, 1560, Art. XXI.

Confession, 'to spoil ourselves of all honour of our own creation and redemption and also of our regeneration and sanctification'.[1] That is the radical nature, and the cutting edge, of Justification.

To bring out the full significance of that a more systematic exposition is necessary.

2 THE NATURE OF JUSTIFICATION

The Greek word *dikaioun*, like the Scots word *to justify*, may mean to condemn as well as to vindicate. The basic meaning, which we find in biblical Greek, is *to put in the right, to put in the truth*. Thus, if a man is guilty he is put in the right by being condemned, for that is the truth of the matter; if he is innocent he is put in the right by being declared guiltless and set free. Justification always involves a fulfilling of the righteousness, or the enacting of the truth.

The Gospel teaches 'the justification of the ungodly', and the astounding thing about it is that it means such a putting of the ungodly man in the right that through fulfilment of his condemnation he is justified, justified in both senses: judged and acquitted, condemned and vindicated, exposed as guilty and made righteous—but that is truth, *aletheia*, concrete reality, only in Jesus Christ.

Let us consider what that means, by thinking of it in terms of *objective justification* and *subjective justification*.

A. *Objective justification* takes place in Christ, before the Father. The *Scots Confession* expounds it in this way. There was 'enmity betwixt the justice of God and our sins',[2] and therefore the Son of God descended to take to himself a body of our body, flesh of our flesh, and bone of our bones, and so to become *Mediator* between God and man. Three conceptions are involved here which we may allow three words of the *Confession* in its Latin edition to express. (*a*) *Frater*. The Son of the Father has made himself our Brother, for through his incarnational union with us, he has established our union with him. By making himself our Brother, he has made us brothers of his and therefore sons of the Father. Through this incarnational fraternity, that which was lost in Adam is restored.[3] (*b*) *Mediator* or *Interpres*. Through his Sonship, that is, through his obedient Life in filial relation toward the Father, and through his brotherhood with us in our estrangement, Christ is the active Agent who reveals God to us and reconciles us to God—and that he does through the whole of his Life lived out in our flesh and bone in which

---

[1] *Scots Confession*, Art. XII. [2] Art. VIII. [3] *Ibid*.

he brought us back to union with God. The positive emphasis here is upon the obedience of the Beloved Son.[1] (c) *Pacificator*. As our Mediator or Redeemer it behoved Jesus Christ to be very God and very Man 'because He was to underlie the punishment due for our transgressions, and to present Himself in the presence of His Father's Judgment, as in our persone, to suffer for our transgression and inobedience be death to overcome him that was the author of death.'[2]

All this could only be done in the hypostatic union, 'the wondrous conjunction betwixt Godhead and Manhood',[3] and out of it issues our justification in resurrection.[4]

This is the doctrine which Reformed theology has called the *Active* and *Passive Obedience* of Christ, and his incarnational *Assumption* and *Sanctification* of our human nature.

1. By *active obedience* of Christ is meant the positive fulfilment in the whole life of Jesus of his Sonship. From the very beginning to the very end he maintained a perfect filial relation to the Father in which he yielded to him a life of utter love and faithfulness, of praise and thanksgiving and confidence and trust, and in which he perfectly fulfilled God's holy will and received and laid hold of the love of the Father. This active obedience was therefore his own loving self-offering to the Father in our name and on our behalf and also his own faithful appropriation of the Father's Word and will in our name and on our behalf.

2. By *passive obedience* is meant the submission of Jesus Christ to the judgment of the Father upon our sin which he assumed in our humanity when he was 'made under the Law' in order to bear it in our name and on our behalf. This is the passion he endured in the expiation of our sins, but it is also his willing acceptance of the divine verdict upon our humanity. The passive obedience is manifested above all in the obedience of Jesus unto the death of the Cross, but that was a passion that began with his very birth, for his whole life, as Calvin says, was in a real sense a bearing of the Cross, but it was in the Cross itself that it had its *telos* or consummation.

This distinction between the active and passive obedience of Christ has been emphasized in Reformed theology not in order to divide or separate them but in order to insist that the whole course of Christ's active obedience is absolutely integral to his work of reconciliation, and that atonement cannot be limited to his passive obedience, that is to his passive submission to the penalty for our sin inflicted upon Christ in his

---

[1] Art. VIII and X.   [2] Art. IX.
[3] Art. VII and VIII.   [4] Art. X.

death. As Calvin put it, immediately he put on the person of the servant he began to pay the price of liberation for our salvation.[1] How could it be otherwise when in the Incarnation there took place a union of God the Judge and the man judged in one Person, so that all through his life, but especially in his death, Jesus bore in himself the infliction and judgment of God upon our sinful humanity, and wrought out in his life and his death expiation and amendment for our sin?

The active and passive obedience of Christ thus do not differ in regard to time, for both extend to the very beginning of the Incarnation, to the birth of Jesus, and both reach out to its fulfilment in his death and resurrection. Nor do they differ in regard to their Subject, for they are both manifestations of the one obedience of the Son of God in our humanity. They are set in mutual unity in the whole life of Christ. Since this is so we must speak of the active obedience as *actio passiva* and the passive obedience as *passio activa*. This mutuality of Christ's active and passive obedience is important, for it means that in our justification we have imputed to us not only the passive righteousness of Christ in which he satisfied for our sins in suffering the judgment of God in his death on the Cross, but the active righteousness of Christ in which he positively fulfilled the Father's holy will in an obedient life. In other words, justification means not simply the non-imputation of our sins through the pardon of Christ, but positive sharing in his divine-human righteousness. We are saved, therefore, not only by the death of Christ which he suffered for our sakes, but by his life which he lived in our flesh for our sakes and which God raised from the dead that we may share in it through the power of the Spirit. It is in that light, of his atoning and justifying life, that we are to understand the Incarnation of the Son in the whole course of his obedience from his birth to his resurrection.

3. By the *sanctification of our human nature* we refer to what was wrought by the Son, not only in his active and passive obedience, but through the *union* he established in his birth, life, death, and resurrection between our fallen human nature and his divine nature. In this union he both assumed our fallen human nature, taking it from the Virgin Mary, and sanctified it in the very act of assumption and all through his holy Life he lived in it from the beginning to the end. Thus our redemption begins from his very birth, so that we must regard the Incarnation, even in its narrower sense, as redeeming event, reaching out to its full *telos* in the death and resurrection. In his holy assumption of our un-

[1] *Inst.* 2.16.5.

holy humanity, his purity wipes away our impurity, his holiness covers our corruption, his nature heals our nature.[1]

If we are to think of the active and passive obedience of Christ as dealing with our actual sin and its penalty, we are to think of the incarnational union of the Holy Son with our unholy nature as dealing with our original sin, or as sanctifying our human nature, through bringing it into a healing and sanctifying union with his own holy nature. That applies, as Calvin insisted in a famous section of his *Institute*, to the whole life of Jesus, his conception, birth, childhood, youth, manhood, for by living his holy life through the whole course of our life he has sanctified our conception, birth, childhood, youth, manhood, and death, in himself.[2]

This is supremely important, for it is only through this union of the human nature with his divine nature that Jesus Christ gives us not only the negative righteousness of the remission of sins but makes us share in the positive righteousness of his obedient and loving life lived in perfect filial relation to the Father from the cradle to the grave. If we neglect this essential element in the obedience of the Son, then not only do the active and the passive obedience of Christ fall apart in our understanding and doctrine, but we are unable to apprehend justification as anything more than a merely forensic non-imputation of sin. Moreover, if we neglect this essential element we are unable to see the Humanity of Jesus Christ in its saving significance, that is, to give the whole life of the historical Jesus its rightful place in the doctrine of the Atonement. It is necessary for us, then, to give the fullest consideration to the place of the union of human and divine natures in the being and life of the incarnate Son, for it is that saving and sanctifying union in which we are given to share that belongs to the very substance of our faith and life in Christ. In other words, what we are concerned with is the *filial relation* which the Son of God lived out in our humanity in perfect holiness and love, achieving that in himself in assuming our human nature into oneness with himself, and on that ground giving us to share in it, providing us with a fulness in his own obedient Sonship from which we may all receive.

B. *Subjective Justification.* It is illuminating to recognize that subjective justification, as well as objective justification, has already taken place in Jesus Christ. Not only was the great divine act of righteousness fulfilled in the flesh of Jesus, in his life and death, but throughout his life

---

[1] See Robert Bruce, *Sermons Preached in the Kirk of Edinburgh*, ed. Cunningham, pp. 268f.   [2] *Inst.* 2.16.19.

and death Jesus stood in our place as our Substitute and Representative who appropriated the divine Act of saving Righteousness for us. He responded to it, yielded to it, accepted it and actively made it his own, for what he was and did in his human nature was not for his own sake but for our sakes. That is true of all that he did. He was the Word of God brought to bear upon man, but he was also man hearing that Word, answering it, trusting it, living by it—by faith. He was the great Believer —vicariously believing in our place and in our name.[1] He was not only the will of God enacted in our flesh, but he was the will of man united to that divine will. In becoming one with us he laid hold upon our way-ward human will, made it his very own, and bent it back into obedience to, and in oneness with, the holy will of God. Likewise in justification, Jesus Christ was not only the embodiment of God's justifying act but the embodiment of our human appropriation of it. In that unity of the divine and the human, justification was fulfilled in Christ from both sides, from the side of the justifying God and from the side of justified man—'He was justified in the Spirit', as St Paul put it.[2] Justification as objective act of the redeeming God and justification as subjective actualization of it in our estranged human existence have once and for all taken place—in Jesus.

The New Testament employs other language to speak of this, *hagiazein*, to sanctify, and *teleioun*, to consecrate, especially in their application to Christ. Thus in the Fourth Gospel, in his great high-priestly prayer, Jesus spoke of sanctifying himself that we also may be sanctified in him, and prayed that we may be consecrated in one with him as he and the Father are one. Similarly the Epistle to the Hebrews spoke of Christ as our High-Priest who has consecrated himself for our sakes, and pointed out that he who sanctifies and those who are sanctified are all one. Once and for all we have been sanctified and consecrated in Christ's vicarious work.

That aspect of justification tended to drop out of sight when Protes-tant scholastic theology began to operate with an *ordo salutis* in which it assigned justification and sanctification to successive and different stages in a process of salvation. In the New Testament itself, however, sancti-fication or consecration in Christ (for the two words express the same thing) is spoken of in the perfect tense. Christ has already consecrated or sanctified himself for our sakes, so that we are already consecrated or

---

[1] This is the significance of the expression 'the merits of Christ' employed in our Reformed Confessions and Catechisms. See *The School of Faith*, pp. lxxxiii f.
[2] I Tim. 3.16.

sanctified in him—therefore sanctification or consecration is imputed to us by his free grace just like justification. But it would be a mistake to think of these as two different things, for in the Johannine literature and in the Epistle to the Hebrews the words 'sanctification' and 'consecration' correspond closely to the Pauline 'justification'—they have their special nuance, without doubt, for they are more closely associated than 'justification' with the priestly work of Christ, but it is the same reality, the same verity, to use Knox's term, which they describe.

This teaching is found deeply embedded in the theology of John Calvin and it is an immense pity that later 'Calvinism' overlaid and obscured it, although it is once more being brought to light and appropriated in our Reformed doctrine.[1] Our concern here is with *subjective justification*, that aspect of it in which the mighty act of God's righteousness and holiness is appropriated and translated into human life—and that is precisely what Calvin spoke of as the consecrated and sanctified flesh or Life of Jesus in which we are given to share. Let us take as a text for our discussion his answer in the *Geneva Catechism* to question 342. 'Since the whole affiance of our salvation rests in the obedience which he has rendered to God, his Father, in order that it may be imputed to us as if it were ours, we must possess him: for his blessings are not ours unless he gives himself to us first.' The same essential point is made by Knox in the *Book of Common Order* in which he says that justification, regeneration, sanctification flow out of *adoption*.

We may single out of this two points immediately relevant for our concern at the moment. 1. It is only through union with Christ that we partake of the blessings of Christ, that is through union with him in his holy and obedient life. Through being united to him we share in his judgment and his exaltation, in his passive and active obedience, in his Death and also in his Resurrection and Ascension—but first of all it is necessary that we be united to him, that is, have part in the union which he wrought out between us in his Incarnation and in the whole course of his Life. Unfortunately this was reversed in the later teaching of the Church of Scotland, as found in the Westminster Standards—for they put justification first, and then spoke of union with Christ and sanctification as following upon the judicial act that took place in justification by faith.[2]

2. But there is a second point we have to note in Calvin's statement,

---

[1] Cf. R. S. Wallace, *Calvin's Doctrine of the Christian Life* (1959), in which Dr Wallace shows that for Calvin Christ's self-consecration on our behalf governs the whole of the Christian life.
[2] See *The School of Faith*, cvi f.

the meaning of 'affiance'. As Calvin used it this term had a covenanted significance, for it referred to the 'fiance' or trust which we have within the covenant mercies of God. A great deal of harm has been occasioned through a sharp distinction between *fides quae creditur* and *fides qua creditur*, or between *credere* and *confidere*, belief and trust. Once this distinction is drawn, faith is separated off from its objective ground and is understood as 'trust', *fiducia*—then justification by faith means justification through our trust in God. Now of course there is a truth here which must not be neglected. The Latin term for trust, *fiducia*, which Calvin often translated *fiance*, was a legal term taken from conveyancing, and referred to the conveying of a property from one person to another without any documented receipt; it is an act of trust that relies solely upon the word of another without any tangible pledge of his deed. As Calvin used the word *affiance*, however, the trust or faith of the believer was regarded as grounded and pledged in the faithfulness of Christ, not only in his spoken promises but in his flesh. He has already received from God all his blessings and has sealed that reception of it for us in his own life and death. Faith is thus a polar concept that reposes upon and derives from the prior faithfulness of God which has been translated permanently into our actual human existence in Jesus Christ. We do not rely, then, upon our act of faith, but upon the faith of Christ which undergirds and upholds our faith. But his faith is not in word only; it has been translated into his life and saving action and set forth in the covenant of his Body and Blood. The text which we have taken from Calvin comes from his account of the Lord's Supper, for it is in our participation in the Supper and our union with Christ which it gives us that we discern what *affiance*, faith depending upon the faithfulness of Christ, really means.

We may summarize this by saying that Jesus Christ was not only the fulfilment and embodiment of God's righteous and holy Act or *dikaioma*, but also the embodiment of our act of faith and trust and obedience toward God. He stood in our place, taking our cause upon him, also as Believer, as the Obedient One who was himself justified before God as his beloved Son in whom he was well pleased. He offered to God a perfect confidence and trust, a perfect faith and response which we are unable to offer, and he appropriated all God's blessings which we are unable to appropriate. Through union with him we share in his faith, in his obedience, in his trust and his appropriation of the Father's blessing; we share in his justification before God. Therefore when we are justified by faith, this does not mean that it is *our* faith that justifies us, far from it—it is the faith of Christ alone that justifies us, but we in faith flee from our own acts even of repentance, confession, trust and response, and take refuge in the obedience and faithfulness of Christ—'Lord I believe, help thou mine unbelief.' That is what it means to be justified by faith.

We may express it in still another way. Justification has been fulfilled subjectively as well as objectively in Jesus Christ, but that objective and subjective justification is objective to us. It is freely imputed to us by grace objectively and we through the Spirit share in it subjectively as we are united to Christ. His subjective justification becomes ours, and it is subjective in us as well as in him, but only subjective in us because it has been made subjectively real in our own human nature, in our own human flesh in Jesus, our Brother, and our Mediator.

When we look at it like this, we understand why John Knox hesitated to use the expression 'justification by faith' and preferred instead concrete expressions which made it clear that we are justified only in Christ, by what he has done alone, and not by any act of ours, even if that act be an act of believing. We believe in Christ in such a way that we flee from ourselves and take refuge in him alone—and therefore we can hardly speak about 'justifying faith' without transferring the emphasis away from Christ and his faithful act to ourselves and our act of trust or believing. At this point Calvin and Knox stood in contrast to Luther who approached the whole question from a point that tended to be anthropocentric: 'How can I get a gracious God?' Luther made it indubitably clear that justification does not derive from the act of the self, but from a righteousness outside of us in Christ, from an *aliena justitia*, as he called it. But his basic question demanded an answer to the self, and inevitably gave the whole question of assurance undue prominence. With Calvin and Knox it was different—assurance had little place, because it was not needed. The very act of faith was pivoted upon Christ and his faith, not upon my faith or my need for this or that answer, and hence the assurance was unshakable, because it was grounded in the solid faithfulness of Christ. It was only later in Scottish theology when the anthropocentric questions emerged, questions of conscience and soul-searching, when the eyes of the believer were turned inward upon his own heart rather than outward upon his Lord and Saviour, that the demand for assurance became clamant. Whenever there is talk of 'justifying faith' then uncertainty creeps in, for all our acts, even of repentance and faith are unworthy before God. If it is upon our repentance and our faith that we have ultimately to rely, who can be saved, not to speak of being sure of his salvation? It is against this false notion of justification and this false notion of faith that Fraser of Brea directed his profound writings, for what disturbed him more than anything else was the new legalism and the new self-righteousness that had crept into the Reformed faith under cover of 'justifying faith'.[1] If we are to use the expression 'justification by faith alone', and there is no reason why we should not, then let it be crystal clear that 'by faith alone' is meant 'by the grace of Christ alone', that faith is but an empty vessel to be filled by the covenant mercies and faithfulness of God in Christ.

3 THE RADICAL CONSEQUENCES OF JUSTIFICATION

Justification means justification by Christ alone—that is the reference of the expressions *sola fide, sola gratia, sola scriptura*, used in Reformed theology. Justification means that we look exclusively to Christ, and therefore that we look away from ourselves altogether in order to live out of him alone. That radical nature of justification is expressed and its radical consequences drawn by the *Scots Confession* in the words we cited earlier: 'we willingly spoil ourselves of all honour and glory of our own salvation and redemption, as we also do of our regeneration and sanctification.'

This is something that very badly needs to be reiterated today within the Churches of the Reformation. Justification by Christ alone means the rejection of *all* forms of self-justification, and all forms of justification by anything or out of any source other than Jesus Christ. Let us consider what this means in several areas of doctrine and life.

(*a*) At the Reformation justification by the grace of Christ alone was seen to set aside all *natural goodness*, and all works-righteousness; but this applies to all goodness, Christian goodness as well, that is, to 'sanctification' as it came to be called. This is powerfully driven home by the *Scots Confession* in several articles, such as the twelfth and the fifteenth. All that we do is unworthy so that we must fall down before you and unfeignedly confess that we are unprofitable servants—and it is precisely justification by the free grace of Christ alone that shows us that all that we are and have done even as believers is called in question. Justification by grace alone remains the sole ground of the Christian life; we never advance beyond it, as if justification were only the beginning of a new self-righteousness, the beginning of a life of sanctification which is what we do in response to justification. Of course we are summoned to

---

[1] James Fraser of Brea, *A Treatise on Justifying Faith*, and *Meditations on Several Subjects in Divinity, Particularly Trusting upon God*, etc.

live out day by day what we already are in Christ through his self-consecration or sanctification, but sanctification is not what we do in addition to what God has done in justification. And yet that is the tendency
of the *Westminster Catechisms*, where we have a return to the Roman
notion of infused sanctification that has to be worked out through strict
obedience to legal precepts—hence the exposition of the Ten Commandments takes up the greater part of the Catechisms. But the *Scots Confession* laid the axe to the root of any such movement when it insisted
that we have to spoil ourselves even of our own regeneration and sanctification as well as justification. What it 'axed' so radically was the notion
of 'co-redemption' which in our day has again become so rampant, not
only in the Roman Church, but in Liberal and Evangelical Protestantism, e.g. the emphasis upon existential decision as the means whereby
we 'make real' for ourselves the *kerygma* of the New Testament, which
means that in the last resort our salvation depends upon our own personal
or existential decision. That is the exact antithesis of the Reformed
doctrine of election, which rests salvation upon the prior and objective
decision of God in Christ. It is justification by grace alone that guards
the Gospel from corruption by 'Evangelicals', 'Liberals' and Romans
alike.

(b) Justification by the grace of Christ alone calls in question not only
all natural goodness but all *natural knowledge*. Natural knowledge is as
much the work of the flesh as natural goodness; it is a work of the
natural man. It is at this point that Karl Barth has made such an immense contribution to the Reformation. We cannot separate knowing
and being for they belong to the same man, and it is the whole man,
with his knowing and his acting, with the whole of his being, who is
called in question by justification. Justification puts us in the right and
truth of God and therefore tells us that we are in untruth. Now, let it be
clear that justification by grace alone does not mean that there is no
natural goodness in man, but that man with his natural goodness is
called in question. Jesus Christ died for the whole man (with his good
and his evil) not for part of him, the evil part, but for the whole man.
He died for all men, the good and the bad, and all alike come under the
total judgment of his Death and Resurrection; all alike have to be born
again in him, and made new creatures. That is the radical nature of the
Gospel, which becomes so clear to us when we communicate at the
Holy Table in the Body and Blood of our Lord, for there we feel
ashamed for our *whole being*, for our good as well as for our evil. But the
same applies to our natural knowledge. Justification by the grace of

Christ alone, does not mean that there is no natural knowledge—what natural man is there who does not know something of God even if he holds it down in unrighteousness or turns the truth into a lie?[1] But it does mean that the whole of that natural knowledge is called in question by Christ who when he comes to us says: 'If any man will come after me, let him deny himself, take up his cross and follow me.' The whole man with his natural knowledge is there questioned down to the root of his being, for man is summoned to look away from all that he is and knows or thinks he knows to Christ who is the Way the Truth and the Life; no one goes to the Father but by him. The theology of Barth can be described, then, as the application of justification to the whole realm of man's life, to the realm of his knowing as well as the realm of his doing. In that he has sought to follow through the radical consequences of the Reformation from which our forefathers resiled when they took refuge again, like the Romans, in the works of the natural man, for justification.

But if we are to take the *Scots Confession* seriously then we have to apply this not only to natural knowledge but to *all* Christian knowledge; we have to learn to spoil ourselves of our own vaunted knowledge, we have to let our own theology be called into radical question, by Christ. If we translate the word 'justification' by the word 'verification' we can see the startling relevance of this to modern theological and philosophical discussions. Justification by grace alone tells us that verification of our faith or knowledge on any other ground, or out of any other source, than Jesus Christ, is to be set aside. Justification has an *epistemological* as well as an ethical reference—epistemologically it insists that the only legitimate demonstration of Christian truth is that which is in accordance with its nature, which is grace, and that to seek justification of it on any other ground is not only fundamentally false in itself but to falsify the Gospel at its very basis. But apart from the contemporary debate on 'verification' justification means that at every point in our theological inquiry we have to let our knowledge, our theology, our formulations, our statements, be called into question by the very Christ toward which they point, for he alone is the Truth. Justification means that our theological statements are of such a kind that they do not claim to have truth in themselves for by their very nature they point away from themselves to Christ as the one Truth of God. Therefore whenever we claim that our theological statements or our formulations have their truth in themselves we are turning back into the way of self-justification. Out of sheer respect for the majesty of the Truth as it is revealed in the Holy

[1] Rom. 1.18 25.

Scriptures, we have to do our utmost to speak correctly and exactly about it—that is the meaning of orthodoxy and the way of humility—but when we have done all this, we have still to confess that we are unfaithful servants, that all our efforts fall far short of the truth. Far from seeking justification on the ground of our 'orthodoxy' we can only serve the Truth faithfully if we point away from ourselves and our statements to Christ himself, and direct all eyes to him alone. He who boasts of orthodoxy thus sins against Justification by Christ alone, for he justifies himself by appeal to his own beliefs or his own formulations of belief and thereby does despite to the truth and grace of Christ. Once a Church begins to boast of its 'orthodoxy' it begins to fall from grace.

(c) Justification by the grace of Christ alone calls in question all *tradition*. The radical consequence of justification was keenly felt in this direction at the Reformation. Concentration upon the Word of God, the self-utterance of the Truth, and the acknowledgment of its primacy, cut the strings of prejudice and prejudgment and made clear the path of faith and obedience. Justification here meant that faith is determined by the objective Word of God as its ultimate authority, and so it was freed from the shackles of every lesser authority, for devotion to the truth of the Word (the whole truth and nothing but the truth) inculcated a readiness to rethink all preconceptions and to put all traditional ideas to the test face to face with the Word. In other words, sheer attachment to the Word of God as the real object of knowledge meant detachment from all other sources and norms of knowledge, and the demand that all traditional ideas and notions had to be tested at the bar of the Word. That did not mean that tradition was to be despised, but that it was to be subjected to the criticism of the Word and the Spirit, and corrected through obedient conformity to Jesus Christ. The Reformation stood, therefore, for the supremacy of the Word over all tradition, and for theological activity as the repentant rethinking of all tradition face to face with the revelation of God in Jesus Christ.

But that applies no less to the Reformed and Evangelical tradition; to our Presbyterian tradition as well as to the Roman tradition. When we examine our own position today, it is astonishing to find how close we have come to the Roman view even in the Church of Scotland. How frequently, for example, we find that appeal is made to 'Christian instinct' or to 'the mind of the Church' over against the plain utterances of Holy Scripture, and often just at those places where the Word of God offends our will, opposes our habits, or cuts against the grain of our desire! And how massive is the effect of our several traditions upon the interpretations of the Bible! How easy it is to allow the Presbyterian tradition to determine our reading of the New Testament especially when it is a question of justifying our tradition before the critique of others! There can be no doubt that every one of the great Churches of the Reformation, the Lutheran, the Anglican, and the Reformed, has developed its own masterful tradition, and that that tradition today exercises massive influence not only over its way of interpreting the Bible and formulating its doctrine but over the whole shape and direction of its life. Those who shut their eyes to this fact are precisely those who are most enslaved to the dominant power of tradition just because it has become an unconscious canon and norm of their thinking. It is high time we asked again whether the Word of God really does have free course amongst us and whether it is not after all bound and fettered by the traditions of men. The tragedy, apparently, is that the very structures of our Churches represent the fossilization of traditions that have grown up by practice and procedure, and have become so hardened in self-justification that even the Word of God can hardly crack them open. There is scarcely a Church that claims to be *ecclesia reformata* that can truthfully claim to be *semper reformanda*.

(*d*) Justification by Christ alone calls in question all *systems* and *orders*, and calls them in question because Jesus Christ alone is central and supreme in the one Church of God. In any true theological system, justification is by reference to Christ alone, for conformity to Christ as the Truth of God for us is the one ultimate principle of unity. Likewise justification in ecclesiastical order or polity ought to be through appeal to Christ alone. Our quarrel with the Church of Rome in doctrinal matters concerns the centrality of Jesus Christ, the primacy and supremacy of Christology which is so obscured and compromised by Roman doctrines of merit and tradition, and above all by Mariology. In our debate with the Church of England over questions of order, we are also concerned with the centrality of Christ, and the primacy of Christology —and therefore the doctrine of the Church as the Body of *Christ* is in the forefront. It is justification by Christ alone that makes it so, for he alone is the ground and Head of the Church, and in him alone is the Church's unity constituted and its order maintained. But for that very reason justification by Christ alone disallows any appeal from one Church to another for recognition of its orders, as it also rebukes the self-justification of a Church in calling in question the orders of another Church. Justification by Christ alone means that we renounce the way of the flesh in seeking honour from men, or justification from one another; and therefore justification by Christ alone means that in any movement for reconciliation between Churches, the question of the recognition of orders cannot have priority without radical betrayal of the Reformation, nay, without radical betrayal of Christ for he is thereby ousted from his place of centrality.

It becomes more and more clear that in the ecumenical movement it is the doctrine of justification by Christ alone that is at stake, and that it can just as easily be sinned against by those who shout loudest that they are upholding the Reformation tradition as by those who make no such boast. He is truest to the Reformation tradition who is always ready to subject it to the ruthless questioning of the Word of God.

(*e*) Nowhere does justification by Christ alone have more radical consequences than in regard to the pastoral ministry. Justification by Christ is grounded upon his mighty Act in which he took our place, substituting himself for us under the divine judgment, and substituting himself for us in the obedient response he rendered to God in worship and thanksgiving and praise. In himself he has opened up a way to the Father, so that we may approach God solely through him and on the ground of what he has done and is—therefore we pray in his Name, and whatever we do, we do in his Name before God. Thus the whole of our worship and ministry reposes upon the substitutionary work of Christ. Now the radical nature of that is apparent from the fact that through substituting himself in our place there takes place a displacement of our humanity by the humanity of Christ—that is why Jesus insists that we can only follow him by denying ourselves, by letting him displace us from a place of centrality, and by letting him take our place.

At the Reformation this doctrine had immediate effect in the overthrow of Roman sacerdotalism—Jesus Christ is our sole Priest. He is the one and only Man who can mediate between us and God, so that we approach God solely through the mediation of the Humanity of Jesus, through his incarnate Priesthood. When the Humanity of Christ is depreciated or whenever it is obscured by the sheer majesty of his Deity then the need for some other human mediation creeps in—hence in the Dark and Middle Ages arose the need for a human priesthood to mediate between sinful humanity and the exalted Christ, the majestic Judge and King. There was of course no denial of the Deity of Christ by the Reformers—on the contrary they restored the purity of faith in Christ as God through overthrowing the accretions that compromised it; but they also restored the place occupied in the New Testament and the Early Church by the Humanity of Christ, as he who took our human nature in order to be our Priest, as he who takes our side and is our Advocate before the judgment of God, and who once and for all has wrought out atonement for us in his sacrifice on the Cross, and therefore as he who eternally stands in for us as our heavenly Mediator and High-Priest.

The Church on earth lives and acts only as it is directed by its heavenly Lord, and only in such a way that his Ministry is reflected in the midst of its ministry and worship. Therefore from first to last the worship and ministry of the Church on earth must be governed by the fact that Christ substitutes himself in our place, and that our humanity with its own acts of worship, is displaced by his, so that we appear before God not in our own name, not in our own significance, not in virtue of our own acts of confession, contrition, worship, and thanksgiving, but solely in the name of Christ and solely in virtue of what he has done in our name and on our behalf, and in our stead. Justification by Christ alone means that from first to last in the worship of God and in the ministry of the Gospel Christ himself is central, and that we draw near in worship and service only through letting him take our place. He only is Priest. He only represents humanity. He only has an offering with which to appear before God and with which God is well-pleased. He only presents our prayers before God, and he only is our praise and thanksgiving and worship as we appear before the face of the Father. Nothing in our hands we bring—simply to his Cross we cling.

But what has happened in Protestant worship and ministry? Is it not too often the case that the whole life and worship of the congregation revolves round the personality of the minister? He is the one who is in the centre; he offers the prayers of the congregation; he it is who mediates 'truth' through his personality, and he it is who mediates between the people and God through conducting the worship entirely on his own. Nowhere is this more apparent than in the case of the popular minister where everything centres on him, and the whole life of the congregation is built round him. What is that but *Protestant sacerdotalism*, sacerdotalism which involves the displacement of the Humanity of Christ by the humanity of the minister, and the obscuring of the Person of Christ by the personality of the minister? How extraordinary that Protestantism should thus develop a new sacerdotalism, to be sure a psychological rather than a sacramental sacerdotalism, but a sacerdotalism nonetheless, in which it is the personality of the minister which both mediates the Word of God to man and mediates the worship of man to God! Protestant Churches are full of these 'psychological priests' and more and more they evolve a psychological cult and develop a form of psychological counselling which displaces the truly pastoral ministry of Christ. How frequently, for example, the minister's prayers are so crammed with his own personality (with all its boring idiosyncrasies!) that the worshipper cannot get past him in order to worship God in the name of Christ—but is forced to worship God in the name of the minister! How frequently the sermon is not an exposition of the Word of God but an exposition of the minister's own views on this or that subject! And how frequently the whole life of the congregation is so built up on the personality of the minister that when he goes the congregation all but collapses or dwindles away!

There can be no doubt that the whole concept of the ministry and of worship in our Reformed Churches needs to be brought back to the criticism of the Word of God in order that we may learn again the meaning of justification by Christ alone in the midst of the Church's life and work. Jesus Christ must be given his rightful place by being set right in the centre, as Head and Lord of the Church, as its sole Prophet and Priest and King, and that means in the midst of our preaching, in the basic notion of the ministerial office, in the fundamental mode of worship, and in the whole life of the congregation as the Body of *Christ alone*.

10

The Roman Doctrine of Grace
from the Point of View of Reformed Theology[1]

THE purpose of this article is to raise the problems which the Roman doctrine of grace poses for Reformed theology, and to throw those problems into high relief in the hope that it will lay bare the areas where real dialogue is badly needed. The differences are deep, but some are due to misunderstanding, some to terminological differences, and some arise from the fact that the doctrine of grace is formulated from different frames of reference. In so far as this is the case, it is to be hoped that frank dialogue may go far to clearing away misunderstanding and bridging the gap. As this is done the basic differences, if there are any, will emerge, but only when they emerge clearly into the open can dialogue really get to grips with them and, by penetrating behind them to a deeper level of common agreement, work out reconciliation in understanding. Hence if the manner of this article is frank, and its statement of the problems abrupt, without much attention to qualifying modifications, the intention is not polemical but irenic.

I

Since this article is written from the *point of view* of Reformed theology with its characteristic emphasis upon the *Word*, let me begin by distinguishing three ways of thinking which have contributed so much to the development of the Western mind, for it may help us to see that some at least of our differences derive from an initial difference in approach.

(*a*) *The way of the Greeks.* In all their thinking, in philosophy or science, the Greeks were concerned with discerning the shape and pattern of things. Thinking was ultimately a kind of *seeing*, and the truth was apprehended in terms of *form*. Vision held the primacy in Greek habits of thought. That is the tradition that lies behind our

[1] Reprinted from *The Eastern Churches Quarterly*, Oct. 1964.

modern understanding of science in which *observation* and *theory* hold such an important place. (We may recall that theory = *theoria* meant 'beholding', 'speculation'.)

(*b*) *The way of the Romans*. The great genius of the Romans was for law and order. They were concerned with ways and means, with getting things done, with management and control of resources, whether of armies, supplies or public life. It is this Latin way of thinking that has left its mark in the legal structures, and the social and political institutions, of the West, but it has also had its influence in the realm of disciplined knowledge and interpretation. The Latin way of thinking has contributed not a little to the place of *control* in modern science, along with observation and theory.

(*c*) *The way of the Hebrews*. This is the kind of thinking we find in the Bible, where we learn through listening and responding, serving and obeying. In the Scriptures where we have to do with the Word of God, the emphasis falls upon hearing that Word, letting it speak to us out of itself, and upon the obedience of the mind in response to it. The principle involved here can be spoken of as knowledge of an object in accordance with its nature.

This Hebrew way of thinking has also made its important contribution to scientific method. Within the realm of theological knowledge itself it involves the primacy of the personal, but when it came to be applied to natural science, particularly after the Reformation (e.g. by Francis Bacon), it gave rise to the concern for *objectivity*, i.e. the determination to know something out of itself, unhindered by anything outside of it, and undistorted by any previous notions we may have acquired. Thus nature is to be understood only by humble learning, by serving it, giving ear to it, and following the clues it gives us of its own secrets, without attempting to force our own patterns upon nature, even when we may have to use violent methods of putting the question to nature.

It can be said that these three ways of thinking, the Greek, the Latin and the Hebrew, contribute the three essential ingredients in our Western habits of mind and modes of knowing. There can be no question of discounting any of them, but in the nature of the case a different balance of the' three will be employed in accordance with the nature of the object being investigated. It is in this way that one can distinguish the fundamental approach of the Reformers from that of the mediaeval theologians. The latter were concerned primarily with a combination of the first two ways of thinking and knowing, whereas the

Reformers gave primacy to the Word, to hearing, and to the obedient response of the mind to God speaking personally through the Scriptures. This effected a real change in understanding and in theological articulation, as one can see in the shift from a more static to a more dynamic set of conceptions, from a more impersonal to a more personal mode of statement. The re-emergence of the personal and dialogical in place of the logical and dialectical in theology carried with it a different stress upon objectivity, for concentration upon the Word of God as the proper object of theological knowledge involved a critical questioning of all preconceptions and a reconstruction of traditional formulations, and therefore involved at the same time a decisive shifting of the locus of authority from the subject of the interpreter (whether the individual subject of the Renaissance man or the corporate subject of the mediaeval Church) to the object of inquiry, the Truth of God declaring himself to us in his Word. This did not entail a rejection of tradition, but a testing and a reforming of it before the self-disclosure of the Word, and therefore the substitution of an objective form of thinking for the objectifying form of thinking which had yielded the masterful tradition in which knowledge of the Truth was subjected to the control of definition.

Such was the intention and method of Reformed theology, but so far as the history of the Evangelical Churches is concerned, this must be modified, for they soon began to develop their own masterful traditions, and then under the impact of Renaissance notions of autonomy and the pietistic stress upon inwardness, they tended to shift the locus of authority back to the individual subject or to the religious self-consciousness of the community. The Roman Church on the other hand now finds itself in the full stream of a rising biblical theology in which objective thinking on the ground of the Word of God more and more assumes a position of primacy. Since the basic approach which we adopt affects our understanding of the Truth, it is not surprising to find that there is much in Neo-Protestantism that corresponds with mediaeval notions of grace, and not a little in modern Roman teaching that corresponds with what the Reformers had to say about grace. As an example of the latter one can point to the fact that the objectivity of the *ex opere operato* can be expounded in such a way that it corresponds closely to the objectivity of the *sola gratia*.

Before we proceed to examine the main difficulties in the Roman doctrine of grace for Reformed theology we must glance at certain historical problems which concern us all, for they have come to affect our understanding of grace in the West quite seriously.

(i) Early in the history of the Church the understanding of grace came to be affected by notions of *charis* long rampant in Hellenism. In classical times 'grace' or *charis* could be thought of as a supernatural quality conferred by the gods on legendary heroes making them 'godlike'; it could even be personified. In hellenistic times it could refer to an objective endowment, to a mystical power affecting even inanimate objects, to a pneumatic potency infused into the soul, or to the divinity that dwells upon Caesar endowing him with the power to confer divine blessings. Even in the writings of Philo *charis* can be used of a cosmic potency at work in nature, or of a special endowment beyond the natural given only on the ground of merit. The impact of these notions was first felt upon popular piety, but more and more they infiltrated theological usage and left their mark on the understanding of the West as well as of the East.

(ii) In the New Testament grace is regularly associated with the Person and work of Christ, and is only twice brought into connection with the Spirit (Heb. 10.29; James 4.6), but later on grace was often used in detachment from the Person of Christ and then thought of as an independent principle or as correlated only with the Spirit. This facilitated its lapse into the hellenistic notion of pneumatic potency, especially when the notion of 'Spirit' came to be influenced by Stoic conceptions of 'spiritual substance'. This was the road sometimes taken on which grace came to be treated as something akin to magical power. The connection of grace with the Spirit is not itself theologically unsound, for grace must surely be understood in relation to the Holy Trinity, but detachment from intimate relation to the personal Being of Christ, along with failure to give the *filioque* its full weight in the doctrine of the Spirit, could, and often did, lead to serious error. Notions of 'spiritual grace' are found in Protestant as well as in Roman pietism.

(iii) Before many centuries there developed in the West the idea of *'means of grace'*—this was greatly encouraged by the Latin way of thinking, and spurred on by the Roman genius for administration. Grace came to be considered within the orbit of ways and means, as something that required to be dispensed and controlled through institutional structures. But even when the primary structures fell into the background the conception of means of grace, grace as something that required *means* for its administration, remained and continued to be a constant source of difficulty. It was carried over into the Churches of the Reformation, and all through their history it has contributed not a little to the pragmatic slant often given to the doctrine of grace. Sometimes it was enunciated in more legalist terms, sometimes in more pietist terms, but the pragmatic slant remained. So long as we talk about *means of grace*, there will always arise in us tendencies to *use* grace for our own ends.

(iv) One further point may be mentioned—and this will serve to lead us on to the major discussion of this article—the development in the debates of St Augustine with the Pelagians of the notion of *irresistible grace*. This was later to affect the Calvinist branch of the Church as much as any, but it carried an internal connection between 'grace' and 'cause' which had a deleterious effect upon the whole of mediaeval teaching on the subject, even when anti-Pelagianism was not in the ascendency. This is particularly apparent when a *pancharistic* view of the universe developed with the supervening of Aristotelian notions of entelechy upon high mediaeval Augustinianism, in which grace came to be regarded as a divine mode of causation at work in the universe, in nature as well as in supernature, and leading from one to the other.

I have singled out these factors in the history of the doctrine of grace for they affected the whole Church of the West, Protestant as well as Roman Catholic, and gave rise to erroneous ways of understanding grace which took distinctively Protestant as well as distinctively Roman forms. I believe it is most important for us to see this, for we have not really understood the error which we may point out in the other side of the Church unless we have seen the form it takes in our own side.

2

We now turn to discuss the *major problems* that arise in the Roman doctrine of grace.

1. We begin with the Augustinian conception of grace. Of all the teachers of the Church throughout its history, after St Paul, it is St Augustine who deserves most the title of supreme doctor of grace. The debt of the Reformation to St Augustine is quite immense, not only for his doctrine of election, for his battle against Pelagius and his followers which set the Church squarely upon the ground of grace alone, or for his doctrine of the Sacrament, but for his discernment of the relation of grace to the Incarnation, and of the way which grace takes with us to the way which it took once and for all in the miraculous birth of Jesus of the Virgin Mary, and in his death and resurrection. We do not and cannot forget all that, but there is another side to Augustine's teaching which had baleful results: his view of grace as the interiorizing of a divine power within us, the inspiring of good will and the implanting

of an ability to will and perform what is commanded in the divine Law. The inflowing of love, of the Spirit and of grace (they are hardly distinguishable here) into man has the effect of healing man of his disabilities and transforming the sinner into a saint in a gradual movement in and through which he enters more fully into communion with God as he fulfils works of righteousness and thereby opens up for himself the possibility of receiving more grace. The intention of Augustine throughout was emphasis upon *sola gratia*, the insistence that it is grace that is the ground of good works, but it was stated in such a way that it carried in spite of his intention a semi-Pelagianism in its heart: *ex utroque fit, id est et voluntate hominis et misericordia dei.*

This led to the peculiar mediaeval and Roman conjunction of grace and merit which ran such a powerful course from Alexander of Hales through Thomists and Scotists alike to the Council of Trent. It lies behind the distinctions in Roman theology between external and internal grace, actual and habitual grace, the grace of operation and the grace of co-operation, sufficient grace and efficacious grace, etc. The intention is clearly to distinguish between grace that is given and grace that is actualized, but in point of fact it works out into a distinction between free grace and conditional grace. The element of co-operation and indeed the seed of co-redemption that this involves is fructified and magnified when it is set in the context of a doctrine of the hierarchy of being or a metaphysic of the relation of nature to supernature in which the relation between the two becomes a sort of inclined plane leading gradually and easily from the one to the other. The difficulty that this involves for Reformed theology is very great, for to say the least it puts a question at once to the radical character and miraculous nature of the Virgin Birth, and of the Death and Resurrection of Christ. It fails to take seriously the abysmal depth of the *Eli, Eli, lema sabachthani*, or the absolute miracle of the new Creation.

Nevertheless Roman theology is here concerned with something of immense importance. The relation between creation and redemption, between nature and grace, cannot be treated merely as a dialectical relationship, in which we are content with discerning the limits of the one pole over against the other. If there is no positive relation, then everything is in vain, and we are yet in our sins. But Reformed theology finds itself compelled to articulate this in Christological terms, for to enunciate it on any other ground than that of the Incarnation inevitably modifies the meaning and substance of the Gospel. We shall have to return to this point again.

2. We come back to the teaching of St Augustine at another point, his acceptance of the radical distinction or disjunction between the *mundus intelligibilis* and the *mundus sensibilis*. This had been rejected by the Athanasian theology in spite of the fact that it was endemic in the Alexandrian tradition, but it came into the West through the influence of Origenism and Neo-platonism. This created a real problem for the Church's understanding of the Incarnation as a real *egeneto sarx* on the part of the Logos, for it inhibited a serious consideration of a real *becoming* of the intelligible in the sensible, or of the eternal in the contingent. Hence even St Augustine could echo the view of Origen that the historical Christ and the historical Gospel were 'shadow' compared to the 'reality' of the eternal Truth in God.

This radical disjunction between the two realms raised a further problem. How are we who continue to live in history and within the sensible and passing world to bridge this gap between our world and that of supernal and eternal realities? It was a problem equally pressing in the realm of knowledge (the passage from *scientia* to *sapientia*) and in the realm of salvation (the passage from nature to supernature). The ultimate answer given by Augustinian theology and metaphysic to this was the doctrine of the Church, for the Church (and here I use the language of later Augustinianism) is established on both sides of the gap, within the intelligible world and within the sensible world. As the mystical Body of Christ the Church is full of grace and truth, indwelt by the Spirit of Christ and illumined by his eternal Light and therefore informed with his Mind. It is therefore within the Church where the fulness of divine grace and truth dwells that we may be enlightened and saved. Grace and truth are here really two aspects of the one divine reality that dwells within the Church bringing deification to all who through the Church participate in it, enabling them to make the passage from the sensible to the intelligible world, like pilgrims who seek and reach the City of God and so pass beyond all that is transient and contingent into the eternal.

In the early Middle Ages this conception of the sacramental universe with the Church as the mystical Body at its heart was greatly elaborated with exaggerated notions of a correspondence and harmony between the earthly patterns of the Church and those of the eternal realm, and it had to be thought through soberly and tamed, as we can see in the labours of St Thomas, but the essential teaching remained the same: grace is the divine power filling the Church, the power by which nature unceasingly transcends itself and is made participant in divine nature.

Grace is the supernatural quality poured into the Church by God, but
it is also that power actualized and embodied in the structured life of
the Church on earth, through which human beings are raised up beyond
their natural capacities to the state of sanctification or deification. The
effect of this can be seen, for example, on the doctrine of the ministry,
as even St Thomas expounds it. After the pattern of Christ who worked
out our salvation as God and Man, the priest is regarded as one who
participates in the divinity of Christ by virtue of the grace of his ordina-
tion. He is thus a 'second Christ' who mediates the divine grace to man,
and brings man to participate in the divine through his ministry of
grace. There is no normal way for man to go to God or to partake of the
divine life except through the priesthood and its mediation of grace.
(This doctrine persists as late as 1935 in the *Ad Catholici Sacerdotii* of
Pius XI.)

The intention of this in the teaching of St Thomas, if I understand
him aright, is thoroughly anti-Pelagian. Within the structure of Roman
tradition and Roman doctrine as he had received it, he sought to make
indubitably clear the evangelical nature of the Gospel which he had to
expound in terms of *sola gratia*, and no theologian has been more
faithful to that than St Thomas. But when the practical effect of this
way of stating things turned out to carry in its bosom an ecclesiastical
form of semi-Pelagianism, then the Reformers were forced to question
the basic notion of the priesthood or even the Church as representing
man before God and as making or forming the bridge that leads man
across from nature to supernature. What disturbed the Reformers and
continues to disturb Reformed theology is the deep and subtle element
of Pelagianism in the Roman doctrine of grace, as it emerges in its
notion of the Church (to use modern terminology) as the extension of
the Incarnation or the prolongation of Redemption, or in its doctrine
of the Priesthood as mediating salvation not only from the side of God
toward man but from the side of man toward God. The teaching of
Reformed theology is made clear in its insistence that while the ministry
is sent to represent Christ, and to act on his authority, it does not represent the people, for only Christ can take man's place, and act for man
before the Father. In other words, it rejects the notion of created grace
or connatural grace, both in its understanding of salvation and in its
understanding of the ministry.

We shall have to return to this notion of 'created grace' again, for in
spite of its rejection, there is an element here that is utterly essential to
salvation and to the ministry, which **Reformed theology** prefers to state

in other ways in order to avoid what it considers to be error. But before we address ourselves to that we have to complete our picture of the Roman doctrine of grace by developing it along other lines.

3. Here we are concerned not so much with Augustinianism, although that forms the essential background of it all, but with a peculiar combination of nominalism and realism that finally fixed the mediaeval doctrine of grace—by 'nominalism' and 'realism', however, reference is made not primarily to the epistemological problems raised by the *via moderna* in the fourteenth and fifteenth centuries, but to the masterful hermeneutic of the canon lawyers and the rational synthesis of legal and institutional definitions and the Augustinian spirituality carried out by the Schoolmen through the application of Aristotelian modes of thought. That is to say, what we are concerned with here is the nominalistic notion of definable, controllable grace, which we find in Gratian for example, with the realist notion of conferring or causing grace *physice ex opere operato*, which we find in the great philosophical theologians of the thirteenth and fourteenth centuries.

In order to set out the problem this mediaeval synthesis involved let us return to the notion of the sacramental universe with its pre-established harmony between the visible and the invisible, the earthly and the heavenly. If the distinction between the *mundus sensibilis* and the *mundus intelligibilis* had not been modified, it would either have led the Church back into Arianism or Gnosticism, or have encouraged it to take flight from this world by soaring up, as it were, through its own creative spirituality, into some quite transcendental realm. That had indeed begun to happen through the allegorizing exegesis that ran riot in the early Middle Ages and the growing power of Hellenic forms of mystical thought, but it was mastered and brought down to earth largely by the genius of St Thomas who made magnificent use of the Aristotelian psychology and philosophy to bring the two worlds together and so prevented them from breaking apart altogether. This gave the Augustinian notion of the sacramental universe a more rational interpretation, with a general form and a particular form.

In its *general form* it stood for a correspondence between active thought and being, and therefore between the form-structure of knowledge and the form-structure of being. That is, it posited an inherent relation between logical forms and the nature of the truth. By means of this conception mediaeval theology worked with an all-embracing system within which it brought its understanding of God and the creature, absolute and finite being, and their relations to one another.

Even the revelation of God in Christ was interpreted within this system, but that tended to mean that revelation was used to fill out a conception of being established independently on the ground of natural theology.

The *particular form* which the principle of the sacramental universe took was the Church regarded as a sacramental institution of grace grounded upon but continuous with the Incarnation, as its extension in space and time. As sacramental institution the Church was related as redemptive microcosm to the macrocosm of the whole universe. Here mediaeval theology posited an intrinsic relation of grace between the being and existence of the Church and the nature of the truth of revelation, so that the institutional Church was held to represent in its forms and dogmas the objectification of the truth in its institutional and rational structure, i.e. in the ordinances, decrees, and dogmatic definitions of the Church. It was on this ground that the Church itself came to assume supreme authority, for the expression of the mind of the Church in its dogmatic definitions was held to be the expression of the nature of the Truth.

The knowledge derived from both these sources was articulated in a grand synthesis through equating the doctrine of grace as the relation of the Divine Being as Cause to the creaturely being as operation, with the doctrine of the inherent relation of likeness between the Truth and the logical forms of the reason. In this way the element of dialogue or personal relationship was played down, and dialectic, that is the manipulation of the norms or forms immanent to thought, came to exercise a determinative power over all the apprehension of the Truth, so that in the last resort Roman theology appeared to be subordinated to a philosophical ontology. Thus it is apparent that there took place in this theology an amalgamation of the Latin way of thinking through controlling definitions with the Hellenic way of thinking through the discernment of eternal forms, to the detriment of the Hebrew way of thinking in which living relationship with God through his Word and the personal response of faith and obedience were primary. A consistent system of ideas tended to displace real and historical conversation with the living God.

The effect of this upon the doctrine of grace was twofold: on the one hand, grace came to be treated in a legalist and impersonal sense, and on the other hand, it came to be understood as something mystical and metaphysical.

(i) The assimilation of grace to the institutional structures of the

Church brought it within the purview of the Latin habit of thinking in terms of means and ends, and the Roman genius for orderly administration. Grace came to be treated as something to be ministered through legal definition and control. As the Vessel of grace, the Ark of salvation, the Church had conferred upon it by divine decrees the power to dispense saving grace. In the thinking of the legalists and nominalists the dispensation of grace was governed by specific decrees or ordinances, and therefore it had to be controlled in actual practice through a multitude of definitions, making clear the exact formulae to be used and the appropriate application in different cases. It was in this way that grace came to be divided up into many kinds of grace, each of which had to be carefully defined in its nature and dispensation. With the growth of nominalism in its epistemological and logical forms this led more and more to the atomization of grace and to inordinate concern for questions of matter and form, and at the same time, as legalism always does, to the growth of Pelagian notions of merit and fulfilled duty. This development was long inhibited by Thomistic theology, but its realist assimilation of grace to being, and therefore of its operation to logico-causal interpretation, had the effect of making grace something almost physical and material and so even of hardening the notion of institutional grace as something to be rationally defined and administered under the control of the Church. It is not surprising, therefore, that the underlying nominalism broke through the more evangelical outlook of the Thomists to dominate the scene at the Council of Trent and to prevent the fathers from understanding what was really going on within the Church at the Reformation. The *ex opere operato* now became the mark of a thoroughly impersonalist and objectivist view of grace, and stood in sharp antithesis to the *sola gratia* of the Reformers, although it was in the interest of *sola gratia* that it had first been formulated in the twelfth century.

(ii) But the mediaeval doctrine of grace had another side to it which was mystical; grace is the divine, supernatural mystery inexplicably at work through the Church and its sacramental ordinances, sanctifying, transforming and elevating nature for its participation in the divine. With the recasting of the Augustinian tradition in realist Aristotelian terms, this grace came to be regarded from a more ontological point of view. No longer was it merely the 'inward grace' mediated by an outward sign, but a divine power at work in human being transforming and changing it invisibly and visibly, grace actualizing itself within the physical as well as the spiritual, metaphysically heightening and exalting creaturely existence. Grace was regarded as acting within the reci-

pient in much the same way as the divine power in transubstantiating
the bread and the wine in the Mass into the realities of the Body and
Blood of Christ. The operation of grace is a divine causation, and there
follows from it a divine effect in the creature. It is almost like a supernatural potency that is infused into human beings, enlightening their
minds, strengthening their wills, and conferring upon them beyond any
natural state a divine quality which more and more transmutes the
sinner into a saint, a being of earth into a being of heaven. This is the
notion of grace inhering in the soul of man and lifting him up to vision
of God, grace affecting even his physical being and at last transforming
and translating him into the heavenly and eternal realm. It is in fact the
notion of *created grace*, grace actualizing itself in the creature and
elevating it to supernatural existence, *ontological grace* at work in man's
very being and raising him to a higher ontological order.

Now admittedly this is a very difficult way of thinking for Reformed
theology, for to think of grace in the categories of nature as a causality
appears to import a confusion between the Creator and the creature;
and to think of grace as deifying man or heightening his being until he
attains the level of a supernatural order appears to do docetic violence
to creaturely human nature. However in their use of this language
Roman theologians do not presumably desire to import any abolition of
essential human nature in its sanctification or deification through grace.
Protestants, on the other hand, often react too violently when they contrast to this 'metaphysical' notion of the work of grace, a conception of
salvation through *faith alone* where 'faith alone' may mean 'mere faith'
as if to be regenerated were simply resolvable into believing. In this
connection Calvin used to comment upon the teaching of St Paul that
Christ dwells in our hearts by faith, to the effect that while it is through
faith that Christ comes to dwell in our hearts, his dwelling in our hearts
involves *a relation in being* beyond faith. Through faith we enter into an
ontological relation with Christ as our Redeemer and Creator, for he
both redeems and recreates our being in him. If this is what Roman
theology means, then it uses unfortunate categories in which to express
it—but there may well be more than a terminological difference here.

3

How, then, are we to state the position of Reformed theology vis-à-vis
the Roman doctrine of grace? That is the question to which we must
address ourselves in the rest of this article.

  1. The Reformed doctrine of grace cannot be isolated from the new

turn that theology took at the Reformation, or rather from the reaction of the Reformers against the impersonal philosophical theology of the mediaeval schoolmen and their return to *positive theology* grounded upon the Word of God and obedient conformity to it in the faith and teaching of the Church. Here we have a conception of theology as the conformity of thought with its object, but the object is God revealing himself in his Word, God speaking to us in history, God encountering us as Person and addressing us as persons over against him and in communion with him. This had the effect of restoring to theology its dialogical character and of restoring the centre of gravity to the objective Truth to which all human thought-forms are therefore subordinated. Theology proceeds by constant reference to its source and sole norm in the Word of God, so that theological terms and formulations are ever brought to the bar of the Word for criticism and creative reorientation.

This involved at least two changes that had their effect on the doctrine of grace. (*a*) In place of the conception of the sacramental universe and the rational synthesis which it involved in its realist interpretation, Reformed theology set the biblical conception of the covenant of grace. The covenant embraces not only man but the whole of creation, visible and invisible, for all that God has made is made to be the theatre of his glory and the sphere of his revelation, but within that universal range of the covenant it is the concrete form which the covenant of grace took in history, with Israel, and its fulfilment in the Incarnation and the foundation of the Church in Christ, that provides the frame of promise and fulfilment within which theology as historical dialogue with God is understood. (*b*) This dialogical theology had the effect of giving the knowing subject full place over against the object, God speaking personally and historically. Man is here posited by God as his partner in the covenant and in conversation, so that personal relations are established and maintained within the covenant of grace. The human partner is both the Church and the individual believer within the Church. This had the effect of restoring to theology its intensely personal character, and therefore of restoring to the understanding of grace the sense of living relationship with the Persons of the Holy Trinity.

Grace is intensely personal. It involves encounter with God who draws personally near to us through his Word and Spirit, and personally acts upon us, creating on our part personal response to him in faith and love. However, this very fact has laid Protestant theology open to a constant snare. Just because the human partner is given his full place by God as knowing subject over against God as his proper object, he is always being tempted to assume the major role in the theological conversation, to convert theological statements into statements of human concern, and to lapse into anthropology or subjectivism. This personalism can make a show for itself by opposing the opposite tendency in Roman theology toward objectivism, but it involves the fatal weakness of being unable to distinguish the objective reality of grace from man's own subjective states. This in turn leads to a humanizing and then a secularizing of grace, and so we have in a different form the old notion of *created grace* all over again with its attendant notions of co-operation and co-redemption. It must indeed be admitted that there is scarcely anything which Protestantism opposes in Romanism for which it does not have its own erroneous counterpart. That does not allow us, however, to shut our eyes to the fact that the notion of grace as an impersonal *res* or *potentia* is to be rejected, as it surely is today by all responsible theologians in the Roman Church.

2. The second major point we have to note in Reformed theology is its application of the *homoousion* to the understanding of *grace*. This fact alone cut off as with a hatchet the Reformed doctrine of grace from the mediaeval proliferation of *graces*, each of which required dogmatic definition and constitutionally determined application. It rejected the notion of grace as a detachable quality which could be made to inhere in creaturely being, thus assuming many forms within it while at the same time divinizing and elevating it. Thus the doctrine of *created grace* could only be regarded as a species of Arianism. The formulation of the *homoousion* in the Early Church taught that the self-communication of God to us in Jesus Christ is identical with God himself in his own eternal Being, that the Gift and the Giver are one. What God is in his acts toward us in Christ he is antecedently and eternally in himself, and this in turn led to the full formulation of the doctrine of the Trinity. Christ is equally Person, *hypostasis*, with the Father and with the Spirit. Hence he cannot in any way be construed as an Image of God, detachable from his Being, and changeable, and somehow semi-divine. He is the Image and the Reality of God, and therefore the sole, exclusive Image of God.

It is the same teaching, according to Reformed theology, that must be applied to the grace of God, for what God communicates to us in his grace is none other than himself. The Gift and the Giver are one. Grace is not something that can be detached from God and made to inhere in creaturely being as 'created grace'; nor is it something that can be proliferated in many forms; nor is it something that we can have more or less of, as if grace could be construed in quantitive terms. This is the Reformation doctrine of *tota gratia*. Grace is whole and indivisible because it is identical with the personal self-giving of God to us in his Son. It is identical with Jesus Christ. Thus it would be just as wrong to speak of many graces as many Christs, or of sacramental grace as of a sacramental Christ, or of created grace as of a created Christ.

We do not forget, of course, that the human nature of Christ was created—we shall return to the import of that for a doctrine of grace— but we must remember that his human nature was enhypostatic in the Son, and was not separated, and therefore not separable or detachable, from the *hypostasis* of the Son. Thus even when we think of the grace of God as coming to us in and through Christ we cannot allow ourselves to think of that except in hypostatic terms—nor must we ever imagine that any hypostatized entity is the equivalent of the self-giving of God in the Person of his Son.

Now if it be admitted that we must apply the doctrine of the *homoousion* to the grace of the Lord Jesus Christ, as surely Roman theologians must agree to do, then what becomes of the many distinctions between this and that kind of grace with which Roman theology operates? Does this mean that these distinctions only serve our modes of thinking and speaking of grace, but have no objective distinctions corresponding to them in grace itself? If this is the case, and this is the way I read not a few works of modern Roman theologians, then are we not here approaching a basic agreement on the ground of Christology? I would hope so. But if disagreement goes deeper, then the disagreement must surely be in the Christology itself that lies behind the doctrine of grace.

3. Reformed theology applies to the understanding of grace not only the *homoousion* of Nicaea but the classical Christology of Chalcedon, with its doctrine of the *hypostatic union*, for if grace is God's self-giving to us in Christ, then grace must be understood in terms of his human as well as his divine nature. It is from this point of view that the notion of deification through grace must be tested. If the human nature of the saint is deified through grace, presumably that applies par excellence to the human nature of Jesus. But what is the relation of this deification to his Deity? If it is said that deification comes through participation in the divine nature, what is the relation of this participation of the human nature of Christ in his Deity to the hypostatic union of his human and divine natures? Is not some attempt being made here to 'go further' than the doctrine of the hypostatic union with its carefully

guarded understanding of the union as taking place *inconfuse, immutabiliter, indivise,* and *inseparabiliter*? Is *grace* not being used here in Western theology as *wisdom* is used by some theologians in Eastern theology, in the so-called 'sophiology', to say something positive where the Chalcedonian fathers would not allow themselves to do so because in the nature of the case the mystery of Christ cannot be defined? If *grace* is being used in this way, then what can it lead to but to some form of monophysite error sinning against the *inconfuse,* for to speak of Christ as divine man is just as much a confusion as to speak of him as human God? Or to express it more concretely, if sacramental grace involves transubstantiation in the Mass, does that not point back to some docetic error in Christology, to a transubstantiation of the human nature of Christ, leaving only a *species* to remain?

Now before we proceed any further let it be said that Reformed theology interprets participation in the divine nature as the union and communion we are given to have with Christ in his human nature, as participation in his Incarnate Sonship, and therefore as sharing in him in the divine Life and Love. That is to say, it interprets 'deification' precisely in the same way as Athanasius in the *Contra Arianos.* It is only through *real and substantial union* (Calvin's expression) with him in his human nature that we partake of all his benefits, such as justification and sanctification and regeneration, but because in him human nature is hypostatically united to divine nature so that the Godhead dwells in him 'bodily', in him we really are made partakers of the eternal Life of God himself. To be united to Christ in this way through the power of the Spirit whom he pours out upon us is to be united to him in the power of his resurrection, and so to partake of his *New Humanity,* to be participant in the *New Creation.* If that is what is intended by 'created grace', then there can be no quarrel with it so far as the reality signified is concerned, but only with an unfortunate use of language.

Yet the difficulty that we are concerned with here seems to lie at a deeper level. It concerns the concept of *participation.* Is it *koinonia* or *methexis* that is meant: a participation governed by the Chalcedonian doctrine of the union of divine and human natures in Christ or by the Greek notion of participation in the eternal realities? Even before Chalcedon Athanasius pointed out that if we interpret the union in Christ in terms of *methexis* we destroy the *homoousion,* and make impossible the faith of the Church that in the communication of himself to us Christ communicates to us the very Life of God. It would appear to be the case that the more Latin theology lost sight of the distinction in Greek between *koinonia* and *methexis*, the more easy it became for a false notion of participation to obscure the understanding of the Church, and for a subtle tendency toward monophysitism to develop. Let me illustrate this by a current doctrine of the Church in Roman theology.

It is often argued that as in Christ himself divine and human natures are united, so in the Church there is a union of divine and human elements. Here there would appear to be a double error. First, this way of paralleling the relationship between the divine and human elements in the Church to the union of divine and human natures in Christ, appears to argue that the union in Christ is comparable to the kind of participation in the Church, in which through grace the Church is participant in the Spirit—which is to obscure the understanding of the hypostatic union. Secondly, this is to make use of a false form of the analogical relationship, which ought to be stated thus: *as divine and human natures are related in Christ, so in the Church Christ and human nature are related*, for the Church is the Body of Christ. The analogy then takes the proper form; *as A is to B, so C is to D*, where C is: *A to B*. Since Christ (C) in whom the Church of believers (D) participates, is one who unites human nature as well as divine nature in himself, the Church participating in him participates in his human nature. But when the false form of the analogy is drawn, as in the statement I have cited, then the human nature of Christ is omitted from it, and that means that C is replaced by A in the form: *as A is to B, so A is to D*. Thus this doctrine of the Church turns out to be monophysite. When we translate the statement that divine and human elements are united in the Church into the language of participation, and speak of the Church as participating in the grace of the Spirit, we can easily see the damage that this does to the doctrine of grace at a very crucial point.

What then is the positive teaching of Reformed theology on this point?

(*a*) Grace is the self-giving of Christ to us in which he both redeems and recreates us, such a self-giving that he unites us to himself and makes us share in his human nature, and in him share in the very Life and Love of God himself. When we remember that Christ is the Incarnation of the Creator-Logos by whom all things have been made and in whom all men cohere, then we can see that this self-giving of Christ to us involves us in an ontological relation with him even in his human nature. It must be granted that this is the point that Protestant theology not infrequently leaves out, and therefore deserves the criticism of Roman theologians.

(*b*) The participation of the Church and, within the Church, of believers, in Christ must be construed in terms of *koinonia* governed by the Chalcedonian doctrine of the union of two natures in Christ. This is a participation in which the human nature of the participant is not deified but reaffirmed and recreated in its essence as human nature, yet one in which the participant is really united to the Incarnate Son of God partaking in him in his own appropriate mode of the oneness of the Son and the Father and the Father and the Son, through the Holy Spirit. In the nature of the case we are unable to describe this participation in positive language any more than we can describe the hypostatic union in positive language—refusal to do so does not by itself import that a real and creative and therefore an ontological relation is not envisaged in this participation, which is what Roman critics of Protestants frequently forget. The mystery of grace is the mystery of Christ; by keeping ourselves within the limits of the great Chalcedonian adverbs we allow that mystery constantly to declare itself to us and impose itself upon us. It would be quite fatal at this point to use grace (through the devising of various distinctions and forms) as a means to say positively what the Chalcedonian fathers so wisely refrained from doing. This is a lesson that Roman theologians can still learn from the Cappadocian divines.

(c) It must not be forgotten that participation in grace, so far as the life of the faithful *in via* is concerned, can be formulated only within the eschatological perspective, i.e. within the real participation here and now in the new creation through the Spirit, and within the time of waiting for the redemption of the body at the *Parousia* of the Lord. Participation in grace involves a real having of grace within our creaturely being and existence, but a having that is yet to be fulfilled or completed when Christ comes to make all things new. It is this eschatological perspective that governs the Pauline and Reformation doctrine of *imputation*, and the Lutheran doctrine of *justus et peccator*. But where this imputation is construed only in a dialectic of having and not having so that participation here and now in the fulfilled reality of the new creation is suspended, then it deserves the criticism that Romans are not slow to level against it.

It is very difficult to believe that Roman theology really intends anything other than what has been set out positively here. It certainly does not intend any form of monophysitism, but intention may be diverted through inappropriate language, and serious error allowed to creep in under its cover.

4. Because grace is Christ giving and communicating himself to us

unconditionally in his own sovereign love and freedom, its mode of activity can be thought of only as intensely and supremely personal. It is grounded in the living relations of the Persons of the Holy Trinity, and its operation is never one that breaks connection with that ground. Rather is it one in and through which God the Father, the Son and the Holy Spirit are operative together in the divine Love. Between its going forth from God and its coming out upon the creature grace at no point ceases to be what it is within the Trinity, in order to become what it was not, some impersonal entity or causality. Grace can never be regarded in an instrumental sense, for from beginning to end in grace God is immediately present and active as living Agent.

In other words, grace has its own *sui generis* mode of operation, akin to the creative activity of God which likewise cannot be described in terms other than itself. For this reason it is not inappropriate to relate the movement of grace to the Holy Spirit, provided we remember the inseparable relation between the Spirit and Christ, and that the Spirit proceeding from the Father operates in and through the Son and thus proceeds from the Son as well as the Father. This connection is not inappropriate for it helps to deliver theology from construing the operation of grace as some form of causality. Grace is as sovereignly free as the Spirit of God and yet as free from arbitrariness as the Persons of the Trinity in whom it is grounded and from whom it cannot be separated. How fatal it is to construe the *sui generis* movement of grace in causal terms is apparent perhaps above all in the doctrine of election, for then it is converted into some form of impersonal determinism the relation of which to the Persons of the Trinity can then appear to be only quite arbitrary.

It is perhaps above all in the very nature of theology itself that it is most important to be faithful to the nature of grace and to respect its own mode of activity. Where grace is related to being and causality then the whole redemptive and creative activity of God can be construed only in the concatenation of logico-causal connections. But where theology is faithful to the nature of grace it is concerned to explicate and articulate its understanding of the redemptive and creative activity of God according to the *logic of grace*, i.e. in accordance with the actual way which the grace of God has taken in the incarnation, life, death and resurrection of Jesus Christ, and in accordance with the sovereignly free and yet divinely compulsive movement of the life of the Incarnate Son on earth, such as comes to view in the biblical statements 'It behoved him', 'Ought not Christ to', 'For the Son of Man must', etc.

All this becomes entirely wrong when it is construed in terms of necessary, logical connections, for then grace is converted into something quite other than it is. That is the difference between the kind of theology pursued in modern dogmatics, and the kind of theology we find in the Summae of the old schoolmen. Yet it must be admitted that the question of more personal statement in theology was already raised in the Middle Ages. That is reflected, for example, in St Thomas' careful avoidance of the *ex opere operato* in the *Summa* which he had earlier used in the *Scriptum super sententiis*, and it was accentuated by Duns Scotus' doctrine of the person which came to its own, not in nominalism, but in the formidable revival of anti-Pelagianism toward the end of the Middle Ages which had such an influence upon the Reformers, and that at certain points was backed up by Bernardine piety and the teaching of Thomas à Kempis.

5. The Reformed doctrine of grace carries with it a radical rejection of nominalism, for nominalism both in its earlier legal and its later terminist forms was essentially Pelagian. There is so much confusion in some Roman polemics against Protestants at this point (e.g. Louis Bouyer) that clarification is required. Nominalism had undoubtedly an influence upon the rise of the Reformation as it had upon the rise of modern science in that it operated with a distinction between intuitive and abstractive knowledge, and so posited a bifurcation between empiricism and formalism. In this way it struck a deep blow at the mediaeval synthesis between the form-structure of abstract knowledge and the form-structure of being which was grounded upon an alleged inherent relation between logical forms and the structure of the truth, even the Truth of God, and so nominalism questioned very radically the mediaeval notion of *deus sive natura*, although within the mediaeval synthesis that could hardly help appearing to be a form of atheism. Nevertheless the rise of nominalism meant the liberation of intuitive knowledge from the shackles of a formalistic logic, and therefore the serious study of the contingent without arbitrary control from behind by metaphysical presuppositions.

This in turn had a double effect upon theology. (*a*) It threw theological inquiry back upon intuitive, and indeed empirical knowledge of God, and (*b*) allowed it to take seriously the operation of the Word of God in history, and the relation of eternal Truth to historical fact. But whereas the nominalists themselves were ready to pursue this empirical and intuitive mode of inquiry within the natural realm, they refused to do so within theology, and so by rejecting empirico-intuitive and therefore directly objective knowledge of God through his Word and Spirit, they posited a fatal disjunction between faith and reason; throwing theology back upon the authority of the Church, and therefore into the arms of the older legal nominalism, and throwing the main weight of thought and activity within the Church upon Pelagian voluntarism and human merit. This had a powerful impact upon late mediaeval Roman theology everywhere evident in the legalism and terminism, the Pelagianism and sophism, with inordinate love of *distinctiones*, evident even in the theology of the fathers of Trent.

It was against this that the humanists like Erasmus and the Reformers like Luther and Calvin revolted alike, Erasmus more against the logical sophistry, and the Reformers equally and sometimes violently against the Pelagian notions of merit. At any rate Reformed theology from the start would have nothing to do either with nominalist logistics or nominalist voluntarism, nor would it have anything to do with the nominalist disjunction of faith from reason, for faith is thrown directly back upon the *Veritas Dei* which the reason apprehends as God speaks personally to man through his Word, for God enables man by the power of his Spirit to hear and respond in the obedience of his mind to the Truth. This is nowhere more apparent than in the first few chapters of Calvin's *Institute* in which he takes the correlation of knowledge of God and the knowledge of the self very seriously, for God addresses man personally, but in which he shows that in theological knowledge man is thrown upon the implacable objectivity of the *Veritas Dei*, much as it is expounded in the teaching of Anselm and Grosseteste.

The upshot of this for the doctrine of grace lies in the opening up of theological understanding for the appreciation of the 'personalogical' movement of grace, the apprehending of it from its connection with the living Persons of the Trinity, as the personal self-giving of God to men in Jesus Christ, creating the community of the faithful, the Body of Christ, within which alone this personal mode of understanding grace arises and takes root. But it also involved the rejection of the nominalistic idea, rooted in the teaching of the canon lawyers, that the definition of the truth becomes part of the truth itself, and that therefore grace becomes effective in and through legal formulations and enactments and the actions of the Church fulfilled strictly in accordance with them. Thus the rejection of nominalism by Calvin and the Reformed theologians involved a return to the *positive theology* of the Catholic fathers, and, in spite of the enormous influence of St Augustine, in actual substance more to the Greek than the Latin fathers (i.e. to Irenaeus,

Athanasius and Cyril of Alexandria, Basil, Nazianzen, and Chrysostom especially, editions of whose works were poured out by the Swiss publishing houses); and in this way involved a radical rethinking of the mediaeval proliferation of graces and their legal definitions and specifications and a return to grace regarded as an indivisible whole and a living reality interpreted through the *homoousion*. Regarded in this way *sola gratia* is to be understood as a form of *solo Christo*, and as corresponding very closely to the *filioque*.

By way of epilogue to this article we may note certain changes in the history of Reformed and Roman doctrines of grace. Reformed doctrine lapsed very sadly from its reform, and fell first into a new Aristotelian scholasticism in the so-called Protestant Orthodoxy, and then into a new pietistic subjectivism which came to its ascendency in Neo-Protestantism. From this long detour the doctrine of grace is now enjoying a great renewal due not a little to fresh investigation of Reformation and patristic teaching, but even more to the emergence of a new biblical dogmatics in which Reformed theology has not been slow to learn from the teaching of other Communions. Roman theology on the other hand has also been engaged and still is engaged in renewing itself on a massive scale through patristic, liturgical and biblical studies, and is advancing everywhere a new kerygmatic theology in which the doctrine of grace is governed from a Christological centre involving a rejection of the nominalistic tradition.

Here in our day we have a remarkable process of rapprochement which penetrates behind scholastic terminology to more biblical and personal modes of thought and speech under the influence of a revived Catholic Christology. Yet the present situation is fraught with great dangers. On the Protestant side the failure to take the *homoousion* seriously has tended to throw up a notion of *event-grace*, in which the centre of gravity is translated to man's own decisions and acts, so that Pelagian notions of co-operation and co-redemption are still rife within Protestantism. This involves a failure to distinguish the objective reality of grace from the individual believer's subjective states, and so a tendency, if it may be so expressed, to replace the *filioque* by a *homineque*. On the Roman side there appears to be a corresponding danger in the so-called *New Theology* when it is tempted to exalt kerygmatic statements at the expense of dogmatic statements, since it is in this way that it finds itself more easily able to overcome the remnants of nominalism in its tradition; but to avoid the hard work of thinking out the profound inner connections of Christian doctrine, which is the task of dogmatics, can only import real weakness. Granted that the kind of logico-causal connection with which the schoolmen worked is not appropriate to the nature of grace, nevertheless the New Theology will not be able to stand the tests ahead of it, unless it is prepared to think through the *logic of grace* to the end, that is, to work out the profound Christological and Trinitarian connections of grace in the whole realm of Christian doctrine.

At no period since the Reformation have Reformed and Roman theology been in such a position to help one another as they are today. If they are to help one another, it will only be through frank conversation in which each side is ready to let itself be called into question by the other, and each is ready to examine itself to see whether what it holds to be error in the other may not have a place within itself even if under quite a different guise. And then they may really go forward together, finding agreement as they go, if they are prepared to submit their thinking to the great verities of the Apostolic and Catholic Faith and to follow the lead of the great Ecumenical Councils in which the Church's dogmatic thinking was so decisively and exclusively made to repose upon Christological and Trinitarian foundations. So far as the doctrine of grace is concerned the following would appear to be of paramount importance: the *homoousion* with equal stress upon the Being of God in his Acts and upon the Act of God in his Being, participation in the new Humanity of Jesus Christ the crucified and risen Saviour, with the rejection of every form of monophysitism, and, behind all, the living and life-giving communion of the Persons of the Holy Trinity, with the rejection of every form of nominalism.

It would be wise to give heed to the call of John XXIII to remember the distinction between the substance of the Faith and its formulations.

II

The Foundation of the Church: Union with Christ through the Spirit[1]

THE Church is grounded in the Being and Life of God, and rooted in the eternal purpose of the Father to send his Son, Jesus Christ, to be the Head and Saviour of all things. The Church does not exist by and for itself, and therefore cannot be known or interpreted out of itself. Both the source and the goal of the Church are in the eternal love of God which has overflowed in the creation and redemption of the world. God has not willed to live alone, but to create and seek others distinct from himself upon whom to pour out his Spirit, that he might share with them his divine life and glory, and as Father, Son and Holy Spirit dwell in their midst for ever. God will not be without his Church; the Church is nothing without God. But in God the Church exists as the supreme object of divine grace, and in the Church God is pleased to live his divine life and manifest his divine glory. That is the mystery and destiny of the Church, hidden from the foundation of the world, but revealed and fulfilled in the Incarnation of the Son of God and in his glorious work of redemption, for in Jesus Christ the Church as the redeemed people of God is the crown of creation living in praise and gratitude to the Creator and reflecting with all things, visible and invisible, the glory of the eternal God.

The Church does not derive from below but from above, but it does not exist apart from the people that make up its membership or apart from the fellowship they have with the life of God. The Church is a divine creation but in the divine economy it did not come into being automatically with the creation of the world or all at once with the establishment in the world of a human society. The Church was formed in history as God called and entered into communion with his people

---

[1] Part of an essay written for the Faith and Order 'Commission on Christ and His Church', of the World Council of Churches; reprinted from *Scottish Journal of Theology*, 16.2, 1963.

and in and through them embodied and worked out by mighty acts of grace his purpose of love which he brought at last to its fulfilment in Jesus Christ. While there is only one people and Church of God throughout all ages from the beginning of creation to the end, there are three stages or phases of its life. It took a preparatory form before the Incarnation as in the covenant mercies of the Father one people was called and separated out as the instrument through which all peoples were to be blessed; it was given a new form in Jesus Christ who gathered up and reconstructed the one people of God in himself, and poured out his Spirit upon broken and divided humanity that through his atoning life and death and resurrection all men might be reconciled to God and to one another, sharing equally in the life and love of the Father as the new undivided race; but it is yet to take on its final and eternal form when Christ comes again to judge and renew his creation, for then, the Church which now lives in the condition of humiliation and in the ambiguous forms of this age, will be manifested as the new creation without spot or wrinkle, eternally serving and sharing in the glory of God.

Because Jesus Christ through the Spirit dwells in the midst of the Church on earth, making it his own Body or his earthly and historical form of existence, it already partakes of the eternal life of God that freely flows out through him to all men. Because its existence is rooted in the sending of the Son by the Father to be the Saviour of the world, the Church lives its divinely given life in history as the servant of Christ sent out by him to proclaim the Gospel of God's love to the whole world and to be in itself as the reconciled people of God the provisional form of the new creation. It is therefore the mission of the Church by the witness of its word and life to bring to all nations and races the message of hope in the darkness and dangers of our times, and to summon them to the obedience of the Gospel, that the love of God in Jesus Christ may be poured out upon them by the Spirit, breaking down all barriers, healing all divisions and gathering them together as one universal flock to meet the coming of the Great Shepherd, the one Lord and Saviour of all.

I THE PEOPLE OF GOD UNDER THE OLD COVENANT

The Church had its earthly beginning in Adam for then it began to subsist in the human society formed by God for immediate communion with himself. But in Adam the whole Church fell through disobedience, and its immediate relation with God was broken and interrupted by the

barrier of sin and guilt. It fell not as a divine institution but in its constituent members, and therefore the Church upheld by the eternal will
of God took on at once a new form under his saving acts in history.

In spite of their sin God did not give up his people but maintained
with them a covenant of grace, in which he allied himself with his
creatures as their God and Saviour, and committing himself to them in
paternal kindness took them into communion with himself as his dear
children. Therefore from generation to generation he sought to reveal
himself to his people as they were able to apprehend him, and called
them by his Word to a life of obedience and faith and righteousness.
In the fulfilment of this purpose for the whole race God chose one people
from among the others as the medium of his revelation and the special
sphere of his redemptive acts leading throughout history to the fulfilment of his promise of salvation. Thus while the covenant of grace
embraced all men, it was when God called Abraham and specifically
promised him 'I will be a God to you and to your seed after you', that
the Church began to be separated out from the nations and brought
into definite form as the appointed sphere in history of God's revealing
and redeeming activity through which all nations and all creation would
be blessed.

It was with the redemption of Israel out of the bondage of Egypt and
its establishment before God as a holy people in the ratification of the
covenant at Sinai that Israel stood forth as the *Ecclesia* or Church of
God. 'I am your God. Walk before me and be perfect. I am holy; therefore be ye holy.' This covenant was sealed with two major 'sacraments':
circumcision, which inscribed the promise of God's blessing in the flesh
and seed of his people and covenanted them to a life of obedience and
faith; and the passover, in which God renewed his covenant promising
redemption from the bondage of sin and the tyranny of the powers of
evil into fellowship with himself through a sacrifice which God himself
would provide. Even in its Sinaitic form the covenant was essentially a
covenant of grace. God knew that his people would be unable to keep
the covenant, and to walk before him in obedience to his holy will, and
so in his faithfulness and mercy he provided within the covenant a way
of obedient response to his loving-kindness, and a way of cleansing and
restoration to fellowship with himself. Not only, therefore, did he give
his people his 'Word and Sacraments' through which he revealed himself familiarly to them and adopted them as his children, but he provided for them a Law which clearly set forth his will, and an order of
worship and sacrifice in the cult which supplied his people in their

weakness with a covenanted way of response to his will. Both of these were a testimony to the fact that mercy and judgment belonged to God alone, and enshrined the promise of messianic salvation.

In this way Israel came to be constituted God's Prophet among the peoples of the earth, that is, his Servant entrusted with the oracles of God and the promises of the Messiah, and to be equipped with ordinances to train it in the ways of righteousness and truth and faith. While the ordinances were temporary, belonging only to the preparatory economy of the divine covenant, the oracles and promises pressed forward throughout the whole history of Israel to their fulfilment in the Incarnation of the Word in Jesus Christ and in the establishment of his messianic Kingdom through a redemption that would embrace all races and nations in a new covenant of the Spirit and in one universal people of God.

When the Christian Church came to refer to itself as the *ecclesia* it was claiming continuity with the *qahal* or the People of God under the old covenant, but in so doing it clearly regarded the people before the Incarnation as the Church under the economy of the old covenant. It was the *ecclesia* or *qahal* that arose and existed through election, that was actively engaged in God's purpose of revelation and salvation, that was caught up in the mighty events whereby God intervened redemptively in history, and became involved in the forward thrust of the covenant toward final and ultimate fulfilment. It was the Church of God in its preparatory form in the tension and struggle of expectation, unable to be yet what it was destined to be when incarnation and reconciliation were fulfilled. Only with the consummation of the mediation between God and man in Jesus Christ could the people of God under the old covenant fully become Church in its permanent form in the Body of Christ. Nevertheless it was that one Church in the process of formation, waiting for its new birth in the resurrection and its universalization at Pentecost, while the mode and structure of its existence in the historico-redemptive movement of God's grace in Old Testament times were determinative of the Christian Church built upon the foundation of the prophets as well as the apostles.

(*a*) Israel was *the chosen people of God*, elected not for its own sake but for God's sake, in the fulfilment of his revealing and redemptive purpose. It was Church, therefore, not in the merely sociological or political sense of *ecclesia*; it was society formed not by human but by divine convocation. It was Church as act of God, as the community called into being by the Word of God, and constituted through union and communion with him. Yet by being separated out as a covenant-community with an ordered life of its own, Israel was also established as a nation among the peoples of the earth. Thus there arose and persisted through the history of Israel a struggle between Israel and its Lord, between its 'ethnic' aspirations to be a nation like the other nations of the earth, and its 'laic' calling to be a people in covenant-communion with God. It was this conflict that plunged Israel into its long ordeal of suffering. Precisely because it was the bearer of divine revelation it could not be a secular nation like the others, and because it was elected for the fulfilment of God's redeeming purpose it had to be the holy people exercising a vicarious mission through which the whole race was to be transformed.

Nevertheless God used the suffering and ordeal of Israel to reveal himself more profoundly and give himself more completely in all his infinite faithfulness and love and his undeflecting will for the salvation of mankind, and at the same time to drive his revelation into the inner existence and understanding and life of this people in order to mould and fashion it into the vessel through which the Word was to be made flesh, reconciliation to be achieved, and the final revelation to be actualized in the midst of humanity. Hence already in the historical experience of Israel before the Incarnation the lineaments of the Church began to become manifest as the worshipping people of God called into being by his Word, with the mystery of divine election hidden behind the events of their history, and laden with the ministry of his revelation, and throughout it becomes more and more clear that as the creation and corporate election of God the Church exists prior to the individual members incorporated into it from generation to generation but that it will be brought to its fulfilment only through the death and resurrection of Israel in the body of the Messiah.

(b) Israel was called to be the *Servant of the Lord*, the one people within the Adamic race set apart for vicarious mission in the redemption of the many. Through the cult Israel had been taught that the covenant could be fulfilled only through an obedient response or sacrifice provided by God himself from within the covenant, but through the prophets Israel learned that such an obedient response had to be translated into its very existence and life and made to issue out of it. The election of the one for the many called for the election within the one people of a Servant chosen of the Lord who would fulfil in his own body and soul the covenant-will of God for his people, and fulfil the covenanted obedience of the people to God's will. This righteous

Servant would mediate the covenant by bearing the sins of the people in himself and being cut off out of the land of the living for the sake of God's people, so that they might be pardoned and healed and restored to fellowship with God. The covenant thus mediated would be transformed to extend far beyond the bounds of Israel, for all nations would come at last under its light and salvation and share in the fellowship it bestowed between God and man.

The whole conception of the Servant represents the activity of God whereby he began to draw together the cords of the covenant in which he had bound Israel to himself as his covenant-partner; it represents the activity in which he began to narrow down the assumption of Israel into union with himself toward the point of the Incarnation where, in the midst of Israel, he was to assume man into oneness with himself in the ultimate act of reconciliation. But because the election of Israel as God's Servant was the election of man in his sinful existence and enmity to God, election involved the judgment of man in his will to isolate himself from God and in his refusal of grace. That was the reason for the suffering of Israel, for it involved the breaking and making of Israel as the Servant of the Lord. Thus the election of Israel as the Servant of the Lord meant that it was elected to be used even in its refusal of grace that through it the ultimate self-giving of God to man in spite of his sin and because of his sin might take place—elected, that is, to act in representative capacity for all peoples in their rejection of God's will; but the election of Israel as the Servant of the Lord meant also that out of Israel there was to come the Mediator to act in a representative capacity for all men, through whose rejection in suffering and sacrifice the redemption was to be achieved for all men, not least for Israel itself.

(c) Israel was called to be *the bearer of the Messiah*, the mother out of which should spring the new race. And so to the end of time it remains true that 'Salvation is of the Jews'. It is not only that Israel was called to be the bearer of the promises of God and therefore to be the messenger of hope, but that throughout her long history in her concrete existence in the flesh Israel always bore within her the seed of the messianic Saviour and of the messianic race. It was not least that organic union of Israel with Christ that constituted it Church and preserved it from extinction throughout all its ordeal of suffering, so that at last when it gave birth to the Messiah its whole historical life was gathered up in him and together with the Church of the Gentiles was constituted one New Man, the Israel of God, the universal Body of Christ.

But the transition from the people of the Old Covenant to the people of the New Covenant was only through the death and resurrection of the Messiah. Church of God though it was, the holy people bearing the Presence of God in its midst, yet Israel was concluded under sin with the Gentiles, in the solidarity of the whole Adamic race, in the one equal grace of God freely extended to all men. By condescending to be made flesh of our flesh in Israel, the holy Son of God incorporated himself into the continuity of man's sinful existence, taking on himself our body of sin under the curse of the law and the judgment of God, and even our body of death, that through his death and resurrection there might take place the death of the old man and the resurrection of the new, the destruction of the temple and the raising of it again, the cutting of Israel down to the very root, and the springing up of the new shoot, the Vine of Truth. Thus in the dying and rising of the body of Christ the old was translated into the new and the new was grafted into the continuity of the old.

The Christian Church must not forget that it has no independent existence, for through Christ it is grafted on to the trunk of Israel, nor must it imagine that God has cast off his ancient people or that the promises made to Israel as a people of divine election and institution have only a spiritualized fulfilment. Israel too as God's first-born son has part in the resurrected body of the Messiah, and together with the Gentiles grafted into it and sharing its riches, forms the one commonwealth of the people of God. All members of the Church are of the race of Abraham, and there is no messianic race but Israel.

At last in the fulness of time when a body had been prepared the Messiah came to do the will of God. John the Baptist as the messenger of the Covenant had been sent ahead of him to prepare the way. He stood on the boundary between the Old Testament and the New, proclaiming that the messianic Kingdom was at hand and that the covenant promises made to Abraham were about to be fulfilled, and through a baptism unto repentance for the remission of sins made ready a people prepared for the Lord. When Jesus submitted himself to John's Baptism and had the seal set on his messianic vocation by the voice from heaven, it meant that as the Servant of the Lord and only Righteous One he identified himself with the people of God concluded under sin that through union with them in one body he might make their sin his own and make them participant in his righteousness. It was his consecration to the whole course of sacrificial obedience in life and death in which he healed and transformed the Church through death and resurrection in his own body. 'Christ loved the Church and gave himself for it; that he might sanctify and cleanse it with the washing of water by the word, that he might present it unto himself a glorious Church, not having spot or wrinkle or any such thing; but that it should be holy and without blemish.'

2 JESUS CHRIST AND HIS MESSIANIC COMMUNITY

From the very start of his public ministry Jesus came proclaiming the Gospel of the Kingdom of God and saying, 'The time is fulfilled, and the Kingdom of God is at hand: repent ye and believe the Gospel,' and set about at once calling people to himself in his mission to gather and redeem the people of God. With his advent and presence the transcendent Kingdom of God that had so long been the object of longing and prophecy had arrived and was active among men for their salvation. In the whole historico-redemptive activity of God in Israel the Kingdom of God and the people of God were essentially correlative conceptions, or rather two different aspects, of the one rule of God grounded in creation and made good in redemption. It was to be fulfilled through the saving acts of God in Israel but on fulfilment it would inevitably transcend the boundaries of Israel and take form as the universal kingship of God over all his creation. That Kingdom was to be ushered in with the coming of the Messiah, the anointed King, through whom it would be grounded on earth in the redeeming and raising up of a people who would enter into the Kingdom as its constituent members and be themselves the instrument through which the Kingdom would extend its rule over the ends of the earth. Small though its beginning was, grouped immediately round the person of the Messiah, it would grow and spread until all nations were brought under its rule. 'Fear not little flock, for it is your Father's good pleasure to give you the Kingdom.'

That is the context in which Jesus Christ and his messianic community are presented to us in the Scriptures—the Kingdom and the People of God alike are concentrated in him, while the life and mission of the Church, the people of the new covenant, are rooted in his sending as the Son from the Father and take their form and shape from his incarnate ministry on earth. It was the kind of person he was and the kind of mission he undertook which determined and gave form and structure to the messianic Kingdom and messianic people.

From his very birth Jesus was hailed as the Son of the Highest to whom the Lord would give the throne of his father David, and of whose reign over the house of Jacob there would be no end. He was born to be

Saviour as well as King, for in his birth God had come to visit and redeem his people, raising up in Jesus a horn of salvation in accordance with his promises to the fathers and prophets since the world began, and in remembrance of his holy covenant. His coming was not only to restore the Kingdom to Israel and Israel to the Lord, but to bring a salvation prepared for all people, a light to lighten the Gentiles as well as the glory of God's people Israel. He was the Lord's Messiah or Christ, anointed to gather the people of God into one and save them from their sins.

That was the mission upon which Jesus publicly embarked at his baptism which was both his consecration as King and his consecration as the righteous Servant to bear the sins of the many. He who was baptized embodied the fulness of the Kingdom and the fulness of God's people in himself. His being was not only individual but also corporate, recapitulating in himself the chosen people and the messianic seed, and embodying in himself also the new humanity of the future. Jesus was not baptized for his own sake but for the sake of the whole people of God with whom he identified himself—on his side it was a vicarious baptism. He as the Son of God did not need to be anointed and endowed with the Spirit, but his baptism, set forth the fact that it was our humanity in him that was baptized and anointed, and that it was in his capacity as a humble representative of the people that he was sanctified and consecrated to a special ministry. As the anointed Servant he was not the Messiah without his people for he existed as Messiah to uphold and serve his people in giving his life a ransom for them, and establishing in them a new way of life. They were not the messianic people apart from him but only as they inhered in him, shared in his anointing, followed him and partook of his redemption. Hence it was for their sakes that he sanctified himself that they also might be sanctified through the truth and in him be consecrated together in one. 'Both he that consecrates and they who are consecrated are all of one: for which cause he is not ashamed to call them brethren.' Thus the goal of his mission to be the Saviour of the world included within it the sanctifying and gathering into one of the people of God, the raising up of the Church in its permanent and final form.

It was in the temptations immediately following his baptism that Jesus made clear the manner in which he was to fulfil his mission: not by acts of open divine majesty and compelling power but, Son of God though he was, by acts of humble service, in which he ranged himself with sinners in their weakness and lostness and bondage under the tyranny of evil and under the judgment of God, acting from their side toward God and only as such acting as God in their midst to save and deliver them. The ministry he had to fulfil before the face of the Father was at the same time the mission of redemption on which the Father had sent him. Hence he insisted on carrying out his ministry as a representative of the people into which he had incorporated himself, and within which he had been consecrated to the vocation of the Messiah, to the office of the *Christos*, the Elect One, the Servant, or the Son of Man, as he called himself. That is to say, he fulfilled his mission on earth as the supreme functionary of the messianic people, as Man holding messianic office and fulfilling a ministerial function.

Hence from his baptism Jesus advanced toward the Cross as the Son of God become Man, to carry out the mighty deeds of our redemption in the weakness of a man among men and in the form of a servant fulfilling a meek and lowly ministry. It was because he was incarnate that his ministry took a human form, and because he subjected himself with us under the Law that it took a servant-form. Because the Messiah and his people are essentially correlative and cannot be separated, the ministry which he came to fulfil he fulfilled as a human office within the conditions of the community he served and sustained by his personal ministry. He was the Son of Man who came not to be ministered unto but to minister. But because that was an office to which he was divinely appointed and consecrated, he exercised it as the Householder in charge of God's household, as the Steward of his people in the mysteries of the Kingdom, giving authority to God's servants within it and to every man his work.

In this way it is apparent that the Church of Christ was not just the holy society founded to perpetuate his memory, or to observe his teachings, or to proclaim his Gospel, but that it inhered in his being as the Incarnate Son, was rooted in his humanity as the historical Jesus, and grew out of the fulfilment of his ministry in the flesh. The Church of the new covenant arose out of the indivisible union of the Messiah and the people of God he came to redeem and raise up; it grew out of the concrete way in which he lived his divine life within their human existence thereby transforming their whole way of life; it took shape and form in every act that he performed, and derived its essential structure from the way in which he fulfilled his ministry on their behalf. This change in the people of God, the new birth or foundation of the Church in the messianic era, had two phases, one before and leading up to the crucifixion, and one after and arising out of the resurrection.

Like the grain of wheat it had to be planted in the ground and had to die before it could spring up and bear abundant fruit.

The rooting of the Church in the Person and Ministry of the historical Jesus

Right from the start of his public ministry Jesus set about to restore the people of God by gathering followers or disciples round himself and building them up as the nucleus of the messianic community in whose midst the Kingdom of God was actively at work. This messianic office he fulfilled personally, not by mighty impersonal deeds, but by direct personal and individual ministry on his part. Hence we have the three arduous years of his personal ministry, in lowly, patient service; in preaching the Kingdom and summoning all to repentance, in seeking and saving the lost, in healing the sick and forgiving sins, in teaching all who had ears to hear and feeding them with the bread of life, in transforming their lives and communicating to them a new righteousness, in instituting in their midst the final Law of God, and moulding them into a structured community with its authoritative centre in himself.

The direct word and action of Jesus himself was essential in all this. As we have traditionally failed to see that the historical ministry of Jesus, his teaching and praying, his living and obeying, his miracles and parables, are an integral part of his atonement, so we have failed to pay sufficient attention to the essential and constitutive nature of his personal and individual ministry in the fulfilment of a special office laid upon him by divine authority for the building of the Church of God among his followers. The only comparison possible is with Moses. It was with divine authority that Moses delivered and reconstituted Israel, instituted the covenant at Sinai, promulgated its laws and installed men in office in the covenanted community. Moses' authority was supreme in Israel. But in Jesus there is not only a new Moses, but the Messiah himself, the Son of Man endowed with authority on earth to forgive sins and utter final commandments. Jesus fulfilled his office with an authority greater than that of Moses or any to which the Scribes and Pharisees appealed. It was the immediate authority of the Father which had been laid on him. He did nothing by himself, but acted only in accordance with the will and mission and Word of the Father who sent him, and therefore he resorted to prayer before all the major acts of his ministry. What he had to do and did was to found the new Israel and inaugurate the new covenant.

He laid the basis for the new Israel when out of the people prepared for the Messiah and out of the band of those he had called to be his disciples he chose twelve to be with him to be the inner nucleus of his Church. It was a tremendous act, for it meant that the longed-for age of salvation had come when the tribes would no longer be scattered but be gathered into one. Hence he formed and instituted them into one Body with himself, calling them to take up his Cross, and deny themselves, that they might have their centre of unity not in themselves but in him. He initiated them into his messianic secret, incorporated them into his messianic mission, sending them out to exercise his own ministry in preaching and healing, and granting them to be baptized with his baptism and to drink the cup which he was to drink, and even to watch and pray with him at the last in the Garden of Gethsemane.

As long before Elijah had gathered together twelve stones representing the twelve tribes of Israel to build an altar for sacrifice, Jesus gathered twelve living stones, such as the rock Peter, and built them round himself the Lamb of God to be offered in sacrifice. They were the many inhering in the one. They had one name in the Son of Man who came to give his life a ransom for the many. In the indissoluble bond between the one and the many, the Messiah and the People, the nucleus of the Church received its fundamental shape and form, and together the little flock went up to Jerusalem where it was to be given the Kingdom. Then there took place the Last Supper where Jesus inaugurated the new covenant in his Body and Blood, renewed the consecration of the disciples in himself, and in covenantal action appointed to them a kingdom making them a royal priesthood to sit with him at last on twelve thrones in his Kingdom.

Then came the crucifixion, the scattering of the disciples, the laying of the axe to the root of Israel, the destruction of the temple, the death of the Messiah. In the ultimate hour he was left alone, dying in lonely substitution on the Cross, the one for many. But in his death, the many who inhered in him died too, and indeed the whole body of sin, the whole company of sinners into which he incorporated himself to make their guilt and their judgment his own, that through his death he might destroy the body of sin, redeem them from the power of guilt and death, and through his resurrection raise them up as the new Israel, the new humanity, the Church of the new covenant, the one universal People of God. The death and resurrection of the Messiah brought the old economy in God's household to an end and inaugurated a new economy through union with himself in his risen body.

The rebirth of the Church in the Body and Spirit of the risen Jesus

The Church did not come into being with the Resurrection or with the pouring out of the Spirit at Pentecost. That was not its birth but its new birth, not its beginning but its transformation into the Body of the risen Lord quickened and filled with his Spirit. Jesus Christ had already gathered and built up the nucleus of the Church round himself, but because he loved it he gave himself for it that he might cleanse it and change it through the mystery of union with himself in death and resurrection. The form he had given it through his ministry was necessarily of a provisional character before the crucifixion and resurrection. He had prepared it for this hour, and therefore far from rejecting it he reaffirmed it, reconstituted it, and recommissioned it, giving it to participate in him now on the ground of his atoning work in a depth and fulness which was not possible before.

The Body had already been prepared, the people and the structure he had given them, remained, but the Body was broken and humbled to the dust—it needed to be quickened by the Breath or Spirit of God. That had already happened to Jesus himself, the Head of the Body, for God had not allowed him to see corruption but had raised him bodily from the dead to be the new life-giving Adam, the Head of the new race. Now first upon the apostolic nucleus he breathed his quickening breath and then poured the Spirit out in fulness upon the whole Church, and so the Body prepared for Christ arose and lived. The Christian Church was born, the one Body of Christ incorporating the faithful of all ages before and after the Incarnation. It is a divine creation, not built by men on earth but deriving from the life of God above, existing prior to its individual members which it incorporates into itself, universal yet appearing in the world in visible form, grounded first upon the college of the Apostles and therefore prior to the local congregations which it assimilates to its order and through which it becomes visible from generation to generation. As such it is the immediate sphere of the operation of the Holy Spirit mediated to it through Christ, the anticipation and manifestation in the history of this ongoing world of the new creation at the end of time.

This Church does not exist by itself as a special creation of the Spirit nor does it have an independent life of its own. It is the Kingdom and Body of Christ and exists solely because of its organic relation to him. There is no Kingdom of the Spirit but only a Kingdom of Christ in and by the Spirit. The Church is not the Body of the Spirit, for there is no Incarnation of the Spirit, but it is the spiritual Body of Christ on earth

and in history. It is the community of men and women with whom he
identifies himself, which he united by the power of the Spirit to himself,
and which in his grace he reckons and makes to be his own earthly and
historical Body. It is what it is because of what Christ, the incarnate and
risen Son of God, is; it is what it is because of its indissoluble bond with
him who will not be without it. There is but one Christ who is both the
Head and the Body, so that the Body cannot exist apart from Christ,
or be divided without dividing Christ. Thus the Church has no independent existence, as if it were anything at all or had any life or power
of its own, apart from what is unceasingly communicated to it through
its union and communion with Christ who dwells in it by the power of
the Spirit and fills it with the eternal life and love of God himself. It is
quickened and born of the Spirit; it is filled and directed by the Spirit,
but in order that the Church may be rooted in Jesus Christ, grounded
in his incarnate Being and mission, and in order that it may be determined in its inner and outer life through participation in his life and
ministry.

This means that through the Spirit the structure and functions of the
messianic community which Jesus had gathered about him in the days
of his ministry in the flesh continued to be determinative for the life and
functions of the Church after the Resurrection and the Ascension. Jesus
and his disciples shared in one messianic mission, but his role in it was
utterly unique for he had a lonely and substitutionary work to fulfil.
Jesus and his disciples formed one messianic Body, but his place in
it was as Mediator, and Head and King, and their place in it was
as the redeemed people, as members and servants. The crucifixion
and resurrection made that likeness and difference completely clear, and
it is that likeness and difference that constitutes the fundamental pattern
of the Church's life and ministry in the world after the resurrection, and
as it is unfolded and comes to view after Pentecost, i.e. in the apostolic
structure of the Church. 'As the Father hath sent me, so send I you.'

Before the crucifixion Jesus took care to initiate his disciples into the
same ministry as he was exercising, incorporating first the Twelve and
then the Seventy into his own mission by sending them out to minister
in the name of the Messiah as he the Messiah had been sent to minister
in the name of the Father. The disciples were permitted to baptize, to
go forth as his representatives bearing the kerygma of the Kingdom on
their lips, and with authority to heal and forgive sins in his name; at the
Last Supper the Twelve were solemnly washed and consecrated as his
servants and prepared for office, and Jesus commanded them at the

Supper to continue to fulfil this ministry until he returned, praying for them, in distinction from the rest, in the fulfilment of their special office; after the resurrection he forgave their failure and recommissioned them as his representatives, sending them out to follow his example in shepherding and feeding the flock, to be teachers and heralds of the Kingdom making disciples of all nations. The records make it clear that Jesus intended to leave behind a community with a structure and form and leadership, a community with a ministry shaped on the pattern of his own, and that while all men were called to be disciples and to engage in a ministry of witness to him, some were given special responsibilities and a special commission of pastoral care over his flock, endowed with an authoritative office to act in his Name. The constituent elements of the Church were all there, but now with the commissioning of the disciples as *Apostles*, and the pouring out of the *Spirit* at Pentecost the Church was given by its risen Lord the permanent form which he intended it to take throughout history until he came again.

The apostles had been specially trained through intimate association with Jesus, through initiation into the secret of the passion, through private instruction, in order that they might be the commissioned and authoritative witnesses to Christ. They were not intended by Jesus to pass on what they had received in precisely the same way they had received it—they had a special function 'in the Word' to perform in the tradition. Where Jesus proclaimed and confronted them with himself, they had to bear witness to him as the Son of God and Saviour. Where Jesus was present in person and acted, and let his presence and acts fulfil as much of his revelation as his words, the Apostles had to gather it all up and pass it on as communicable word. What is at stake here is the essential difference between Jesus, the unique Son of God, the only Saviour and Mediator, and those he came to save. The supreme importance of the Apostles lies in the fact that they were the chosen and trained instruments, endowed with the Spirit, to pass on the self-witness of Jesus (in word and act) translated into witness to him by men in history, for men in history. In the apostolic witness there took place once and for all, under the power of the Spirit, who quickened their understanding and opened their mouths, who brought all things to their remembrance add led them into the truth, that translation in an inspired act which has for ever since been the means of Christ's own self-revelation and communication to men. Thus the Apostles cannot be separated from what they passed on, or what they passed on from their function in passing it on. At the same time it is very clear that the power and authority of the witness of the Apostles do not lie in the Apostles themselves but in the self-witness of Christ which through the power of the Spirit operates in the apostolic witness to him as Saviour and Lord. This being so, we cannot separate the structure of the Church in history from the ministry of Christ's self-revelation through the Apostles.

What the Apostles had to do in regard to the Witness, in translating the self-witness of Jesus into witness about him, required a corresponding change in the functioning of the ministry which Jesus had built up and left behind him, a change which he intended it to take. Thus as we are to see the relation of the witness of the Apostles to Jesus' self-witness, so we are to see the relation between the apostolic ministry to Jesus' own ministry in which it was rooted. Jesus intended the Apostles to become the wise master-builders or architects who would shape and build the mind and life and worship of the Church in him, and so lay once and for all the foundations of the historical Church in the life and ministry of Christ.

The important point here is to discern both the rooting of the apostolic ministry in the ministry of Jesus, and to discern the difference which comes about when the self-ministry of Jesus is translated into ministry in his name. It is the vicarious mediation of Jesus which is of fundamental importance here and explains why the Early Church worshipped the Father and ministered only in the name of Christ, and why they regarded Christ in the absolute and proper sense, as the only Minister of the Church before God, the only One who was appointed and anointed (*Christos*) for office in the Kingdom of God, the only One endowed with all authority in heaven and earth, the supreme Householder in God's Kingdom who at the end would hand over everything to the Father.

Grounded upon the Apostles and determined by their ministry, the ministry of the Church is both like and unlike the ministry of the historical Jesus. It is rooted in it and patterned after it, and in a real sense shares in it. But the ministry of the Church is also utterly different from that of Jesus, for it is directly related to Jesus as his ministry is directly related to the Father, and it is a ministry of redeemed sinners, whereas his ministry is that of the Redeemer. This essential and fundamental translation in the form of the ministry was carried out by the Apostles, so that all true Christian ministry is ever after determined at its root by the special function of the Apostles in their immediate relation to Jesus' ministry on the one hand and to the historical Church of forgiven sinners and its mission in the world on the other hand.

Thus it becomes apparent that in the new form given to the Church by the risen Lord, the ministry is part of the structure of the Church in a way similar to that in which the Messiah is indivisibly united to the structure of the People of God. The Christian Church is what it is because of its indissoluble union with Christ through the Spirit, for in him is concentrated the Church and all ministry. Because Christ fulfilled his ministry by sharing the life of the people of God, the Church is what it is through sharing in his life and ministry, living by the very Gospel it proclaims. Because the Person and Work of Christ, what he was and what he did, are inseparable, what the Church is in him and what it does in proclaiming him, its being and its ministry, are inseparable. As there is only one Christ and only one Body, so there is only one ministry, that of Christ in his Body. But Christ shares in it in his utterly unique way, as vicarious Redeemer, and Lord; the Church shares in it in an utterly different way as the redeemed people who as servants and heralds point away from themselves to Christ alone.

12

Spiritus Creator:
A consideration of the teaching of St Athanasius and St Basil

IT is significant that in the earliest tradition of the Church there was little or no controversy about the deity of the Spirit. It was everywhere acknowledged that God is Spirit and taken for granted that the Spirit of God is God. The main aspects of this tradition are as follows. (*a*) The Holy Spirit is inseparably united with the Father and the Son in the work of our salvation and recreation, for it is into the one Name of God, Father, Son and Holy Spirit that we are baptized. This is the persistent ground theme, out of which understanding and formulation developed. (*b*) The Holy Spirit is worshipped and honoured together with the Father and the Son, which is the consistent reiteration of numerous doxological formulae. Typical is the prayer of Polycarp. 'For this reason I praise thee for all things, I bless thee, I glorify thee through the ever-lasting and heavenly High Priest, Jesus Christ, thy beloved Child, through whom be glory to thee with him and the Holy Spirit both now and for the ages that are to come, Amen' (*Polc. Martyr.* 14.3). (*c*) The Holy Spirit is intimately related to the eternal Word of God, and is the prophetic Spirit by whom God spoke to the prophets and has now spoken to us in Jesus Christ his Son—typical here are the statements of Justin Martyr and Irenaeus. And as Justin says, this prophetic Spirit is worshipped and adored and honoured with the Father and the Son (*Apol.* I, 6). (*d*) Very early the Church understood the biblical teaching about the Spirit in a Trinitarian sense. Athenagoras could speak of 'The Son being in the Father and the Father in the Son by the unity and power of the Spirit' (*Leg.* 10 and 24). This was even more explicit in Tertullian (see espec. *Adv. Prax.* 2, 4, 8, 25, 30).

Two further characteristics of early teaching must be mentioned: we take our examples from Novatian. First, the fact that Christ sends the

TIR O

Holy Spirit, the Paraclete, is powerful evidence for the deity of Christ (*De Trin.* 16). Secondly, Spirit refers to what God is in his Being, but 'what he is cannot be uttered in human speech, nor perceived by human ears, nor grasped by human senses' (*De Trin.* 7). In other words, it belongs to the early tradition of the Church that Spirit expresses the unapproachableness, the ineffability, the unutterable majesty of God. It is this fact that can never be forgotten in the doctrine of the knowledge of the Holy Spirit, or in the relation of the doctrine of the Spirit to any other doctrine, of God or of his works, and this fact which makes precise and clear-cut statements so difficult.

All these aspects of the doctrine of the Spirit are found clearly and firmly brought together in the teaching of Cyril of Jerusalem, and formulated. 'As there is but one Father and one Son, so there is but one Holy Spirit. No other spirit is to be honoured equally with him. He is supremely Great Power, divine and unsearchable, living and rational, and it belongs to him to sanctify all things that were made by God through Christ.... We preach one God through one Son, together with the Holy Spirit. We neither separate the Trinity, as some do, nor confuse the Persons, as Sabellius did, but we devoutly acknowledge one Father who sent his Son, the one Son who promised to send the Paraclete from the Father, and the Holy Spirit who descended at Pentecost here in Jerusalem' (*Cat.* 16.1-4). 'Learn then that this Holy Spirit is one and indivisible, yet of manifold powers, working with many operations, yet not himself broken into parts. It is the Holy Spirit who knows the mysteries, searching all things, even the depths of God; who descended on the Lord Jesus Christ in the form of a dove, who wrought in the Law and Prophets; who even now seals your soul at the time of Baptism, of whose holiness every rational nature has need; against whom if any dare to blaspheme, he has no forgiveness either in this world or in that which is to come; who receives a like honour of dignity with Father and Son, of whom also thrones and lordships, principalities and powers have need. For there is one God . . . one Lord . . . and one Holy Spirit who has power to sanctify and deify all, who spoke in the Law and Prophets, in Old and New Testaments alike' (*Cat.* 40.16).

In view of the very nature of the Spirit, Cyril felt that 'to define accurately the *hypostasis* of the Holy Spirit is impossible; we must be content to guard against errors on various sides' (*Cat.* 16.11). While this respect for the ineffable nature of the Spirit remained, the Church was soon forced to elucidate its faith more explicitly, and to affirm the *homoousion* of the Spirit as it had affirmed it of the Son, if only to guard the truth from error. The problems with which we are especially concerned in this essay are those which arose from error on both sides, from the Sabellians, and from the Arians or semi-Arians. From each side there came attacks upon the originality and the exaltedness of the Son and of the Spirit above and beyond all creatureliness. According to the Sabellians the Son and the Spirit had no part in the creation, for they were not yet, and according to the Arians and semi-Arians the Son and the Spirit had no part in creation, for they were ultimately creatures themselves. Sabellianism and Arianism were different forms of a unitarian or unipersonal theory of God. The same basic error lay behind both, and in their view of the Spirit as in their view of the Son.

There are two elements embedded in the tradition of this error which we must note, and here we take our examples from the Commentary of Origen on St John's Gospel. First, he clearly taught there that the Spirit came into being through the Word, although he is revered more than any other creature that has come into being through the Word of the Father. Secondly, Origen carried over, as an axiomatic assumption into his teaching, the hellenistic disjunction between the real world of the intelligible and the phenomenal or shadowy world of the sensible, i.e. the *chorismos* between the *kosmos noetos* and the *kosmos aisthetos* (*In Ioann.* 1.25f.). While Origen himself appeared to apply to his doctrine of the Spirit the notion of eternal derivation from the Logos which he had applied to his doctrine of the Son in his eternal generation from the Father, nevertheless the axiomatic assumption of the *chorismos* between the intelligible and sensible worlds, together with his stress upon the immutability of God which that assumption was meant to guard, was bound to provoke the question: on which side of this dichotomy are we to think of the being of Christ, and therefore of the Son or Word of God? On which side of this dichotomy are we to think of the being of the Spirit? In answer to this basic question the Arians insisted on the creatureliness of the Son even if he were in some way the image and power of God; and the semi-Arians went on to teach the creatureliness of the Spirit. However, when the Council of Nicaea formulated the doctrine of the *homoousion*, it rejected the assumption of a radical dichotomy between the two worlds (i.e. of the *real* and the *phenomenal*), and set in its place the very different biblical distinction between the Creator and the creature, and the freedom of the Creator to be present and active in his creation, which gave *reality*, but not eternity, to the creature, and at the same time it taught that in Jesus Christ God the Son in his own divine Being and Person has come into

our creaturely existence, revealing himself to us and reconciling us to
the Father.

This had the effect of establishing a doctrine of the deity of the Son
in his inner and natural relation to the Father and therefore in his in-
dependence from and transcendence to the creation. Hence it also had
the effect of destroying the philosophical idea that the Logos or Spirit is
to be understood as a cosmological principle and as having 'eternity',
if at all, only in a lower sense as a correlate of the timeless omnipotence
of the Creator. This elucidation of the Church's faith in Jesus Christ
involved the assertion that he belongs to the eternal and uncreated
Reality of God, and the further elucidation of the Church's faith in the
Spirit involved the same assertion of the Holy Spirit, for as both Cyril
of Jerusalem and Dionysius of Alexandria insisted, the Spirit cannot be
separated from the Father or from the Son (Athanasius, *De sent. Dion.*
17), for he personally or hypostatically subsists in and is always present
with the Father and the Son and indivisibly one with them in the
economy of salvation (*Cat.* 17.5).

This movement of thought within the Church involved the questioning and correction of a dangerous tendency that had arisen through the
apologetic literature of the second and third centuries, namely the
tendency to think of an immanent *Logos* and/or an immanent *Pneuma*
emanating from God but as co-existing with the *kosmos*. The problem
this gave rise to can be indicated by contrasting it with the similar problem that arose in Western mediaeval theology when out of the notion of
correlation between the world and the mind of God there arose the
notion of timeless co-existence of the world with God and hence the
notion of the *aeternitas mundi*. Here, however, the notion of a co-existence of the Logos or the Spirit with the world led to the notion of their
creatureliness. That fatal error the Church destroyed by a twofold line
of thought which brought into clear articulation two basic affirmations
of the Faith. (*a*) The doctrine of the Creator Spirit which snaps the
notion of mutual correlation between the Spirit and the created world,
and therefore snaps at the same time any connection of mutuality between divine revelation and creaturely understanding. This is the
doctrine of the lordly freedom of God in his Spirit and Word over
against all that is not-God. (*b*) The doctrine of the economy of God, the
economy of the Son and the economy of the Spirit, in which God in his
sovereign freedom makes himself present to the creature, giving it being
and sustaining it in being, in relation to himself and yet in its utter
distinctness from himself, and in which God in his sovereign freedom

condescends in incredible mercy to enter man's creaturely existence as one of us, yet without ceasing to be eternal God, in order to fulfil his purposes of redemption and sanctification in us. At the very heart of this movement of thought in its positive construction lay the doctrine of the *homoousion*; in its full articulation it became clear that the doctrine of the Son requires the doctrine of the Spirit, and the doctrine of the Spirit requires the doctrine of the Son. It is only by the Spirit that we know that Jesus is Lord and can assert the *homoousion* of him, but apart from the Son, and the inseparable relation of the Spirit to the Son, the Spirit is unknowable, and the content of the doctrine of the Spirit cannot be articulated.

This is the doctrine of the Spirit that had to be established in the mind of the Church beyond doubt. It was carried through by Athanasius the Great and Basil the Great in their treatises on the Spirit, in which they were ably supported in the East by the work of Didymus and Epiphanius on the one hand and by Gregory of Nyssa and Gregory of Nazianzus on the other hand, and in which they were fortified in the West by the work of Hilary of Poitiers, and of course by Augustine himself, among others. We cannot here range over that whole field, nor concern ourselves with the differences that emerged within the unity of patristic teaching in East and West, but shall confine our discussion largely to the letters of Athanasius *Ad Serapionem* and Basil's *De Spiritu Sancto* with a view to our particular theme on the relation of the Spirit to creation. In the nature of the case, however, we will not be able to avoid discussion of certain epistemological and Christological issues for they are basic to our concern.

When we turn to Athanasius' teaching we are soon made aware of the fact that the Holy Spirit is not cognoscible in himself. In the doctrine of the Spirit we are concerned with the ultimate Being of God before whom the very cherubim veil their faces, for here God the Spirit hides himself not only by the very mode of his Being as Spirit, but by his exaltedness, his greatness and his majesty, that is, by his infinite holiness. Because he is infinitely greater than we can conceive, we can think and speak of him in his revelation to us only with awe and awareness of the weakness of our minds to apprehend him and of the impropriety of the language we use to speak of him (*Ad Serapionem* 1.17-20). Creatures of course are cognoscible in themselves, and are known in their diversities and in their parts and therefore known through analogies with one another. But it is quite otherwise with the Holy Spirit, who is one and indivisible and cannot be known by our dividing and compounding and comparing, for in his uniqueness he is exalted above everything else and is absolutely incomparable (*Ad Serapionem* 1.13; cf. *C. Arianos* 2.18-31, and Basil, *De Spiritu Sancto* 6.13f.; 9.22f.). Thus the very unknowableness of the Spirit by the world (John 14.17, *Ad Serapionem* 4.1f.) means that he belongs to the other side of the *chorismos* that bounds the existence of the creature, that is, to the side of the Creator himself. Hence the very knowledge of the Spirit carries with it the knowledge that he is in no sense creature, but is himself on the active, creative side of reality which gives, imparts, and maintains all other being, and who is known only in and through his own creative activity upon us. To be concerned with the Spirit, to know him, to be acted on by him, is immediately to be concerned with the Being or *ousia* of God the Creator. That, as I understand it, is the import of the patristic notion of *theosis* or 'deification'.

When we ask how Athanasius comes to speak like this of the Spirit we find that he does so by moving from the knowledge of the Son, and the affirmation of him as *homoousios* to the Father, to the knowledge of the Spirit, and the affirmation of him as *homoousios* to the Son and the Father.

In examining the movement of his own argument, Athanasius says, 'It is natural that I should have spoken and written first about the Son of God that from our knowledge of the Son we may be able to have proper knowledge of the Spirit' (*Ad Ser.* 3.1). In meeting the objections of the Tropici to the deity of the Spirit he argued in the first book that we are bound to hold of the Son what we hold of the Spirit of the Son— if the Spirit is a creature, so is the Son. But the deity of the Son has already been established. Hence from the doctrine of the *homoousion* of the Son he goes on to insist that what we hold of the Son we must also hold of the Spirit of the Son (*Ad Ser.* 1.22ff.). This does not mean that Athanasius begins with the doctrine of the Son, merely because that has already been established, but that this is the only proper procedure because of the propriety of the Spirit to the Son, and because it is only in and through the Son or the Word that God has revealed himself. The Spirit does not utter himself but the Word and is known only as he enlightens us to understand the Word. The Son is the only *logos*, the only *eidos* of Godhead (see *C. Arianos* 3.15, and *Ad Ser.* 1.19). Only at that point where in Jesus Christ the Incarnate Word is *homoousios* with us in our human nature and *homoousios* with God in his divine Being, is there a real revelation and therefore a knowing of God which really derives from the eternal Being of God as he is in himself. There is no other 'word', no other '*eidos*' of God, and no other way of knowing God or source of knowledge of him. The Holy Spirit, who is not knowable independently in himself, is known through this one self-revelation and self-communication of God in Jesus Christ. Nevertheless it is only *in the Spirit* that we may thus know the Son, and know that he is antecedently and eternally in himself in God what he is toward us in revelation and redemption. Only he who is *of God (ek Theou)* and consubstantial with him can thus impart knowledge of God *in* himself. It is from the Son that the Spirit *shines forth (eklampei, Ad Ser.* 1.18), and *in the Spirit (en Pneumati)* that God is known.

Two points follow immediately from this. (*a*) The Spirit is no more a creature than the Son, but with the Son belongs to the Being of God, for he is from God. The Spirit is ἐκ τοῦ θεοῦ and not ἐκ τοῦ μὴ ὄντος, as the creatures are, indeed ἐκ τῆς τοῦ Πατρὸς οὐσίας and not ἐξ οὐκ ὄντων (*Ad Ser.* 3.2). Moreover the Spirit belongs to the oneness of God and is inseparable from the Son and the Father. 'If the Son is not a creature because he does not belong to the many, but is one as the Father is one: then the Spirit likewise—for we must take our knowledge of the Spirit from the Son—cannot be a creature. For he does not belong to the many but is himself one' (*Ad Ser.* 3.3). There can only be one such ultimate Being, one who is one God, and so the Spirit participates in all the operations of the one God as co-essential with the Godhead. (*b*) The Spirit is the creative activity of God—far from being creaturely and contingent process, the Spirit is *atrepton* and *analloioton*, for he belongs to the unchangingly divine, the active and creative side of the Creator-creature relationship, in contrast to the creatures who are changeable and alterable, and belong to the passive and recipient side of that relationship (*Ad Ser.* 1.22ff.). This is backed up by the place of the Spirit in the unity of the Trinity, for the Trinity is not a creature, and cannot be composed of both Creator and creature but is wholly Creator. 'There is, then, a Triad, holy and complete, confessed to be God, Father, Son and Holy Spirit, having nothing foreign or alien mixed with him, not composed of one who creates, and one who is originated, but *all creative*; and he is consistent and in nature indivisible, and his activity is one. The Father does all things through the Word in the Holy Spirit' (*Ad Ser.* 1.28).

The Spirit is thus explicitly included by Athanasius in the work of the creation, along with the Son, for where the Word is there is the Spirit also (*Ad Ser.* 3.4f.)—that applies to the original works of creation and to all God's works and gifts in sanctification and recreation, for there is only one divine *energeia* in which all three Persons engage (*Ad Ser.* 1.20ff., 28ff.). The main aspects of Athanasius' teaching about the creative work of the Spirit may be summarized as follows: (*a*) All the activity of God is *from* the Father, *through* the Son and *in* the Holy Spirit. The divine operation is not divided between the Persons, but there is a distinction of mode of operation indicated by the prepositions, *ek*, *dia* and *en* (*Ad Ser.* 1.30). 'Him therefore who is no creature but is one with the Son as the Son is one with the Father, who is glorified with the Father and the Son, who is confessed as God with the Word, who is active in the works which the Father works through the Son— is not the man who calls him creature guilty of a direct impiety against the Son himself? For there is nothing that is not originated and actuated through the Word in the Spirit' (*Ad Ser* 1.31). (*b*) The Holy Spirit is the power of God, the *energeia* of the Son, through whom God realizes and actualizes his works (*Ad Ser.* 1.20, 30f.; see *C. Arianos* 3.5). As such the Spirit fills the universe, joining the creation to the Word, and is therefore he in whom the Father through the Word perfects and renews all things (*Ad Ser.* 1.9, 24-26). (*c*) The emphasis, however, is in line with the traditional teaching of the Church upon the creative work of the Spirit in *renewing or sanctifying* the creature, and consummating (or bringing to its *telos*) the relation of the creature to the Godhead. The Spirit is thus quickening Spirit, the Lord who is *Autozoe*, the Author of Life (*Ad Ser.* 1.22). He is creative source of life in himself, proceeding from the Father as co-essential with him, and not just as one participant in him in some supreme way. (*d*) The Spirit exists in inseparable relation to the Son, and indeed is inseparable from the Incarnate Son, for it is in and through him that his work is fulfilled. 'When the Word visited the holy Virgin Mary, the Spirit came to her with him, and the Word in the Spirit moulded the body and conformed it to himself, desiring to join and present all creation to the Father through himself, and in it to reconcile all things, having made peace, whether things in heaven or things upon the earth' (*Ad Ser.* 1.31). (*e*) But Athanasius insists to the end that we must respect the ineffability of the Spirit. Early in the first letter he reminded Serapion that we must learn not to think falsely of the Spirit by a wrong use of human terms and analogies, but think of him only as our minds are renewed in Christ (*Ad Ser.* 1.4f., 9). This way of thinking and speaking is particularly evident in the awe and restraint with which Athanasius speaks of the inner relations of the Trinity, but it is no less evident in his statements about the specific mode of the Spirit's hypostasis and creative activity. In the fourth letter (as it is called) he takes up the theme of the kind of questions we have to ask in an inquiry appropriate to the Spirit, and points out that our questions have themselves to be questioned. It is thus that we are restrained, when we follow through the biblical witness as to the distinction between the Spirit and the Son and their respective relations to the Father, from pressing human terms and analogies, such as that of generation, beyond their limited range (*Ad Ser.* 4.1ff., 6). They can serve God only by pointing beyond and above themselves as *paradeigmata*. It is surely for this reason that Athanasius will not allow himself to specify in human statements how we are pre-cisely to conceive of the creative work of the Spirit, for it is appropriate to his nature that we can not do so. He will not have us to think of the Spirit's creative work independently of that of the Son, and this means that he does not think of the work of the Spirit in creation itself except within the context of his sanctifying or renewing, or perfecting opera-tion. The creative work of the Spirit is, so to speak, proleptically con-ditioned by that of redemption.

This is a point of immense importance. It is often remarked that in the *Contra Gentes* and *De Incarnatione* Athanasius only spoke of the creative activity of God as through the Word, and that he came to modify that when he wrote the letters to Serapion, as he had to extend his basic analogies of the source-river and light-radiance to include application to the Spirit, but it is not so often recalled that when he came to speak clearly and fully of *deification* in the *Contra Arianos* (cf. 3; 25.19-25; 36.33-35, etc.), he insisted that this takes place through our participation in the *human nature* of Christ by the power of the Spirit. In other words, Athanasius never rejected his teaching about the creation through the Word, but deepened it through reflection on the relation between the Spirit and the Incarnation. This resulted in a twofold doctrine: (*a*) an ontological relation between all men and the human nature of Christ, for the Incarnation of the creating Word posited a creative relation between Christ and all creation; and (*b*) the presence of the Spirit throughout all creation consummating its relation to God through the Word, and therefore fulfilling cosmic redemption and sanctification. Thus the inseparable relation between the Spirit and the Son is basic not only to revelation but also to operation, and therefore essential to a doctrine of the knowledge of God and to a doctrine of creation.

When all is said and done, and all the important points raised by the East against the *filioque* clause are taken into account, it is this doctrine of the inseparable relation of the Spirit to Christ in creation and redemption that must be conserved, whether the *filioque* clause, which was intended ultimately to say just this, is formally accepted or not. If the *filioque* clause arose out of this Athanasian doctrine, why did he not state it in so many terms, but insisted in speaking only of *from* the Father and *through* the Son? Surely for the reason that the human analogies he used, source-river and light-radiance, when extended to take in the Spirit in the form of source-river-water, and light-radiance-enlightenment, could not be pressed beyond their proper scope. As they stood they confined statement of the procession to a series through the Son and from the Father, and a double procession could only mean a double source, which is impossible, apart from the fact that a doctrine of procession of the Spirit from the Son could only have been interpreted in an Arian or at best in an Origenist sense to imply the creatureliness of the Spirit. But Athanasius could not have gone on to say that the Spirit proceeded from the Father *only* for it would have contradicted his basic theology, and have involved the epistemological mistake of making the two analogies *archetypal* instead of merely *ectypal* or, to use his own expression, *paradeigmatic*, in their function—and that would have meant yielding to the Arian principle that that only is true which we can conceive in terms of our own analogies, which Athanasius rejected from end to end of the letters to Serapion. Because *analogies* by their very nature refer us to realities that utterly transcend them, we can never argue to those realities from analogical forms of speech, for that would mean giving them a determinative and formative function over the truth which they do not have. Rather do we use them as divinely-provided aids to our weakness in saying something about realities which cannot be reduced to speech, and as means of pointing out those realities which may well shine through analogical forms but are to be known apart from them and as independent of them. However, the fact remains that the *homoousion* of the Spirit to the Son and to the Father carries with it the inescapable conclusion that what the Spirit is in his mission from the Son he is antecedently and eternally in himself in God. If that conclusion is not valid then the whole Athanasian argument breaks down.

It is surely in this light that we are to interpret the teaching of all the great Eastern fathers up to Theodoret (who was the first to teach that the Spirit proceeds from the Father only), and not least the well-known passages often adduced in favour of the *filioque*, notably: Epiphanius, *Anchoratus* 70f., 75; Didymus, *De Trinitate* 2.5; Ephraem, *Hymnus de defunctis et Trinitate* 11; Cyril of Alexandria, *Thesaurus de Trinitate* 34. The teaching behind these passages involves the following:

(*a*) the unity of the divine *ousia* in the Holy Trinity, and therefore of the *energeia* of the three Persons; (*b*) the inseparability of the Spirit from the Son with whom and with the Father he stands in a relation of consubstantial communion; (*c*) the impossibility of conceiving of the Spirit absolutely in his own eternal *hypostasis* apart from the revelation of God in Christ, and except on the ground of the mission of the Spirit from Christ. (This seems to be the point of the strange Athanasian idea that the Spirit is the *Image* of the Son.) This being so we can forget about the *filioque* clause—it was entirely wrong to introduce it into the Ecumenical Creed without the authority of an Ecumenical Council—but we cannot allow to slip away from us the Athanasian teaching of the *homoousion* of the Spirit, and therefore of his full place in the one creative and redemptive activity of God through Jesus Christ. As Gregory Nazianzen put it, 'The Creator Spirit does all that God does' (*Oration on the Spirit* 29). Nor can we forget the lesson Athanasius taught us in showing how a scientific doctrine is thought out and formulated on the ultimate basis and in accordance with the ultimate logic of the relation between the Incarnate Son and the Father and the Father and the Incarnate Son (cf. not least *In illud omnia*). It was on that ground that he built up and formulated not only the faith of the Church against the Arians, but also the doctrine of the Spirit against the semi-Arians. As H. B. Swete has said, 'He placed the whole subject of the interior relations in the life of the Holy Trinity on a scientific basis, so that the doctrine of the Father, the Son, and the Holy Spirit can be seen to form a coherent whole, no part of which can be abandoned without a general collapse of faith' (*The Holy Spirit in the Ancient Church*, 1912, p. 220).

When we turn to the *De Spiritu Sancto* of St Basil we find that he offers substantially the same teaching as St Athanasius, although he does not explicitly assert the *homoousion* of the Spirit (like Gregory Nazianzen, *Oration on the Spirit* 29). He maintains the indivisible unity of the Trinity and of all divine operations, the inseparable relation of the Spirit and the Son, the essential relation of the Spirit to the *Koinonia* of the Father and the Son, and the immense power and range of the Spirit's operation in creation and in recreation. There are distinctive features and some difficult elements, and on the whole the approach is more from the side of 'ascetic theology' than from the side of Christology after the Athanasian manner.

The epistemology is very similar to that of Athanasius in his refusal to use ordinary language univocally of divine things and his recognition that we can think and formulate our theological knowledge only on the ground of the economic condescension of God in the Incarnation and on the ground of the *reception* by Christ of the Spirit (18.44) and his growth in knowledge toward the Father (5-9). Thus it is not surprising that as soon as Basil approaches the question of the Spirit's activity and its specific nature, and of the power of renewal which he brings, he reminds us that 'the cause is ineffable and hidden in mystery' (12.28; see also 8.18; 18.44; 22.53). We shall expect from Basil, therefore, the same reverent awe and self-restraint (cf. Nazianzen, *Oration* 32), yet he does carry the argument forward in certain more explicit ways.

Basil's basic premisses are taken from the traditional doxologies in which unrestricted divine worship is offered to the Spirit, from the intrinsic holiness of the Spirit which is his divine exaltedness, majesty and greatness, and from the sacrament of Baptism into the Name of the Father, Son and Holy Spirit. From these he draws the conclusions that 'The Spirit is ranked together with God, not on account of the emergency of the moment but on account of his community of nature (διὰ τὴν ἐκ φύσεως κοινωνίαν)' (13.30), that the Spirit is the giver and dispenser of life, the source of our renewal and recreation (15.35f.), and that 'in every operation the Spirit is conjoined with and inseparable from the Father and the Son' (16.39). He insists that the Spirit is sovereignly free and supreme above all creation—'think of his operations, their countless number, their unspeakable greatness, and their boundless range, before creation, in the creature, in the ages to come' (20.51).

What then are, according to Basil, the chief aspects of the doctrine of the *Spiritus Creator*?

(*a*) Since the Holy Spirit is inseparably and wholly incapable of being parted from the Father and the Son, he is united to them also in the source (*pege*) and cause (*aitia*) of all things. Indeed it is precisely from the original creation that we may see the *koinonia* of the Spirit with the Father and the Son (*De Spiritu Sancto* 16.37f.). This fellowship in creative activity extends to the creation of perceptible things, invisible powers, the dispensing and distributing of gifts, and the control of human affairs, from the creation to the final judgment. There are many operations but in every operation the Spirit is closely conjoined with and inseparable from the Father and the Son, and is present and active throughout *of his own will* (*autexousios*, 16.37). Within this unity of operation Basil distinguishes the work of the Father as 'the original cause of all things that are made' (τὴν προκαταρκτικὴν αἰτίαν), and the work of the Son as 'the operative cause' (τὴν δημιουργικὴν αἰτίαν), and the work of the Spirit as 'the perfecting cause' (τὴν τελειωτικὴν αἰτίαν). For example, the ministering spirits of which the Epistle to the Hebrews speaks, Basil says, are to be understood as 'brought into being by the operation of the Son, and perfected by the presence of the Spirit'. It is thus that they subsist by the will of the Father (16.38). 'The first principle of existing things is one, creating through the Son and perfecting through the Spirit.' And Basil explains that this 'perfecting' or *teleiosis* of the Spirit is to be understood both as *hagiasm.* and as *diamone* in it (*ibid.*).

In this way of stating things Basil was ably followed by his brother Gregory, who taught that in God there is no separate action on the part of the three Persons, for there is one power in the Father, Son and Holy Spirit, issuing from the Father as from a fountain, set into operation by the Son and perfecting its grace by the power of the Spirit. That applies to every operation extending from God to creation (*Quod non sint tres dii*).

According to St Basil the creative work of the Spirit is to be understood as the royal freedom of God to be present to the creature to realize and bring to completion the creative purpose of God in which creatures are established in enduring relations with the holiness and majesty of God—hence Basil can speak of the Spirit as τὸν στερεοῦντα τὸ πνεῦμα. An important corollary arises here. If the creative work of the Spirit is essentially holy, then the fulfilment of that creative work, that is, the bringing of it to its proper *telos*, must involve judgment and salvation for the sinner, while in the original creation itself, it involves the conferring of grace (16.38-40). In the language we used earlier of Athanasius' teaching, the creative work of the Spirit is proleptically conditioned by redemption. Final judgement in this case would mean, as St Basil says, complete separation from the Holy Spirit.

(*b*) The creative and redemptive work of the Holy Spirit is to be thought of in terms of his inseparable relation from Christ—indeed he is spoken of in the Scripture as 'the Spirit of Christ' since he is by nature (*kata physin*) closely related to him (18.46). Not only does the Spirit have *koinonia kata physin* with the Father and the Son, but he is peculiarly closely related to the nature of the Son, and it is in this connection that his operations are to be discerned and understood. This relation of the Spirit to the Son is seen above all in the birth of the Lord in the flesh, in his life and work; indeed 'all things done in the economy of the coming of our Lord in the flesh—all is through the Spirit' (16.39). There took place uniquely and fully in his birth and growth and life in our human nature, and in his unction and sanctification by the Spirit, the perfecting work of the Spirit in creation, for it is through that economic condescension of the Son of God in coming into our creaturely existence that the saving and sanctifying work of God for all is wrought out. Not only is the work of the Spirit in Christ the norm of his work in all creation, but the saving means of it, and the sole way through which it is fulfilled by God; i.e. *through* the Son and *in* the Spirit. In the Spirit's activity there is expressed the goodness, greatness and majesty of him who sent him, Christ the power and wisdom of God—but what he is in this mission from the Son he is in himself in God, for it is *in himself* that the Spirit fulfils this work of Christ, of revelation and salvation, upon us (18.46f.). If he were not essentially and intrinsically holy and divine in himself, he would not be able to fulfil this work in making us participate in the Son and in the Father. He is thus, co-ordinate with the Son and the Father, himself creative source of our life and sanctification and recreation (19.48).

(*c*) If we go further, and ask what are the distinctive characteristics of the Spirit's work in sustaining and perfecting creation, Basil points to the grace and the gifts of the Spirit which flow from him (16.38; 19.48ff.). In other words, the Holy Spirit adds something special, whether it be in creation, revelation, or redemption—that is not to say that the creative work of the Father or of the Son is imperfect without him, for we cannot think like that when we are concerned with the one indivisible *ousia* and *energeia* of the Holy Trinity (16.38; 19.48). This special act would seem to be the creation of life as distinct from mere existence, and the conferring through the *parousia* of the Spirit on the creation of the gift of the grace of continuance in consummating creaturely relations with the Godhead, or the conferring of enlightenment and sanctification in the renewal of creation by bringing to their completion the relations of creatures to the saving work of the Son. 'There is indeed not one single gift which reaches creation without the Holy Spirit' (24.55).

More explicit statements are found in two letters traditionally attributed to Basil, but whose authenticity is disputed. According to a letter to the Caesareans in 360, there are 'three creations'. 'The first is the passage from non-being into being. The second is a change from the worse to the better. The third is the resurrection from the dead. In these

you will find the Holy Spirit co-operating with the Father and the Son'
(*Ep.* 8.11). It is thus shown that the Spirit was at work in the creating
of the heavens and all their host, in the recreation of man in Jesus Christ,
and in the resurrection of the dead, alike. In all this he is of one essence
and substance with the Father, and of the same nature as the Father and
the Son, himself God, and as God participant in the creation. According
to the other letter, said to be written by Basil to his brother Gregory
(who was, however, its real author) the distinctive thing of this creative
work of the Spirit is that he is the *source* from which flows all good
things for the creation (*Ep.* 38.4).

(*d*) We may summarize the characteristic work of the Spirit by
pointing to what Basil speaks of as the royal *freedom* of the Spirit
(*C. Macedonium*), who though he is exalted infinitely above and beyond
all creatures and all the powers of heaven (19.49) is yet free to be present
to the creature and to fulfil from the side of the creature the perfecting
work which binds the creature in relationship to the Creator, and so to
realize its life. He is the Lord the Spirit (20.51; 31.52). It is through
him that the economies of God are carried out from beginning to end,
creation, old covenant, the Incarnation itself, the ministry of the Church,
and the future Advent of Christ (16.39, 49). The Holy Spirit is the Lord
acting out of the free ground of his own divine Being, in the total
sovereignty and power of his presence. This is so important for Basil
that it is rather strange (though understandable in view of his delicate
political situation—cf. H. Chadwick's review of Dörries, *De Spiritu
Sancto, Zeitschrift für Kirchenges.* 1958, 69/3, 4, p. 335) that for a while
at least, as in the *De Spiritu Sancto*, Basil refrained from asserting outright that the Spirit is very God (unless *Ep.* 8.2-3 is genuinely Basil's)
or even from affirming in the actual word the *homoousion* of the Spirit
to the Son and to the Father (but see again *Ep.* 8.9). For this timid
deference to others Basil was chided by Nazianzen, but nonetheless he
does succeed in giving us a clear and definite account of his convictions.
The doctrine of the lordly freedom of the Spirit to be present to the
creation and bring its creaturely relations to their proper *telos* in the
Creator, means that the creature does not have a continuity in relation
to God that belongs to the creature in itself, for this is continuously given
and sustained by the presence of the Spirit.

There are several aspects of the Basilian doctrine that call for a little
discussion.

1. In arguing from the fact that it is *in* the Spirit that we know God
to the deity of the Spirit, for he must be himself what he gives us to

know of God in himself (see also Nyssen, *C. Macedonium*), Basil says,
'Thus the way of knowledge of God lies from the one Spirit through
the one Son to the one Father' (18.47; cf. also *Ep.* 38.4). This series of
'before' and 'after' is difficult, for it would appear to imply a creative act
of the Spirit first and independently of the act of the Son. Is this due to
Basil's ascetical interest, his concentration upon the work of the Spirit
in his own heart and life? If so, how can it be distinguished from an
anthropocentric starting-point? This is worth mentioning, for it is along
this line that the doctrine of the Spirit, as we see in nineteenth-century
theology, is easily led astray. The stronger Christological perspective of
Athanasius is theologically sounder. But if we take a leaf out of Basil's
own argument when he insists that the light cannot be divorced from
visible objects, and that the cause of vision is seen at the same time as
visible objects (26.64), then we would have to argue for the simultaneity
of knowledge of God in his Son and the enlightenment of the Spirit.
(This is a point that is conceded in *Ep.* 38.4.)

Gregory of Nyssa could also speak like Basil of the way in which we
know God in the Spirit through the Son, but insisted that this does not
argue for a 'before' and 'after' in the subsistence of God. It has its place
only in our thought, for periods of time have no place in a life which was
before the world began (*C. Eunomium* 1.42). This is so even in Gregory's
rather difficult distinction between the Father as *aition* and the Son and
Spirit as each *aitiaton* for no difference of time or nature, but only of
mode of being, is intended here (*Quod non sint tres dii*). If it is argued
that to speak of the Spirit as 'caused' in relation to the Father, even if
that is an eternal relationship, takes him out of the creative activity of
God, then the same thing must be said of the Son, but clearly no such
thing is intended by Gregory.

2. Similar to this question is another, as to what Basil means by
'form' in the statement: 'Inasmuch as the Holy Spirit perfects rational
beings, completing their excellence, τὸν τοῦ εἴδους λόγον ἐπέχει' (26.61).
Is there here some notion that the Spirit is the entelechy, so to speak, of
rational creation, informing it with order, giving it to participate in form
and so in rational being? If so, this would be a very difficult notion to
integrate with the doctrine of the ineffability of the Spirit, for it would
mean that the Spirit imparts form to the creation out of himself, and
could presumably be brought to expression through the forms he creates
within rational minds. But if it means that it is through the Spirit that
the mind is filled with the form of the Logos, that the Spirit, for example
imparts to the Church its true form in Christ as his Body, then it is

compatible with Basil's insistence that the Spirit is inseparable from the *Logos* in *koinonia* and *energeia*. But again, this would be strengthened with the Athanasian doctrine of the Son as the only *eidos* and *logos* of Godhead.

3. A third point relates to Basil's connection of grace with the Spirit, and in particular his suggestion that human souls who have grace conferred on them by the Spirit may themselves emit grace to others (9.23). If this were valid, it would surely invalidate the Athanasian argument which Basil himself shares, that if the Holy Spirit were a creature he could not mediate to us any participation (*metousia*) in the grace of God. If he is to mediate divine grace he must be fully divine in himself, for only God is a source of grace. This passage in Basil is worth pointing out for it appears to indicate a weakening of the doctrine of grace in the direction which ultimately forced upon the Church of the West the Reformation insistence that in grace God communicates to us himself, and that grace is God's self-giving. In other words, against the Church of Rome and its doctrine of different forms of 'created grace' communicable from some human beings to others, the Reformation insisted on applying the *homoousion* to grace, interpreting it as the one indivisible self-giving of God in Christ. As the Fathers of Nicaea had laid the stress upon the Being of God in the act of his self-communication in Christ, so the reforming fathers found they had to lay the stress upon the *homoousion* of the Spirit in order to teach clearly that in Christ we are confronted not only by the Being of God in his Act, but by his Act in his Being. That is to say, they found out again the truth of the patristic doctrine that the *homoousion* of the Son could not be fully maintained apart from the *homoousion* of the Spirit—that is part, at least, of the significance of the application of the *homoousion* to the grace of God. If grace is related to the Lord the Spirit who is sovereignly free to be present to the creature, though infinitely exalted above it, in order to bring its relations with God to their *telos*, then the notion of mutuality between the creature and God is snapped, and with it all the Arian and Pelagian notions of created grace and merited grace that go along with it. But that is precisely the doctrine of the *Spiritus Creator* who is at work in redemption as much as in creation. The doctrine of the *filioque*, rightly taken, could have led the Roman Church to avoid the development of these erroneous notions, but it was through a return of the Reformers to the teaching of the post-Nicene fathers as to the inseparable relation of the Spirit, and therefore of grace, to Christ, that correction eventually came.

By way of gathering up this discussion of the doctrine of the Spirit in the Greek fathers we may make the following points.

1. He who grants that the Holy Spirit is God, as Gregory of Nyssa expressed it, has granted all the rest. If the Spirit is God he cannot be thought of as idle or inactive in the creation, so that the Macedonian idea that the Spirit is quite disconnected with the creative force of God is to be rejected altogether (*C. Macedonium*). The Spirit is the creative Power of God. 'The fountain of power is the Father, and the power of the Father is the Son, and the spirit of that power is the Holy Spirit; and creation entirely, in all its visible and spiritual extent, is the finished work of that divine Power' (*ibid.*).

2. When we come to distinguish the Spirit from the Father and the Son, and ask for the notes peculiar to the Spirit, we may speak negatively by saying that he is none of those things which are rightly believed to be proper to the Father and the Son, for he is neither Unbegotten nor Only-Begotten. He is one with the Father in so far as he is increate, and one with the Son both as increate and as deriving his subsistence from the God of all, but when we ask what he is in himself, *in the nature of the case*, we can only say, '*He simply is what he is*' (Nyssen, *C. Eunom.* 1.22). We know who he is, because he creates in us, beyond all creaturely or human capacities, the ability to know the unknowable God, and because he makes us actually know God the Creator, we know that it is *in* the Spirit that we know the Creator—were the Spirit not himself the Creator, we could not know God in this way. But since he is the Spirit, and neither the Father nor the Son, we must beware of thinking of him after the mode of Being of the Father or of the Son, but know him in accordance with his own mode of Being, as he who utters the Word and illumines the Son of the Father, creating in us the capacity to hear and see him. In the nature of the case the Spirit hides, as it were, his own *hypostasis* from us and reveals himself to us by revealing the Father through the Son. But though he stands, as it were, behind the Father and the Son, throwing his light upon us and enlightening our minds to know the one Triune God, he confronts us with all the unknowable ultimateness and infiniteness of the Godhead before whom we can only bow in worship and adoration, and with all the reverence and obedience of our minds. We know him as no less Lord God, the Creator, than the Father and the Son, for he is the sheer Power of all creation and re-creation and confronts us with the limitless majesty of God's eternal Being in it all. The difficulty of the doctrine of the Spirit derives from this hiding of himself on the part of the Spirit behind the Face of the

Father in the Son and the Heart of the Son in the Father; or rather the difficulty lies with our wrong movement of thought in trying to think of him after the mode of Being of the Father or after the mode of Being of the Son, instead of knowing him in accordance with his own mode of Being as *Spirit*, of the Father and of the Son. It is when we make that wrong movement of thought that we have difficulty in thinking and speaking of him as *Spiritus Creator*.

3. It is most important that we think of the Spirit in his indissoluble relation to the Son, as the Spirit of God who has uttered the Word and incarnated the Son, as the Spirit who in and through the crucified and risen Christ sustains from beginning to end and brings to its completion the creative and redemptive work of the Holy Trinity. Though proceeding from the Father he comes to us *in the Name* of the Son and as sent by him. Hence he is known as 'the Spirit of Christ' (Rom. 8.9), 'the Spirit of Jesus Christ' (Phil. 1.19), 'the Spirit of the Son' (Gal. 4.6), 'the Spirit of the Lord' (II Cor. 3.17), 'the Spirit of Jesus' (Acts 16.7), etc. It belongs to the nature of his operation, and to the mode of his Being that the Holy Spirit comes to us not in his own Name but in the Name of Christ, he who is God and Man in one Person, the one Mediator between God and man. If this is the way in which the Spirit comes to us, proceeding from the Father and sent by the Son, then this is the way in which we are to know him, and think and speak of him.

If we do not do this, then because the Holy Spirit in accordance with his Nature and mode of Being hides himself, we lapse into the error of confounding him either with the Church within whose sphere we meet the Spirit or with the human heart, for it is within us that the Spirit is sent by Christ to bear witness that we with him are sons of God. One of the major lessons we learn from Athanasius and his attack upon Arians and semi-Arians alike is that unless we know the Holy Spirit through the objectivity of the *homoousion* of the Son in whom and by whom our minds are directed away from ourselves to the one Fountain and Principle of Godhead, then we inevitably become engrossed with ourselves, confusing the Holy Spirit with our own spirits, and confounding the one Truth of God with notions of our own devising. In other words, apart from the indissoluble relation of the Spirit and the Incarnate Son, we are unable to distinguish the objective reality of the Lord God, the Creator of the ends of the earth, from our own subjective states and conditions, or from our own creative spirituality.

This has been the persistent error of Romanism and Protestantism; the one confounds the Spirit with the spirit of the Church, and substitutes, so to speak for the *filioque* an *ecclesiaque*, and the other confounds the Spirit of God with the human spirit. Thus knowledge of the Spirit is dissolved in the subjectivities of the consciousness of the Church or of the individual, and the products of this consciousness, in its collective or individual genius, are put forward as operations of the Holy Spirit. Against all that the Athanasian doctrine of the Spirit stands like a great Rock in our path against which our own notions and inventions can only shatter themselves again and again. It is only as that happens, and we are delivered from being engrossed with ourselves, and are flung upon the infinite glory and majesty of God revealed in Jesus Christ, that we are able to distinguish the Holy Spirit from our spirits, and to know him in all his transcendent freedom and power as *Creator Spiritus*.

13

The Relevance of the Doctrine of the Spirit
for Ecumenical Theology[1]

I T is one of the curious features of church history that the Western
Church which had officially championed the addition of the *filioque*
clause to the Nicene-Constantinopolitan Creed has tended in practice
to ignore it, whereas the Eastern Church which decidedly rejected it has
tended to uphold the emphases which it was designed to safeguard—
without of course ever agreeing to the formal statement that the Spirit
proceeds from the Son as well as the Father.

There were understandable reasons for the original divergence of the
East and the West on this issue. It was supremely important for the
Eastern Church to insist upon the procession of the Spirit from the
Father, the one Source (*arche*) and Fount (*pege*) of the Godhead and to
avoid a procession from the Son, in view of the assertions of the Arians,
Macedonians and Tropici, that the Spirit was a creature of the Son
since he came into being through his mediation. For the Western
Church, however, it was of the utmost importance to insist that the
Spirit was truly the Spirit of the Son as of the Father, for unless the
Father and the Son were held to be fully equal the doctrine of the
homoousion could hardly be maintained. Nevertheless the Eastern
Church upheld the doctrine of the Spirit propounded by Athanasius,
'from the Father, through the Son, in the Spirit', and continued to
maintain and develop a doctrine of the Spirit in the closest association
with the doctrine of the Son.

The *filioque* clause in the West had been intended to make clear the
Lordship of the Spirit and the propriety of the Spirit to the Son, that
is, the transcendent presence of God over the whole of his creation
whereby he governs and disposes all things according to his goodness,
power and wisdom, and the intensely personal presence of God to his

---

[1] German text, *Oekumenische Rundschau*, 1963; French text, *Verbum Caro*
17.66, 1963: written in honour of Professor Edmund Schlink of Heidelberg.

people through the Incarnate Person of the Son and his life-giving
Word. But in the West there arose a tendency toward the depersonaliza-
tion of the Spirit regarded as the instrument in the hands of God, and
toward an interpretation of the operation of the Spirit in terms of
immanent principles or norms within the creaturely processes. This
allowed Western theologians to develop a powerful natural theology,
although the *filioque* clause clearly implies a renunciation of so-called
natural revelation, since it insists that we cannot speak of the operation
of the Spirit in the world as if the Incarnation had not taken place, as
if the Incarnation and the Atonement made no difference to his work,
or as if he may now operate as it were behind the back of Jesus Christ.
In fact the *filioque* is the earliest and profoundest way of saying *solo
Christo, solo verbo, sola gratia, sola fide*. The extent to which the Reformation had to recall the Western Church to the centrality of Christ is
the measure of its departure from the *homoousion* of the Spirit.

There is every reason to say that this is still a crucial question for the
East and for the West. Perhaps it does not matter very much today
whether the formal statement that the Spirit proceeds from the Son as
well as from the Father is adopted or not, but what does matter is
whether ecumenical theology is fully prepared to maintain the *homoousion*
both of the Son and of the Spirit for they belong inseparably together.
It is only through basic agreement at this point that there can be agreement on the vexed doctrine of the Church, and only through staunch
support of the *homoousion*, that there can be prevented a dissolution of
the work of Christ into timeless events, and a dissolution of the operation of the Spirit into timeless processes. It is only through thinking out
carefully within the doctrine of the Trinity the doctrine of the Spirit
and the doctrine of the Son in the closest interrelationship that we can
recover and preserve the proper understanding of the Being of God in
his Acts (the emphasis of the fathers) and of the Acts of God in his
Being (the emphasis of the Reformers). It is as we take seriously the
utter lordship and deity of the Spirit, i.e. the presence of God in all his
glory, majesty and sheer Godness in the Person and mode of Being of
the Spirit, that we take seriously the very Being of God in his self-
giving to us in the Incarnation; and it is as we take seriously the utter
lordship and deity of Christ, i.e. the presence of God in all his transcendent grace, condescension and nearness in the Person and mode of
Being of the Son, that we take seriously the direct and intensely personal activity of God in his self-giving to us at Pentecost.

One of the principal aspects of this doctrine, which is of special significance for ecumenical theology today, is the transcendently personal yet implacable objectivity of God's presence and activity in the Church. The importance of this for the West can be seen if it is said, with a little exaggeration, that there has been in it a persistent tendency to substitute for the *filioque* either an *ecclesiaque*, the error of Romanism, or a *homineque*, the error of Neo-Protestantism. In other words, there has been a marked failure to distinguish the Holy Spirit from the spirit of the Church or the spirit of religious man, that is, from the self-consciousness of the Church or the self-consciousness of the believer. In Protestantism this has a long history, deriving ultimately from mediaeval spiritualism and subjectivism, but in which popular piety and idealist philosophy have combined to lay the stress upon religious inwardness and immediacy. As a result we have the great error of modernism which finds the truth of salvation in the religious subject himself, and which identifies the Holy Spirit with the depths of man's own spirituality and personality. This has been accentuated in German thought by the fact that the word *Geist* stands both for the Spirit and for the reason, so that for a great deal of modern Protestant theology the Spirit of God means little more than subjective awareness of God or religious self-understanding and has very little to do with the objective reality of the Being and presence and power of God himself.

This is extremely grave for it means that modern religious man is afflicted with a deep-seated mental disease. Failure to distinguish between objective realities and subjective conditions, or a confusion between them, is the primary mark of irrational behaviour or mental disorder. But this is precisely the kind of madness that has infected so much modern theology. That is why the obsession with self-understanding and the reduction of the great Christian doctrines of the Incarnation and Atonement to the self-understanding for their explanation, indicates that religious man is in desperate need of some kind of spiritual psychiatry.

Let us state the problem in another way—the way in which we are bound to look at it in the world of careful, scientific thought, because we cannot hold a conception of rationality which obtains for religion and ethics and art and does not obtain for science. In every sphere of our life, in reflection, in action, and in worship, *reason is our capacity for objectivity*. That was one of the great lessons of the Reformation, when face to face with the majestic Word of God men learned that the way to true knowledge of God or of nature is the way of obedience in which we submit our knowing to the given reality and act in accordance with

its nature unfettered by preconceptions. But this is a lesson which we
theologians are being forced to learn once again today under the
pressure of the empirical science that surrounds us on every side.

In the language of Professor John Macmurray, reason is our capacity
to behave consciously in terms of the nature of what is not ourselves,
that is to say, the capacity to act in accordance with the nature of the
object. Hence true thoughts are thoughts which refer properly to
reality and which are thought in accordance with the nature of the
object to which they refer. They are not true if they refer to certain
objects in a mode that is determined by the nature of other and different
objects; they cannot be true, for example, if they refer to personal beings
as if they were merely things. Persons must be treated as persons if our
thoughts of them are to be properly objective. Reason is our capacity
for objectivity in this sense. To be rational, therefore, means to behave
not in terms of our own nature, but in terms of our knowledge of the
world outside of us, of things and persons, in accordance with their own
natures. Clearly this objectivity or reason cannot be confined to the
intellect alone, but characterizes every aspect of our human life and
activity as rational persons—indeed it is the essential characteristic of
personal consciousness. It is what distinguishes rational, personal
activity from all inorganic, impersonal activity. Genuine *objectivity*
must never be confused with *objectivism*—that would be a form of
irrationality. It is of the nature of persons to be reasonable, to relate
themselves objectively to the world around them, in action as well as in
reflection, in emotion as well as in volition. Thus if in natural science
we develop a knowledge of things in their objective reality by learning
to act in accordance with the nature of the world around us, so in the
sphere of the ethical and social life we develop a capacity to act objectively in relation to other persons, by behaving towards them in
accordance with their natures, not in terms of the natures of things and
not in terms of our own subjective determinations. That is why love
occupies such an essential place in these inter-personal relations, for
the capacity to love objectively is the capacity in which we live as
persons. Indeed, it is the ultimate source of our capacity to behave in
terms of the nature of the object. Hence it would also be irrational to
treat things as persons. Strict respect for the nature of what is other than
ourselves is the very core of rationality.

Why should it be different in religion? Why should it be otherwise in
theology? The nature of the object is certainly different, for here we are
confronted with the Lord God, not just with things and other creaturely

persons, but with the God who gives himself in the transcendent freedom and power of the divine love, for God *is* love. For that very reason it is precisely here that we know what true rationality and true objectivity are, as we learn to act toward God in accordance with his nature as Lord, and develop the capacity to relate ourselves objectively to him, and so to one another, and even to the world around us, in encounter with the relentless objectivity of the divine love. Hence it is here more than anywhere else that to be rational means to act, not in terms of our own nature, but in terms of the nature of the reality of God himself, not in terms of our own self-understanding but in terms of our knowledge of the Being and Activity of God independent of us yet acting upon us in his grace. But it is here more than anywhere else that failure to think and act objectively, failure to distinguish what is objectively real from our own subjective conditions and states, is a grave form of mental and spiritual disorder. It is at once the betrayal of the objective reality of God and the falsification of our own rationality in a distorted mode of thinking and acting in which objectivism and subjectivism coincide.

What is required is a recovery of complete objectivity, but that depends upon our being objectively related in worship, action and reflection, to the transcendent objectivity of God. It can take place only when we allow God in the sheer majesty and transcendence of his divine Being and Act to press upon us within the structured objectivities of things and other persons in which we have our human existence in space and time, and open us up for truly objective relation toward himself, in which we are reconciled to him and healed of our mental alienation and estrangement. That is not something we can achieve, but we can let it happen to us. What we may do is to reflect upon his self-communication in Jesus Christ and pray that in the pouring out of his Spirit upon us we may fall under the overwhelming mastery of his divine Being and come under the determination of his saving grace. This cannot but involve the reconstitution of our relations with one another in the objectivity of God's love, for it will plant in their midst the healing source of all true objectivity, '*from the Father, through the Son, in the Spirit*'. It is then that the true nature of the Church becomes manifest, as the work of the three divine Persons, as the holy place appointed by God where diseased and sinful men are healed and saved through encountering the ultimate objectivity of God himself in Incarnation and Atonement.

What then is the bearing of the Incarnation and of the Atonement to the objectivity of God in the freedom and presence of his Holy Spirit, and to our objective relationship to him in and through the Spirit?

The Incarnation is the self-objectification of God for us men within the same sphere of existence and reality to which we belong. It means that God does not hold himself aloof from us but draws near to us, that he does not relate himself to us by some sort of tangential relation between the other-worldly and the this-worldly, but is active and at work within creaturely being and within the objectivities of space and time. All this is not to deny that God remains God, he who is Lord and transcendent over all creaturely and contingent existence, but it does mean that in his love and self-revelation God takes seriously our human existence in space and time, and relates himself to us in such a way as to act in accordance with our human nature, and it does mean that God continues in his relations toward us and the world in which we exist to be the Creator and Redeemer and not just some ultimate Being who is only deistically and paradoxically related to us and our world. There is no need to go into this in detail, but we may note several basic aspects of the divine objectivity in the Incarnation that have a bearing upon the doctrine of the Spirit.

It is the objectivity of God's love, in which the divine objectivity meets our human objectivity, and far from demolishing it or asking men to transcend it, respects it, and acts in accordance with its nature. It is precisely because God acts objectively with us in this way that we are enabled to relate ourselves objectively to him, in the divine love. That is surely the irreducible objectivity of the Holy Spirit which is inseparable from the fact that God loved us and sent his Son to be the Saviour of the world, for it is as participating and effecting that movement of the divine love that the Spirit acts upon us, and enables us to act toward God in terms of his action upon us.

But that objectivity takes concrete form in the historical humanity of Jesus Christ, and therefore confronts us historical human beings right in the midst of our objectivities with the very Being and majesty of God himself, in all his ultimate lordship. This is not a divine objectivity that stands behind some radical dichotomy between the objectifiable and the non-objectifiable, between the given and the not-given (in relation to which we can only have a feeling of absolute dependence), but an objectivity that meets us in the particularity of Jesus Christ where God himself has really given himself to us within the structures of our intramundane and inter-personal relationships. It is a completely obdurate objectivity which we cannot avoid and cannot remove, both because it meets us within our own existence and life and because it is backed up by God's own ultimate Being and Person. As such, however, it is an objectivity that objects to, and resists, every attempt on our part to master or domesticate it, or to side-step or transcend it, or to ignore it. No more than the Jewish authorities could ignore Jesus can we ignore him: we have either to follow those who crucify him, or take up his Cross and follow him. The Incarnation, as Kierkegaard used to say, is God's attack upon man—it is the full resistance of the divine Being and nature to the will of man to isolate himself from God, to man's determination to act in terms of his own nature instead of in accordance with the revelation of the divine nature. It is an attack completely unavoidable because it is incarnated in our flesh and blood in Jesus. It is that divine resistance on God's part to man's self-will, his judgment upon man's desire to be wise in his own eyes, his questioning of man's vaunted self-understanding, that encounters us in the self-objectification of God in Jesus Christ making the objectivity of God all the more implacable by its relentless objection to our self-chosen ways.

That is the context in which an adequate doctrine of the Spirit is to be formulated, for it is in that context that we are not allowed to confound the objective reality of God with our own subjective states, or to resolve it away as the symbolic counterpart of our human concerns. It is when we encounter the very Person and presence of God in the exclusive particularity of Jesus Christ, and come up against the relentless attack upon us of God's love incarnated in him, that we are prevented from evaporating the Spirit into the immanent processes of nature or from confusing the Spirit with our own spirits. It is when face to face with Jesus we are questioned down to the very roots of our existence that we yield ourselves to the overwhelming mastery of the divine Being, and are able to distinguish the objective divine reality from our own self-understanding.

That is the epistemological relevance of the doctrine of the Spirit. Certainly the history of Christian doctrine makes it clear that wherever the Church has allowed the reality of the historical Jesus Christ to be depreciated there it has also lost a doctrine of the Holy Spirit, through the dissolving of the Spirit into the immanent reason or into man's own attempts at understanding. The doctrine of the Spirit, i.e. of the objective reality and personal Being of the Spirit, stands or falls with the acknowledgment of the active coming and activity of the Being of God himself within our space and time in Jesus Christ. Failure to relate ourselves objectively to the Being and Act of God in Jesus Christ, results in failure to discern the objective reality of the Holy Spirit in his presence and power. But with this unforgivable sin the basic structure of the Gospel is discarded, and we are of all men most miserable.

It is high time, perhaps, to add a note about the cry which one hears only too often today, that in the interpretation and understanding of the New Testament and its message one must transcend and set aside the subject-object relationship. Since our traditional understanding of that relationship is bound up with classical physics, the implications of this demand should become clear if we look at it in the light of modern science. It is certainly true that we have had to advance beyond classical physics to nuclear physics, and have had to modify the criterion of perceptibility which was so central to it, but far from rejecting classical physics nuclear physics has shown its limited range, and has at the same time established it all the more securely on its own proper foundations within that limited range. It has made indubitably clear that apart from its foundations in classical physics, nuclear physics could not take place, for all the experimental questioning and learning it employs is set up on the basis of classical physics. On this ground, then, it must be declared very firmly that any suggestion that we have to transcend the subject-object relationship would be just as stupid as to say that we must set aside classical physics, for without the subject-object relationship of classical physics there would be no science at all. No doubt the subject-object relationship must be modified, when applied to the interpretation and understanding of the New Testament and its message, but modified appropriately in accordance with the nature of the object and never in some alleged identity of subject and object. But that means that the demands of objectivity here are not less but all the greater and all the stricter. That is as it should be, for here we are up against the ultimate objectivity of the Lord God, in all his divine majesty and grace, in Jesus Christ, summoning us to relate ourselves to him correspondingly in the utter objectivity of love.

It is when we come to consider the Atonement, however, that we can discern how understanding of the divine objectivity has to be modified in accordance with the activity of God in his saving love. It is objectivity so positive that the divine objection to man's disobedience leads to the re-establishment of true objectivity from the side of man toward God, in faith and love.

John Craig, the sixteenth-century Scottish theologian, used to speak of the difference between the Gospel and the Law by pointing out that the Spirit is joined with the Gospel and not with the Law. That is not to deny that the Spirit is at work in the order of nature and that he governs and rules over all things, executing the divine decrees, but that there is a fundamental difference between the general work of the Spirit in creation and providence and the pouring out of the Spirit at Pentecost due to the fulfilment of the divine judgment and the establishment of reconciliation and peace. With the Fall of man the relation between the creation and God had been thrown into tension, man's disobedience against God met with the divine resistance. That does not mean that God has given man up and turned his back upon the creation, but that he holds himself at a distance from man and keeps man at a distance from himself, precisely for man's sake. With the Fall of man the presence of God's Spirit to his creatures brings the judgment of God to bear upon them, so that if the creatures are to have continued existence and are not to be destroyed, God must mercifully withhold the fulness of his presence from them, while nevertheless maintaining them in being and order in his creation. It is only with the reconciliation of the world, and the removal of the enmity between man and God, that the Spirit of God may be poured out upon his creatures without consuming them in judgment. But with the Incarnation in which God no longer holds himself at a distance from man but draws so near to him that he enters within his creaturely life, and with the completion of the atoning work of Christ in which the divine judgment is fulfilled and all enmity removed, there takes place such a pouring out of the Spirit of God upon human flesh that the Church is created as the sphere within which reconciliation is actualized and God himself is present with men in the acute and intimate personalization of his love. Thus the doctrine of the Church as the community in which men and women are objectively related to God and to one another in love is grounded upon the relation of the Holy Spirit to the Incarnation and the Atonement.

All-important here, however, is the fact that there takes place in the Atonement the final action of God in which with all his ultimate objectivity he penetrates into the depths of human existence, fulfilling his judgment against our sin, overcoming the barriers of guilt and estrangement, and restoring man to such communion with God that both divine nature and human nature are fully respected and maintained in the pure objectivity of love. God does not override man but recreates, reaffirms him and stands him up before himself as his dear child, and man does not seek to use or manipulate knowledge of God for the fulfilment of his own ends in self-will and self-understanding, but loves him objectively for his own sake and is so liberated from himself that he can love his neighbour objectively also.

Thus far from having anything to do with an infinite separation between God and man or a radical dichotomy between the non-objectifiable and the objectifiable, the Gospel is the message that through Incarnation and Atonement God has opened up the earth for heaven and
hence by Resurrection and Ascension opened up heaven for earth,
establishing such a communion between them, that God, in all the
ultimate objectivity of his divine Being and majesty, is free really to give
himself to man, to be present with him and to act for his salvation within
his existence in space and time, and man is emancipated from his own
subjectivities, from imprisonment in his own preconceptions or prior
understanding, to know and love God truly in accordance with his own
divine nature. By coming *into* man the Holy Spirit opens him *out* for
God. But at the very heart of this movement is the act of God in which
he became man in order to take man's place, and give man a place within the communion of the divine life. It is the act of the divine love taking
the way of *substitution*, and opening up the way for a corresponding act
on the part of man in which he renounces himself for God's sake that
the divine love may have its way with him in a self-less objectivity.
Hence when we speak of the Spirit as pouring out the love of God in our
hearts, we are to think of his activity in strict correlativity to the atoning
substitution in the life, death and resurrection of Jesus Christ—that is
to say, we are to think of the work of the Spirit not simply as the actualizing within us of what God has already wrought for us in Jesus Christ
once and for all, but as opening us up within our subjectivities for Christ
in such a radical way that we find our life *not in ourselves but out of ourselves, objectively in him.*

This is in some respects the most crucial point for us today in a doctrine of the Spirit, its relation to the objective *pro me* (we bear in mind
here Iwand's castigation of the subjectivist distortion of *pro me* in existentialist exegesis). This is the objectivity that will not allow us to
confuse the Holy Spirit with our own spirits, or to confound his objective activity with our own subjective states, for it turns us inside out.
It is an objectivity that demands the renunciation of ourselves, with all
their pre-understanding, and requires of us the readiness to hear and
learn what contradicts our preconceived self-understanding in order
that we may develop a way of understanding appropriate to the nature
of God's redeeming love and therefore genuinely objective. It is precisely by taking in all its terrible seriousness the objection of God to our
sin, and the fulfilment of that objection in the Incarnation and Atonement, and therefore the opening up of a way of true love in objective

relations with God, that we are healed of the mental and spiritual disease in which we fail to distinguish our own subjective conditions from objective realities. Only at this point are we in a position to formulate a proper doctrine of the Holy Spirit, in all the Godness and majesty of God, and yet in his distinctness of Person and mode of Being from those of the Son and of the Father. And only on that ground is it possible to formulate adequately the doctrine of the Church. Unless we can gain a clear understanding of the objectivity of the Holy Spirit, it will be difficult to formulate a doctrine of the Church without lapsing back into the confusion between the Mind of the Spirit and the historical self-consciousness of the Church which characterized alike the teaching of Schleiermacher and the first Vatican Council, or, to put it the other way round, without losing the Spirit in the depths of man's own self-understanding in its corporate or in its individualist forms.

We may state the problem with which we are faced in modern theology in another way, by recalling the statements of the New Testament that we may *grieve* the Spirit of God, or *quench* his presence and power in the Church. If our understanding of the Holy Spirit is determined by our understanding of the self-giving of God in the Incarnation and by his atoning reconciliation in Jesus Christ, then it is precisely at these basic points that we may fail, and grieve or quench the Spirit both in our understanding of the truth and in the life of the Church. Is that not what we are up against in the rejection of the Incarnation as the actual coming and presence of the Being of God himself in space and time, and the rejection of the objective Act of God for us men and our salvation in the death and resurrection of his Son? Or, to be quite frank, what can quench among us the presence and power of the Spirit of God more than the so-called 'demythologization' of the Gospel, or grieve the Holy Spirit more than persistence in the division of the Church, for each in its own way, by theory or by practice, calls in question the very activity of God whereby he so gives himself to us objectively and overcomes our estrangement that we are granted a communion in the Spirit in which we may love God objectively, not for our own sakes, but for his sake, and love our neighbour as ourselves? So long as we are thrown back upon ourselves, on our own preconceptions and predeterminations, we are plunged by sheer self-centredness into ruinous dissension and division, and sin against the Holy Spirit, but in so far as we allow the relentless objectivity of God to break into the circle of our self-enclosure in understanding and life we may really be emancipated for the communion of the Spirit in the fulness of his power and love.

14

Come, Creator Spirit,
for the Renewal of Worship and Witness[1]

W H A T do we mean by the prayer, *Come, Creator Spirit*? It cannot mean
that the Holy Spirit should come and act as in the original creation of
the world or in its creative preservation, and yet it is a prayer for his
creative power. It is a prayer for the Holy Spirit in accordance with his
new coming and acting as on the day of Pentecost. On that day the
Holy Spirit came into the world and entered into the experience of men
in a way that had never happened before. Certainly the Spirit continued to operate in the world and to be at work among men as he had
been from the beginning, but at Pentecost something quite new happened, as new and distinct and indeed as unique as the Incarnation
itself. Along with the birth, life, death, resurrection and ascension of
Christ the pouring out of his Spirit at Pentecost belongs to the series of
God's mighty acts which brought salvation to mankind and inaugurated
the new age. They are acts which cannot be repeated and cannot be
undone, for they have entirely altered the relation of the world to God.
From that point all history presses relentlessly forward to its consummation when Christ will come again to judge the quick and the dead
and make all things new. We live on this side of Pentecost and are on
our way to meet the Advent Christ. We live, therefore, after the new
thing has happened, within the new age in which the Creator Spirit of
God is abroad among men and actively at work among them in a new
and distinctive way, in addition to his original and continuing operation
in the world. *Come, Creator Spirit* is a prayer of participation in this
new happening, a prayer in which we allow it to overtake us; it is a
prayer in which we ask that the new mode of the Spirit's entry into the
lives of men at Pentecost may not be obstructed in our own experience.

[1] Address delivered to the World Alliance of Reformed Churches, Frankfurt,
5th August, 1964. I wish to acknowledge my indebtedness in this essay to the
teaching of the Scottish divines from Knox, Craig and Boyd to Milligan,
Wotherspoon and Manson.

How, then, are we to understand this distinctively new mode of the Holy Spirit's activity in the experience of men?

The meaning of Pentecost is determined by the great evangelical facts that lie behind it, for they made possible this new mode of the Spirit's activity. It is in the *Incarnation* and the *Atonement* that we learn the secret of Pentecost. With the Incarnation, God the eternal Son became Man, without ceasing to be God and without breaking the communion of the Holy Trinity within which God lives his own divine life. In the birth and life of Jesus on earth human nature and divine nature were inseparably united in the eternal Person of God the Son. Therefore in him the closed circle of the inner life of God was made to overlap with human life, and human nature was taken up to share in the eternal communion of the Father and the Son in the Holy Spirit. In this one Man the divine life and love overflowed into creaturely and human being, so that Jesus, Man on earth, received the Spirit of God without measure, for the fulness of the Godhead dwelt in him bodily. Jesus became the Bearer of the Holy Spirit among men.

But who was Jesus? He was very Man, our Brother. In him the Holy Son of God was grafted on to the stock of our fallen human existence, and in him our mortal and corrupt human nature was assumed into union with the Holy Son of God, so that in Jesus, in his birth and sinless life, in his death and resurrection, there took place a holy and awful judgment on our flesh of sin, and an atoning sanctification of our unholy human existence. It was only through such atonement that God in all his Godness and holiness came to dwell in the midst of mortal, sinful man. Because that took place in Jesus who made our flesh of sin his very own and who wrought out in himself peace and reconciliation between man and God, he became not only the Bearer but the Mediator of the Holy Spirit to men.

Now we may understand the distinctively new mode of the Spirit's coming into the experience of men. The inner life of the Holy Trinity which is private to God alone is extended to include human nature in and through Jesus. This is possible because of the atonement that took place in him, for now that the enmity between God and man has been abolished, God the Holy Spirit may dwell in the midst of mortal sinful man. This is the way that the divine love has taken to redeem man, by making him share in the holy power in which God lives his own divine life. The pouring out of that power from on high took place at Pentecost, with the entry of the Holy Spirit in his new mode of presence and activity into the experience of mortal men. On our lips the prayer, *Come,*

Creator Spirit, is a prayer of commitment to what God has already done in Jesus Christ, and a prayer of participation in the divine nature, in the faith that it is only the power of God which can redeem fallen man, and that nothing short of the very life and breath of God himself can renew the life of his people. Hence for the Church to worship God is to draw into itself the holy breath of the life of God, and to live out that divine life on earth is to live a life of praise and witness to his glory.

That is the Church's belief in the Holy Spirit which it confessed in the Nicene Creed: 'And I believe in the Holy Spirit, the Lord and Giver of Life, who proceeds from the Father and the Son, who with the Father and the Son together is worshipped and glorified, who spoke by the prophets.' It is worth noting that it is in the Nicene (Constantinopolitan) Creed which is essentially a doxological act, in which worship and witness combine inseparably together, that the Church's faith in the Holy Spirit first came into clear articulation. By his very nature the Holy Spirit not only proceeds from the Father but lifts up to the Father; he is not only the Spirit sent by Christ but the Spirit of response to Christ, the Spirit in whom and by whom and with whom we worship and glorify the Father and the Son. Not only is he God the Holy Spirit descending to us, the Spirit by whom God bears witness to himself, but God the Holy Spirit lifting up all creation in praise and rejoicing in God, himself the Spirit of worship and witness by whom the Church lives and fulfils its mission to the glory of God.

THE NEW COMING OF THE HOLY SPIRIT AT PENTECOST WAS A COMING IN THE UTTER GODNESS OF GOD

We have become accustomed to think of the coming of the Holy Spirit far too much as the interiorizing in our hearts of divine salvation, with the result that the presence of the Spirit is so often identified with inward moral and religious states. Creator Spirit and our own creative spirituality tend to become confused. This way of thinking arose early in the history of the Church, gathered momentum in monastic piety and broke out again in Protestant pietism in its emphasis upon religious *inwardness* and *immediacy*, but all this has been greatly accentuated by modern habits in psychological and personalistic thinking. Certainly the Holy Spirit is sent into our hearts where he begets enlightenment and conviction, and bears witness with our spirit that we are the children of God, but the psychologizing and subjectivizing of this is entirely, or almost entirely, absent from the New Testament. The emphasis of the

Apostolic Church was placed elsewhere. Pentecost meant the living presence of God among men in all his transcendent power and holiness as very God, for only God can give God and lift men up to himself. Hence the descent of the Holy Spirit upon the Apostolic Church lifted it out of itself and made it participate in the undiluted acts of Almighty God and in the uncreated life of the Holy Trinity. The emphasis is not upon man receiving but upon God giving, for man receives only as he falls under the transcendent power of the Creator Spirit who is not limited by man's lack of capacity for he gives himself and presents himself to man even when he has no power to receive so that man's reception of the Holy Spirit is itself a creative work of God.

At this point let me plead for a reconsideration by the Reformed Church of what the Greek fathers called *theosis*. This is usually unfortunately translated *deification*, but it has nothing to do with the *divinization* of man any more than the Incarnation has to do with the humanization of God. *Theosis* was the term the Fathers used to emphasize the fact that through the Spirit we have to do with God in his utter sublimity, his sheer Godness or holiness; creatures though we are, men on earth, in the Spirit we are made to participate in saving acts that are abruptly and absolutely divine, election, adoption, regeneration or sanctification and we participate in them by grace alone. *Theosis* describes man's involvement in such a mighty act of God upon him that he is raised up to find the true centre of his existence not in himself but in Holy God, where he lives and moves and has his being in the uncreated but creative energy of the Holy Spirit. By *theosis* the Greek fathers wished to express the fact that in the new coming of the Holy Spirit we are up against *God* in the most absolute sense, God in his ultimate holiness or Godness.[1]

As I understand it, this is the antithesis of the nineteenth-century notion of 'the divine in man' which imprisons him in the depth of his own being, or of the man-centred emphasis of so many modern Protestants upon their own existential decisions or their own creative spirituality. Let us not quarrel about the word *theosis*, offensive though it may be to us, but follow its intention, not to allege any divinization of man but to speak of the fact that man in the weakness and lowliness of creaturely human being is by God made free for God through the power of the Creator Spirit who is not and will not be limited in his acts by man's weakness or creaturehood or his lack of capacity. *Theosis* is an

[1] See the essays of Nissiotis and Philippou in *The Orthodox Ethos*, ed. A. J. Philippou, 1964.

attempt to express the staggering significance of Pentecost as the coming from on high, from outside of us and beyond us, of divine power, or rather as the coming of Almighty God, the Maker of heaven and earth, to dwell with sinful mortal man, and therefore as the emancipation of man from imprisonment in himself and the lifting of him up to partake of the living presence and saving acts of God the Creator and Redeemer. Is there anything we need to regain more than this faith in the utter Godness of God the Holy Spirit?

Let us apply this to the Church. And here let us ask a double question. Does Pentecost mean that the Church is endowed with the Spirit as a gift for its possession and as the animating principle of its development? Or does it mean that through the coming of the Spirit the Church in its earthly and historical pilgrimage is made to participate in a perfected reality so that it lives out of a fulness above and beyond itself? Put bluntly and crudely: Does the Church possess the Spirit or is the Church possessed by the Spirit?

If we take the first alternative, then we have a doctrine of the Church as the extending of the Incarnation, a Church that is still evolving and is yet to reach its completeness and will do so only when it brings to its completion the redemptive work of Christ, a Church which through Christ's testamentary disposition to it of the Spirit is so invested with authority and endowed with grace that it fulfils its mission in history as the divine society authoritatively administering grace to all who will own obedience to its ways, and a Church which develops its worship and theology as the manifestations of its own rich vitality and the self-expression of its own individuality and tradition. You may think I have been describing the Roman Church, but actually I have been trying to speak of the whole Western Church which everywhere has the same basic tendencies. They certainly assume distinctively Roman forms, but these all have their recognizably Protestant counterparts. For example, where more than in the Protestant West do we get the notion of the Church as the community instinct with the Spirit of Christ which develops from age to age forms of life and worship in which it manifests its own rich and manifold vitality, and where more than in the Protestant multitudes do men believe in bringing in the Kingdom of God through co-redemption? Foolish Protestants, having begun in the Spirit we now think we are made perfect by the works of the flesh.

At the back of all this there lies deep down a confusion between the Creator Spirit of Holy God and the creative spirituality of Christian man, and therefore we think we can develop out of ourselves ways and

means of translating the new coming of the Spirit and the new creation
he brings into the forms of our own natural vitality. The terminology of
Romans and Protestants may differ: what Romans call 'created grace'
Protestants call 'the Christian spirit', but in both the supernatural
energy and life of the Creator Spirit falls under the disposal of man. In
Romanism and Protestantism alike the Church has domesticated the
grace and Spirit of God in its own spiritual subjectivity instead of being
the sphere of the divine freedom where the Lord the Giver of Life is at
work as Creator Spirit. Protestantism may not have a legal centre and
an articulated *magisterium* like Romanism, but it perpetuates in its own
ways the same basic error, and therefore like the Roman Church is
more and more imprisoned in its own developments.

If our worship and witness are conspicuous for their lack of Holy
Spirit, it is surely because we Protestants, whatever we may confess in
our creeds, have diminished belief in the transcendent power and
utter Godness of the Creator Spirit, and have become engrossed in our
own subjectivities and the development of our own inherent potentialities. Hence the first thing that must happen tò us is a glad subjection
to the lordly freedom and majesty of God the Holy Spirit, and a humble
readiness for miraculous divine acts that transcend all human possibilities and break through the limitations of anything we can conceive.
Come Creator Spirit, is a prayer of open surrender to the absolute
creativity of God.

IN HIS NEW COMING THE HOLY SPIRIT IS MEDIATED BY CHRIST AND AT THE SAME TIME MEDIATES CHRIST TO US

It is in grasping this mutual relation between the work of Christ and
the work of the Spirit that we may understand what worship and its
renewal really mean.

What, then, are the determining facts about this mutuality between
Christ and the Spirit?

(a) The Holy Spirit in his new coming is mediated to us through
Christ in his divine and human natures. It behoved Christ to be God
that he might give his Spirit to men, for only God can give God. It
behoved Christ also to be Man that he might receive the Spirit of God
in our human nature and mediate it to his brethren through himself.
We are concerned here not primarily with the continuing presence and
operation of the Spirit in the world which have been since the beginning
of creation, but with the new coming of the Spirit in the profounder and

more intimate mode of presence made possible by the Incarnation, and which the world cannot know or receive apart from Jesus Christ and what happened to our human nature in him.

Jesus Christ was born of the Virgin Mary into our human nature through the power of the Spirit; at his Baptism the Holy Spirit descended upon him and anointed him as the Christ. He was never without the Spirit for as the eternal Son he ever remained in the unity of the Spirit and of the Father, but as the Incarnate Son on earth he was given the Spirit without measure and consecrated in his human nature for his mission as the vicarious Servant. He came through the temptations in the wilderness clothed with the power of the Spirit and went forth to bring in the Kingdom of God by meeting and defeating the powers of darkness entrenched in human flesh. He struggled and prayed in the Spirit with unspeakable cries of agony, and bore in his Spirit the full burden of human evil and woe. Through the eternal Spirit he offered himself without spot to the Father in sacrifice for sin; according to the Spirit of Holiness he was raised from the dead, and ascended to the right hand of the Father to receive all power in heaven and earth. There he attained the ground from which he could pour out the Spirit of God upon all flesh. As Lamb of God and Priest of our human nature he sent down from the throne of the Most High the gift of the Holy Spirit upon his Church that through the same Spirit the Father and the Son might dwell with men.

Jesus Christ, true God and true Man, is thus the Mediator of the Holy Spirit. Since he is himself both the God who gives and the Man who receives in one Person he is in a position to transfer in a profound and intimate way what belongs to us in our human nature to himself and to transfer what is his to our human nature in him. That applies above all to the gift of the Holy Spirit whom he received fully and completely in his human nature for us. Hence in the union of divine and human natures in the Son the eternal Spirit of the living God has composed himself, as it were, to dwell with human nature, and human nature has been adapted and become accustomed to receive and bear that same Holy Spirit. In his new coming, therefore, the Spirit came not simply as the one Spirit who proceeds eternally from the Father but as the Spirit mediated through the human nature and experience of the Incarnate Son. He came as the Spirit of Jesus, in whom the Son sent by the Father lived out his divine life in a human form, in whom the Son of Man lived out his human life on earth in perfect union with the Father above. He came as the Spirit who in Jesus has penetrated into a new intimacy with our human nature, for he came as the Spirit in whom Jesus lived through our human life from end to end, from birth to death, and beyond into the resurrection. And therefore he came not as isolated and naked Spirit, but as Spirit charged with all the experience of Jesus as he shared to the full our mortal nature and weakness, and endured its temptation and grief and suffering and death, and with the experience of Jesus as he struggled and prayed, and worshipped and obeyed, and poured out his life in compassion for mankind. It is still in the Name of Jesus Christ that the Holy Spirit comes to us, and in no other name.

(*b*) The Holy Spirit is mediated to us only through the glorification of Christ. Jesus Christ was himself the Bearer in our human nature of the fulness of the Spirit, but the Spirit in this his new mode of presence and activity could not be transmitted to others when they were yet in their sins or be received by others until atonement for sin was completed and the Mediator took his place on the throne of God in his consecrated and glorified Humanity.

It was only at infinite cost that Jesus Christ gained for us the gift of the Holy Spirit, receiving him in all his consuming holiness into the human nature which he took from our fallen and alienated condition. We shall never fathom the depth of the humiliation and passion that were his or the indescribable tension into which he entered for our sakes. In himself, in his Incarnate Person, he was both God the Judge and Man under God's judgment. Atonement had to be worked out within the union of his divine and human natures, in the inner determination of his Being in life and in death, in the fulfilling of judgment, in the expiation of guilt, in the perfection of obedience, and in the effecting of peace and reconciliation with God. Until he had sanctified himself and perfected in our human nature his one offering for all men, until he had made once and for all the sacrifice to take away sin, until he had vanquished the powers of darkness and overcome the sharpness of death, until he had ascended to present himself in propitiation before the Father, the Kingdom of Heaven could not be opened to believers and the blessing of the divine Spirit could not be poured out upon human flesh or be received by sinful mortal men. Only with the enthronement of the Lamb, only with the presence of our Surety and the continual intercession of our High Priest before the face of the Father, only with the taking up of the glorified Humanity of Christ our Brother into the unity of the Blessed Trinity, could the Holy Spirit be released in all his sanctifying and renewing agency to dwell with man. Then he came down freely upon the Body that had been prepared, the Church purchased by the blood of Christ, and lifted it up, unhindered by guilt and sin or the divine judgment, to participate freely in the very life of God.

There is one Mediator between God and Man, the Man Christ Jesus. The Holy Spirit comes to us only through him as the Spirit of Holiness, the Spirit of Redemption, and the Spirit of Glory. He comes to us from the inner life of Jesus as the Spirit in which he gained the victory over sin and temptation, as the Spirit in which he brought the divine holiness to bear upon our flesh of sin, sanctifying and perfecting in himself the very nature which he took from us, and therefore he comes in all the richness of the divine human holiness of Christ. He comes to us from the triumphant obedience and victory of Christ in his Cross and Resurrection, as the Spirit clothed with mighty, redemptive acts transmitting the energy of Christ's risen and glorified Humanity, and as the Spirit of him who has entered into the new life and inherited all the promises of God, and therefore he comes in all the transforming power of the Saviour and Redeemer of men. He comes to us from the whole life of Christ constituted in death and resurrection as the one, all-sufficient and eternal oblation of mankind, as the Spirit in which Christ lifted up our human nature in worship and prayer and adoration to God, in which at last he presented himself in spotless sacrifice to the Father as the Head of Humanity and through this one offering presented us to him as those whom he had perfected in himself. And therefore the Spirit comes as the Spirit of a Manhood wholly offered to God in perpetual glorification and worship and praise.

What do we learn from this about the renewal of the Church's worship?

The Holy Spirit is God in his freedom not only to give being to the creation but through his presence in it to bring its relations with himself to their end and perfection. He is the Spirit who goes forth from God and returns to God. This answers to the twofold work of the Son when he came down for us and for our salvation and was made Man, and when he ascended again to the Father, presenting to him the humanity which he had sanctified and redeemed in the atoning oblation of himself. It is the same twofold work which took place at Pentecost in the man-ward and in the God-ward movement of the Holy Spirit, supervening upon the Church and lifting it upward in its faith and rejoicing in God.

It was through the power of the Spirit that Christ himself was born among us, lived his life of holy obedience and worship, gave himself in sacrifice for the sin of the world, rose again and ascended to the Father to be for ever the one offering and prayer that prevails for all mankind. It is through the power of the same Spirit who came down at Pentecost that we are united to Christ in his identification with us, and joined to him in his self-consecration and self-offering for us once and for all on earth and eternally prevalent in heaven. Jesus Christ who took our nature upon him has given to God an account for us, making atonement in our place, and in our name has yielded himself in sacrifice and worship and praise and thanksgiving to the Father. We have no other answer to the will of God, no other offering, no other response or worship, for without Christ we can do nothing. Jesus Christ is our worship, the essence of it and the whole of it, and we may worship God in Spirit and in Truth only as we are made partakers in his worship. The Spirit which Christ breathes upon us then becomes the Spirit of our response to him and through him to the Father.

We may express this in another way. The Holy Spirit was first given to Christ, and only transmitted from him to us through his intercession. He prayed the Father for the gift of the Paraclete upon those whom he loved, that they might be with him where he was, they in him and he in them, and he was heard in his prayer. He prayed with his life, and prayed with his death; to the supplication of his lips with strong crying and tears he added the pleading of his awful passion, and offered himself up in expiatory intercession in order to gain for us also the gift of the Holy Spirit. Pentecost was the counterpart on earth to wonderful things done within the veil, for Jesus Christ prevailed with God and the Spirit was poured out on human flesh. And the Holy Spirit continues to be given because the Lamb of God who bore away the sin of the world is for ever enthroned above, because the Atonement he made once for all is eternally valid with the Father, because Jesus Christ our High Priest ever lives to make intercession for us.

In coming upon the Church the Holy Spirit constitutes it the Body of Christ on earth in union with its Head, the risen and ascended Lord. But he comes upon it and dwells in it as the other Paraclete answering to the Paraclete above, as the Spirit of all prayer echoing in us the continual intercession of Christ. We do not know how to pray as we ought but the Holy Spirit intervenes in our stammering and weakness, and with groanings that cannot be uttered makes the prayer of heaven to resound on earth. All our prayer and praise and worship are sinful and unworthy but through the Holy Spirit breathed upon us they are cleansed in the sacrifice of Christ and absorbed into intercession and praise and worship within the veil. Indeed the Holy Spirit so unites earth to heaven and heaven to earth that in his coming Christ himself returns to take up his dwelling in the Church, and he it is who intercedes in its midst, who stands among us as our prayer and worship and praise, offering and presenting himself in our place to the Father, so that it is in him and through him and by him, in his name alone, that we appear before the Face of God with the one offering of his beloved Son in whom he is well pleased.

All true worship is therefore both *epiclesis* and *paraclesis*, i.e. the invocation of the Paraclete Spirit and the coming of the Paraclete to help us. We come with empty hands and empty mouth, and he puts into our grasp the Cross of Christ and into our mouth the prayer of the Lord. He assimilates us into the one all-sufficient worship of Christ, and the Father looks upon us only as we are found in him, consecrated through his self-sanctification and self-offering for us. The Holy Spirit is not to be thought of as acting in the place of, as if in the absence of, the exalted Lord, for in his coming and presence Christ himself is with us, acting for us not only from the side of God toward man but acting in us from the side of man toward God. It is through the agency of the Spirit that this takes place. Thus in our worship the Holy Spirit comes forth from God, uniting us to the response and obedience and faith and prayer of Jesus, and returns to God, raising us up in Jesus to participate in the worship of heaven and in the eternal communion of the Holy Trinity.

If the Holy Spirit is himself the immediate Agent of our worship, he is also the immediate Agent of its renewal, he who realizes in us the re-creative power of the risen and glorified Humanity of Christ. Now it cannot be emphasized sufficiently that it is through Atonement that we are renewed, through the obedience of the Holy One in our flesh and through the Blood of Christ shed for us; and that it is only after the completion of Christ's sacrifice for sin, his self-presentation before the Father and the pouring out of the Holy Spirit upon us, that the Atonement became effective for the remission of our sins and the cleansing of our conscience. From beginning to end it is through the *holiness* of Jesus that we are redeemed and regenerated. Therefore when the Holy Spirit comes to us as the Agent of our renewal he comes not only as the Holy Spirit of the one eternal God but as the Spirit mediated through Christ Jesus and charged with his divine-human holiness. He renews us by drawing us within the self-consecration of Christ made on our behalf and by assimilating us into his holiness. The Holy Spirit renews only through sanctification. If Jesus himself was raised from the dead according to the Spirit of Holiness, it cannot be otherwise with us.

It cannot be otherwise with our worship: renewal may come only through holiness, regeneration only through sanctification. What else can renewed worship be but that which through the Spirit is united to Christ's oblation of himself and is assimilated to his self-sanctification in the Truth? We worship God in drawing near to him by the new and living way which Jesus has consecrated for us, the way of his flesh, for he who sanctifies and we who are sanctified are all of one, Christ in us and we in him through one and the same Holy Spirit. We pray in the Name of Christ and he prays in our place, displacing our acts of devotion by his own self-offering, covering them with his holiness and absorbing them into his own intercession. Who then can disentangle our prayer from the prayer of Christ, for our worship is Christ's own presentation of himself and of us in him before the Father?

If this is the way of divine worship through our great High Priest, then conformity to the holiness and humanity of Jesus Christ is the test that must be applied to all our forms of worship. Are they really expressions of the holy mind and will of God incarnate in Jesus, or are they after all but forms of our own self-expression? Is our worship a constant participation in the holiness of Christ, in his own inner victory over sin and temptation, in his perfect oneness in mind and will with God? Is it the lifting up of our hearts through the Son in the Spirit to the Father? Is it a holding up of Christ in his finished work before Heaven as our only offering and prayer? Or is it the manifestation of our own piety adapted to the pattern of this present world in forms of our own choosing? Have we not obtruded upon God will-worship of our own which is little more in the last analysis than the worship of self or the holding up of our own spirituality? And is not the deepest reason for this that we have lost touch with the Spirit of Holiness? Surely degeneration in worship springs from a weakening in our sense of the utter holiness and majesty of the Most High and an estrangement from the creative source of holiness among men, the sanctified and sanctifying Humanity of Jesus.

IN HIS NEW COMING THE HOLY SPIRIT FOCUSSES
ATTENTION UPON JESUS CHRIST, AND ENABLES
US TO BELIEVE IN HIM AND BEAR FAITHFUL
WITNESS TO HIM AS SAVIOUR OF THE WORLD

If the vicarious life and mediatorial work of Christ led to the supreme gift of the Holy Spirit, the function of the Spirit was not to bear witness to himself but to bear witness to Christ as God and Saviour, and through his glorification to gather all who believe in him into the unity and communion of Father, Son and Holy Spirit.

The Holy Spirit is not knowable independently in himself, but he is known through the one Word or self-revelation of God in Jesus Christ.

In himself the Spirit hides himself from us by his very mode of Being as Spirit, and effaces himself in his very mode of Activity as Spirit, throwing his eternal Light upon the Father through the Son and upon the Son in the Father. We know who he is because he creates in us beyond all creaturely or human capacities the ability to know the Unknowable, and therein reveals himself as Creator Spirit of the living God. The Spirit does not utter himself but utters the Word. He does not incarnate himself but incarnates the Son. He does not show his own Face, but shows us the Father in the Face of the Son. Yet as he comes to us from the Father and from the Son, he confronts us in himself with all the ultimate Godness of the Godhead, before whom we can only bow in worship and adoration, and with all the reverence and obedience of our minds. We know him as no less Lord God, the Creator, than the Father and the Son, for he is the limitless power of all creation and re-creation, God the Holy Spirit in all the freedom and majesty of the eternal Being.

Such is the Spirit who bears witness to Christ, for Christ is not known and believed on the ground of human testimony but only on the ground of testimony that comes from God himself. He is not only the Spirit who comes forth from God and returns to God, but the Spirit sent to us by Christ and who directs us back to Christ, the Spirit of Testimony and the Spirit of Truth. It was through his agency that the Word of God was uttered in the Incarnation, by him that Christ was anointed to preach the Gospel, and in his power that the whole work of divine revelation and redemption was fulfilled. But so long as the Holy Spirit was not yet abroad among men, even the disciples were dull of hearing and slow in their understanding, and could not grasp the bewildering miracle of Jesus, for they stumbled and groped like men blinded by light. The Spirit was not yet because Christ was not yet glorified, for until the consummation of Atonement the Holy Spirit could not come upon them and they could not receive him without being consumed. Until Atonement was made and the Spirit was poured out they were incapable of becoming the habitation of the Holy One, and Christ could not open up their minds to grasp him for he could not be in them.

But the promise of the Paraclete was given: the Spirit of Truth would be sent to them and then they would know. What Christ said to them when he was yet present with them would not be lost, even if they did not understand it yet, for the Paraclete would teach them all things and bring to their remembrance all that Christ had said to them. He had still much more to say but they could not bear it yet. However when the Spirit of Truth would come he would guide them into all the Truth. He would not speak from himself but speak what he heard and make known to them things that were still to take place. He would glorify Christ for everything that he would make known he would receive from Christ himself. All that belonged to the Father belonged to Christ, and therefore what the Spirit of Truth would show them would be from Christ even when it was of the Father.

And the promise was fulfilled, in the gift of the Holy Spirit. They had to wait for the coming of the Spirit, continuing in prayer and in unity with one another and in obedience to such teaching of Christ as they had been able to follow. But when the Spirit came upon them they received power, for the Spirit both testified to them of Christ, creating in them understanding and faith, and made them witnesses themselves to Christ before the world, creating in them the sphere where Christ continues to be heard and to be believed. Thus through the coming of the Spirit God brings his self-revelation to its fulfilment, for the Spirit is the creative Subject of God's revelation to us and the creative Subject in our reception and understanding of that revelation. The Holy Spirit does not do this by continuing a work begun by Christ and now left off by him, as if we now passed from the economy of the Son into the economy of the Spirit. On the contrary through the Spirit, in and with his coming, Christ himself returns to be present among us, living and speaking and operating in the Church which through the Spirit is constituted his Body on earth and in history. The presence of the Holy Spirit in the Church means that it is the living Lord himself who is here in his redeeming and sanctifying activity. The office of the Holy Spirit in the Church is not to call attention to himself apart from Christ but to focus all attention on Christ, to glorify him, to bear witness to his deity, to testify to his mind and will, and in him and through him to lead us to the Father. He is God the Spirit by whom we know God, for he is God the Spirit by whom God bears witness to himself. Transparence and self-effacement thus belong to the very nature and office of the Holy Spirit, as the Spirit of the Father and the Spirit of the Son, who is known only as the Father is known through the Son and the Son

is known in the Father, and who together with the Father and the Son
is worshipped and glorified as himself very God.

On earth there is no Kingdom of the Spirit, and no Body of the
Spirit, but only a Kingdom of Christ and a Body of Christ through the
Spirit, for the Spirit is present and at work among us in his transparent
and self-effacing nature. It is his office constantly to call the Church out
of the world and to create it as the sphere within which he realizes and
perpetuates among men God's own witness to himself. In the Church,
as we have seen, the Holy Spirit exercises a God-ward ministry as he
acts from the side of men uplifting their worship in Christ to the
heavenly Father, but in the Church he also exercises that God-ward
ministry in that he creates and empowers from the side of men a witness
to Christ as God and Saviour of mankind, and so constitutes the corporate witness of the whole Church as the mode of God's own witness to
himself among men. This does not mean that the Church now takes the
place of Christ in his absence, continuing or extending the work which
he began to do when he was with us in the flesh, but that the Church is
chosen to be the locus of his presence among men and that he himself
the risen Lord is at work in and through it, yet transcending it in the
freedom and power of his Spirit, for in spite of the constant failure and
inadequacy of the Church Christ fulfils through it his one ministry as
prophet, priest and king, on earth as in heaven.

In order to see the bearing of this upon the renewal of the Church's
witness, we must consider further the *creativity* and the *transparency*
of the Holy Spirit, for in his regenerative and recreative work the Holy
Spirit remains the Creative Agent of all God's ways and works, and the
uncreated transparent light of his self-revelation.

With the coming of the Holy Spirit at Pentecost God's redemptive
and his creative acts merged together. It was a movement of recreation
through atoning sanctification, for through the *Holy* Spirit the full
creative impact of the divine Word broke in upon the apostolic Church
constituting it a new creation in Christ, fulfilling in it the sanctifying
and regenerating of our human nature that had already taken place in
Christ, and so bringing it into a new state of being in which it was renewed after the image of God. The Holy Spirit was the quickening
breath of this new creation, breathed out by God upon the Church and
breathed in by the Church as it came to life under his power. He was the
Spirit speaking the Word of God to the Church and creating within it
faithful hearing and understanding of the Word, the Spirit testifying to
the mighty acts of God in Christ and the Spirit of response to Christ in

the Church forming it unto the obedience of faith in him. Not only did he act creatively upon the Church in the giving of life and the distributing of his manifold gifts but he brought his creative work to its completion or end in the establishment of the Church as the Body of Christ, the new sphere of existence in him. He was the Creator Spirit acting always both from the side of God toward man and from the side of man toward God.

What does it mean for us to come up against the creative activity of the Spirit in this way? What does it mean for our witness in the Church that the Creator Spirit should dwell with fallen man and recreate him in his knowledge and understanding of God? Fallen man is described in the Scriptures as man attempting to emancipate himself from the Creator, man snatching the very freedom God has given him in order to make himself and reproduce his own image, and therefore as man who even imposes the images of his own devising and fashioning upon God. In this way he changes the truth of God into a lie and worships and serves the creature more than the Creator, for he changes the glory of the uncorruptible God into an image made like to corruptible man. That is to say, man carries the sin whereby he fell into his continuing relations with God, and substitutes his own creativity for that of the Creator Spirit even in the realm of the knowledge and worship of God. Indeed it is in religion that man is most tempted to do this, so that religious forms can become the supreme expression of his sin.

Now the coming of the Creator Spirit as at Pentecost is the point where man's own sinful creativity has to be broken, where man in his Adamic existence, man as he created himself, is stripped of his own image and come to an end, for in the coming of the Spirit fallen man is brought up against the final power of the Creator himself. At that point he is either re-created and emancipated from himself for genuine faith in God, or he lapses back in conflict with the Spirit into his own self-willed existence and becomes even more securely imprisoned within his own inventions. Then the light that is in him is darkness indeed.

Is that not the story of the recalcitrant Jews face to face with Jesus? Out of their own distinctive piety and attitude to existence they had forged their own conception of the Messiah. They even bent the oracles and ordinances of grace to serve their end, and projected their own man-made traditions upon the Word of God making it of none effect. And so they strove to become masters of their own destiny. Then when at last the Messiah actually came the conflict between their own image of God and that mediated by the Messiah was so intense that instead of surrendering to the creative impact of his Spirit upon them, they cruci-fied the Messiah, and in a desperate attempt to force the hand of God they even resisted his Holy Spirit. Was that not the verdict of the martyr Stephen? 'Ye do always resist the Holy Spirit: as your fathers did, so do you.' And they stoned him to death.

Must we not ask whether this is not also the story of the Christian Church, even in modern times? Have we also not been at work forging our own image of God out of our own vaunted prior understanding or out of the depth of our own being, out of our own existential decisions and our own creative spirituality? Have we not also constructed our own conceptions of Christ to suit our own self-willed attitude to exis-tence in the twentieth century? And then have we not been trying to justify ourselves by projecting this way of thinking back upon the Apostolic Church, alleging that its image of Christ is little more than the product of its own creative spirituality or the expression of its atti-tude to existence? And so have we not been busy crucifying again the Christ of the apostolic witness and resisting the Creator Spirit of Pente-cost, substituting the creativity of men in place of the Holy Creativity of God?

The supreme questions must be asked once again. Do we really believe in the Holy Spirit? Do we believe that at Pentecost he came upon the apostolic witnesses as the Creator Spirit and, in spite of the distorting preconceptions of the human heart and the creative pro-jections of the human spirit, transformed their understanding to receive God's own witness to himself in Jesus Christ and so empowered them to become faithful witnesses to Christ themselves? Do we believe the *kerygma* of Jesus Christ to be the creation of God's Spirit or the out-growth of man's own religious consciousness? In short, do we really believe in Jesus Christ as God and Saviour?

Surely the New Testament makes it abundantly clear that the Holy Spirit is given to those who believe in Jesus and that we grow in the grace and knowledge of Christ as we surrender to the creative impact of the Holy Spirit upon us but that unbelief grieves the presence of the Spirit and quenches his power among us. What else is unbelief but resistance to the Holy Spirit, and what can obstruct the renewal of the Church and destroy its witness more than just unbelief? Let it be said quite bluntly that what we need urgently is a renewal of faith: of belief in Jesus Christ as in reality God himself incarnate among men, of belief in the Cross as indeed the objective intervention of God in human existence for the salvation of mankind, and of belief in the resurrection of Jesus Christ from the dead in body as the first-fruits of the new creation. The renewal of our witness will only come as we surrender ourselves to the miraculous divine power of the Creator Spirit, and commit ourselves to faith in Jesus Christ as God and Saviour.

Now if this faith is to be strong and our witness is to be clear we must guard against the impurities that arise when we seek to perfect the operation of the Spirit by our own works and so obtrude ourselves into the evangelical message. This is where the transparency of the Spirit comes in, for to be genuine our witness must be shot through and through with the uncreated light of God's self-revelation. Then alone can it be the means of God's own witness to himself among men.

In all our knowledge and proclamation of God in worship and witness we make use of human and earthly forms of thought and speech, cognitive, linguistic or liturgical forms, but in themselves these forms are quite opaque as far as their reference to God himself is concerned. In themselves they are merely expressions of human and earthly activity and reveal not God but man. If they are really to serve their purpose they must be made to point beyond themselves to the divine realities they are meant to signify. That can happen only through the power of the Holy Spirit as he himself testifies of God in and through them, for he alone can make the forms of faith and witness transparent by making the Reality of God shine through them. Only through the sanctifying presence of the Holy Spirit emancipating us from ourselves is Jesus Christ the Incarnate Word allowed to sound through to us and to take control of our proclamation, and therefore to confront men directly and personally through our witness.

Consider, for example, the Holy Scripture or the Sacrament of Baptism. The Scriptures are human documents written by men of earth and history, expressing the attitudes and thoughts and limitations of their writers, and can therefore be interpreted in their human reference. But they are much more than that for they have been adapted by God under the impact of his Spirit for his own self-testimony, and therefore they are interpreted aright only as we allow the living Word of God himself to sound through them to us, and as through the Holy Spirit the Reality of God in Christ shines through to us—that is what our Reformers called the *perspicuity* of the Scriptures. Or take the Sacrament of Baptism, which is certainly a rite to be performed by men in visible, historical acts. But if we interpret Baptism by looking for its meaning in the rite itself or in its human celebration, then it becomes quite opaque. However, the meaning of Baptism does not lie in the ex-

TIR R

ternal rite or simply its performance but solely in Jesus Christ himself, for Baptism directs us and our children to the saving act of God's love which he has already fulfilled for us in Jesus Christ. Therefore we interpret Baptism not by looking at what we do but by looking through the rite to Christ and his Gospel and by allowing Christ and his Gospel through the power of the Spirit to break through to us. Without sacramental transparence Baptism becomes blind and meaningless.

We recall too that this transparence comes from the Holy Spirit, from his own self-effacing nature and office in hiding himself, as it were, behind the Face of the Father in the Son and behind the Heart of the Son in the Father, yet revealing the one Triune God by letting his eternal light shine through himself to us. It is in his light alone that we see light, and through that light that we are confronted with the ultimate Being of God before whom the very cherubim veil their faces. It is the same Holy Spirit who is present and active in the *witness* of the Church testifying to Christ in fulfilment of the Lord's own promise. But if we turn our attention to the Spirit independently instead of turning our attention with the Spirit to Christ, or try to make the Spirit visible through perfecting his operation by our own works, then we violate the holiness of the Spirit by resisting him in his self-effacing office and confusing him with our own spirits. Thus everything becomes opaque, for we fail to distinguish him in whom we believe from our own believing, and in our proclamation we confound the earthen vessel with the heavenly treasure. We mix up ourselves with Christ and so darken witness and obscure vision of the Saviour.

Renewal of witness will come surely through the holiness of Jesus and renewal of our worship in him, that is, through the sanctifying and recreating power of the Holy Spirit lifting us again out of ourselves in Christ to worship the Father. Only the Spirit of Holiness can purge us from the falsification of the Good News by mixing up with it our own subjectivities and unrealities. Only the Creator Spirit begetting in us the simplicity of faith can make us free from ourselves and the distortion in our understanding of the Gospel through our own preconceptions and inventions. Yet it is against the Holy Spirit that we have sinned, in substituting our own creativity for his, and in resisting his truth in the apostolic witness. We need to be cleansed anew by the Blood of Christ and receive afresh the Spirit he mediates to us through his atonement. Without the transparence of the Spirit we cannot exercise the kind of witness in which God in Christ bears witness to himself, but it is only when God's own self-witness is heard that the world will believe.

15

A New Reformation?

THERE is no doubt that the Christian Churches are everywhere in ferment. The classical creeds are being subjected to rigorous testing, old venerable institutions are being shaken to their foundations, and unbelievable changes are taking place where they were least expected. We are surely in the midst of a new Reformation in which, as David Edwards says,[1] we have been led to see that Christian truth is infinitely greater than our understanding of it. It is this conviction that serves to emancipate us from the narrow and restricted conceptions we have often inherited from this or that particular tradition or in this or that country, and therefore, as I see it, it must be a Reformation into a greater and deeper fulness of the Faith rather than a redacting or restricting of it. I do not mean that there is not much that might well be cut away, for the Church has too many customs and trappings that may have served their end once but serve little purpose in relation to its essential convictions today. Hence I like the insistence that Reformation implies a continuity with the past, for we cannot abandon the history of the Church throughout the ages. Yet this does mean that we must sit loose to our prejudices and stand fast by our foundations.

This Reformation has been going on steadily for the last thirty years, but what worries me about the present outcry is that rather crude and naive notions have obtruded themselves vociferously upon this new Reformation and threaten to submerge it in a flood of muddy water in which clear and steady thinking is not made easy and in which many people are becoming more and more confused. It is alarming to find churchmen sitting loose to the essential convictions of the Faith while standing fast by their prejudices, and indulging in the same kind of pathological iconoclasm which we see in teenagers in other ways. It is so easy to be destructive, to offer cheap remedies for our troubles and to climb on to the various 'band-wagons' of the times in a misguided

[1] *The London Holborn and Quarterly Review*, Oct. 1964.

idea that this is to engage in communication and reformation. What we need is constructive thinking, the kind of thinking that takes place within a frame of continuous historical development where rigorous self-criticism can be taken together with great advances in understanding and action. This is actually going on today, not just among a few theologians, nor merely in the ecumenical movement, but within the Evangelical, Roman and Orthodox Churches, and is already showing signs of far-reaching and exciting change. The upheaval and reform may well be greater than anything we have seen since the early centuries of the Christian era, for it involves the relation of the Church with all history and the whole world of nature.

In order to help understanding of what is happening let me try to put it in the perspective of the great movements of the past, especially of the Reformation.

1. The Church is being forced to think through her convictions today in a way that she has had to do only twice before, in the great periods of change in cosmological outlook: (*a*) in the change from a primitive to a Ptolemaic cosmology that took place between the second and the fourth century, and (*b*) in the change from a Ptolemaic to a Copernican and Newtonian cosmology that took place in the sixteenth and seventeenth centuries. We ourselves are in the midst of just such a vast shift in the thinking of mankind. In each of these periods basic epistemological and theological questions have been raised regarding similar if not identically the same issues, and in each there has taken place a considerable mutation in the forms of thought and speech that resulted from the changes in man's understanding of the universe.

Now there are people today who insist that the advances of modern science in the understanding of the universe make it necessary for us to discard the fundamental framework of the Christian faith as one that is bound up with obsolete cosmology. Even the basic concepts of the classical creeds have to be changed for they are alleged to be but constructs of an objectifying kind of thought that makes use of transitory patterns in man's understanding of the cosmos in order to establish itself. Hence we must dispense with the objective forms in which faith is cast and find new conceptual forms congenial to modern man in which to express our attitude to the universe, and so on.

If this is what is called the 'new Reformation' then it is a disastrous misunderstanding. Certainly the Church can never stand aside from what is going on in the world, for it is only within the world, and not outside of it, that she lives and acts and speaks, and fulfils her mission.

But let us see what actually happened in the eras of great cosmological change in the past. In each of them theological foundations underwent their due measure of adaptation and restatement, yet in each the essential imagery and the basic conceptuality of Christian doctrine did not change, and the Church adjusted herself remarkably well. There were certainly great struggles but the apostolic and catholic faith proved adequate for all that was required of it in the change and advance in the understanding of the universe.

In actual fact it was not change in science or cosmology that constituted the real difficulty for theological statement. It was an unbiblical element in the culture and thought of the times, the axiomatic assumption of a radical disjunction between the sensible and the intelligible worlds, between the world of the creature and the world of God. Within the Ptolemaic cosmology this gave rise to Gnosticism and Arianism which divided God the Redeemer from God the Creator, and made both the Son of God and the Holy Spirit creatures who had their being only on this side of the radical disjunction. The Church found itself struggling with two powerful ideas that threatened to destroy its existence: (*a*) the idea that God himself does not intervene in the actual life of men in time and space for he is immutable and changeless, and (*b*) that the Word of God revealed in Christ is not grounded in the eternal Being of God but is detached and separated from him and therefore mutable and changeable. This means (*a*) that redemption is only to be conceived mythologically for it is never actualized in creation, and (*b*) that all the Christian imagery and conceptuality of God are essentially correlative to creaturely existence and have no objective truth in God corresponding to them.

The answer of the Church to this menace was the Nicene Creed and the doctrine of the *homoousion*—that is, the doctrine that Jesus Christ as the Word and Son of God belongs to the divine side of reality, and is himself very God come into our world to redeem and recreate us. With this doctrine the Church rejected the pagan separation of redemption from creation, and showed the absolute relevance of the Incarnation (including the life and passion of Christ) for the salvation of mankind. The Nicene theologians rendered a valuable service, for which the whole Church is indebted to them, in that they revealed the inner structure of Christian faith in its profound 'logical simplicity' and laid the basis for all subsequent theological advance.

Basically the same problems faced the Church again in the Reformation, but they were necessarily different because cast in a different idioum owing to a different understanding of the universe. Ptolemaic cosmology with a powerful ingredient of Neo-platonism and Christian theology had long been blended in a remarkable way to produce the notion of a sacramental universe in which the visible and physical creation was held to be the counterpart in time to eternal and heavenly patterns. This outlook had taken up into itself the old Hellenic disjunction between the sensible world and the intelligible world, the earthly and the heavenly, but had sought to span the hiatus between the two by Augustine's theory of illumination and his doctrine of the Church as sacramental organism full of grace. Deep in the Middle Ages changes began to be made. St Thomas rejected the theory of illumination and turned to Aristotelian philosophy for tools to effect a new synthesis. Within his own principles he brought about a profound integration between faith and reason, revealed and natural theology, but this in turn began to break up as a result of Ockham's attack upon the physics and metaphysics embedded in it. Then under a destructive nominalism the two worlds began to fall apart again with a widening disruption between faith and reason, the Church and the world.

That was the setting in which the Reformation took place in the sixteenth century when it sought to return to the biblical doctrine of God the Creator, who intervenes actively in the history of men in redemption and recreation, and who has vitally objectified himself for our knowledge in Jesus Christ. This had the effect of liberating nature for investigation by empirical science and of throwing Christian theology back upon its own positive foundations in the Word of God. Once again it was not science and cosmology that were the real difficulty, but the assumption of a relation between God and the world in which God was not regarded as actively and personally at work in the affairs of human history, or intuitively knowable in a living and personal way, and in which there was produced a static and sterile view of nature as timelessly reflecting the changelessness and eternity of God. The Reformation met the double difficulty of Romanism and nominalism by reconstructing the mediaeval doctrine of God on a biblical basis and reconstructing the mediaeval doctrine of grace by the help of classical Christology. It thus did two things: it restored the active relevance of the biblical doctrine of salvation for man in his ignorance, need and sin in historical existence, and emancipated nature from the domination of a rationalist theology for independent scientific investigation. In so doing, it not only adjusted itself to the changing outlook on the universe but contributed to it. I shall return to the doctrinal content of this reform below, but meantime it is worth noting that the Reformation met its difficulties through returning to the Nicene doctrine of the *homoousion* and the biblical conceptions of creation and redemption that it involved.

Now I believe that the real problems which the Church has to face today are not those created by science and the changes in cosmological theory, but in the recrudescence of the old pagan disjunction between God and the world, in which redemption is divorced from creation and the mighty acts of God are removed from actual history; in which a radical dichotomy is posited between the non-objectifiable and the objectifiable, and the conceptuality and imagery mediated to us in the traditional Christ are regarded as detached from God and changeable. In other words, theological knowledge is not regarded as rooted and grounded in an objective Word from God to man, but as something thrown up by man himself in the form of mythological constructs as he seeks to express his attitude to the universe or even to existence. Thus in itself the knowledge of faith is non-conceptual and only symbolic, for God is not strictly 'knowable', and requires to be rationalized by borrowing conceptuality from philosophy or science. Once this radical dichotomy is posited, then, as for example in a Schleiermacher or a Bultmann, the basic affirmation of the Christian Faith, namely that in Jesus Christ we have none other than the Being of God himself in our human existence in space and time, is called in question as a rational statement in its own right and must be 're-edited' or 'reinterpreted' as a correlate to human being or man's attitude to existence. Indeed all the basic affirmations of the Christian Faith are processed in such a way that from being primarily and essentially theological statements they become statements of human concern with varying degrees of ultimacy. What is at stake here then is in a modern form the same problem that the Church faced when it battled with Gnostics and Arians in the early centuries. The great dividing line is once again the doctrine of the *Incarnation*, or if you will, the *homoousion*, i.e. the doctrine that Christ is not an expression of the attitude to the universe thrown up by the creative spirituality of the early Christians but that in Jesus Christ in our flesh and history we have in person the eternal Word of God, who has come to us from the Being of God himself and who communicates to us a knowledge of God that derives from God and is objectively rooted in him. As anyone can see from the opening chapters of Calvin's *Institute*, it was through recovering and maintaining this that the Reformers were able to carry through the reform of the Church which God laid upon them.

I cannot believe that a genuine reformation of the Church can take any other line, for a reformation involves a reconstructing of the forms of the Church's life and thought on its own proper foundations, not the hacking away of those foundations. Let me illustrate what I mean from an analogous movement in modern science, in the advance we have been making from classical physics to nuclear physics. This has involved a logical reconstruction of classical physics, and indeed a limitation of its range, but far from calling it in question it involves the establishing of classical physics all the more securely on its own proper foundations. That is the way also of scientific advance and reform in theology and Church in which great advances can be taken and are being taken because they do not mean that the classical foundations are rendered obsolete but are clarified and understood in such a way that we can build upon them a fuller and ampler edifice of thought which will serve the mission of the Church in the Gospel to the modern world.

2. Let us now come to the doctrinal content of the Reformation in the sixteenth century, and in the light of it try to discern what is or ought to be the pattern of reform today—and here I wish to expand what was said above about the centrality of the *homoousion* in the Nicene theology. As I understand the Reformation it was an attempt to carry through in the sixteenth century a movement of rethinking that corresponded very closely to that of the Early Church. Let us consider it in four steps.

(*a*) At Nicaea, as Athanasius and Hilary tell us, the Fathers were confronted with so many different conceptions and notions thrown up in the debates with Valentinians and Arians that they set themselves to seek out and sift through the basic biblical images and conceptions and to reduce them to their fundamental essence in such a way that the basic logical structure or simplicity that was thus revealed would serve to throw light upon all the other forms of thought and speech, and serve at the same time as a criterion for accurate assessment of them. The result was the *homoousion*, for in Jesus Christ who is not only the image but the reality or *hypostasis* of God we have the one objective standard by which all else is to be understood. He is the *scope of the Scriptures* and the *scope of the faith*. It is in Him that we have to do, not with a man-fashioned, but with a divinely-provided Form (the only *Eidos* of Godhead) to which all else must be conform in the life and thought and worship and mission of the Church. It is that central relation of Christ to the Holy Scriptures that was revived at the Reformation—where is that more clear than in the preaching and teaching of Martin Luther?

(*b*) It remains a fact of history, however, that the Early Church did not carry through the results of its work in Christology into the whole round of the Church's thought and life. Thus in the West many aspects of the Church were allowed a luxuriant growth that was unchecked and un-criticized by the central dogma of Christ. The Reformation represents an attempt to carry through a Christological correction of the whole life and thought of the Church. It was an attempt to put Christ and his Gospel once again into the very centre and to carry through ex-tensive reform by bringing everything into conformity to him and his Gospel.

(*c*) In carrying through this programme of reform the Church had to push the development of Christian theology beyond the point which it reached in the ecumenical councils, especially into the realm of soterio-logy, Church and mission. The movement of the Reformation was not contrary to but complementary to that of Nicaea, Ephesus, Chalcedon, etc. Look at it in this way. The fathers in the Early Church were con-cerned in the *homoousion* to affirm their faith in the deity of Christ, be-lieving that what God is to us in the saving acts of Christ he is eternally in his own divine Being. They thus stressed the *Being* of God in his Acts— they were concerned with theological ontology, the being and nature of the person of the incarnate Son. That did not stand in question with the Reformers, but what they were concerned to do was to stress the *Acts* of God in his Being—they focussed attention on the saving work of the Son. We can state this in another way. The fathers of the Early Church were concerned in the *homoousion* to assert the belief that when God communicates himself to us in Christ it is none other than God himself in his own divine Being that is revealed. The fathers of the Reformation were concerned to apply the *homoousion* to salvation in Christ, insisting that when God gives himself to us in him it is none other than God himself who is at work. God himself is active in his saving gifts and benefits—that is to say, they applied the *homoousion* to the doctrine of *grace*. Mediaeval theology had evolved all sorts of distinctions here, proliferating many kinds of grace; grace was *something* that God communicated, something that was detachable from God and that could assume different forms in the creatures to whom it was communi-cated, as habitual grace or created grace or connatural grace, etc. But when the Reformers applied to grace the *homoousion* they cut all these distinctions completely away and carried through a radical simplification of mediaeval theology, for grace is none other than Christ, God com-municating himself to us, the unconditional and sovereignly free self-giving of God the Lord and Saviour of men. Grace is total, and personal or hypostatic—Jesus Christ himself.

This carried with it, of course, a rethinking of the doctrines of salvation and sanctification and of the Church and sacraments. Accepting fully the patristic doctrine of the Being of God in His Acts in Christ, the Reformation insisted on stressing the Acts of God in the Being of Christ, and in so doing carried through a great transition in theological thinking from a more static mode to a more dynamic mode. This corresponded in its way to the great shift in the whole thinking of the sixteenth and seventeenth centuries from a static to a more dynamic movement of scientific thought which has left its mark even upon the language and style that characterize the modern world in contrast to that of the ancient or mediaeval world. It was indeed this stress upon the mighty living active God who intervenes in history creatively and redemptively and who has himself come to us in history in Jesus Christ that helped to emancipate all thought from the still and sterile notion of *deus sive natura* in the Latin conception of God, and set in motion the great advances of modern times.

(*d*) Along with this came a recovery of the doctrine of the Spirit. The doctrine of Christ had hardly been set upon a proper foundation at Nicaea with the doctrine of the *homoousion* than the Church found itself faced with the same struggle with regard to the Holy Spirit, for the semi-Arians and Macedonians insisted on thinking of him as a creature. But the Nicene theology found it was bound to go on in faithfulness to the biblical teaching to affirm the *homoousion* of the Spirit also, and so laid the foundation for the doctrine of the Trinity. A full doctrine of Christ and a full doctrine of the Spirit stand or fall together. Hence at the Reformation there took place a recovery of the doctrine of the Spirit, of the living presence and personal action of God in the world, released to mankind in fullness on the ground of the reconciling work of Christ. The doctrine of the Spirit and the stress upon the *Acts* of God in his Being went together. This also involved a recovery of the doctrine of the Church. Right up to the Council of Trent the Roman Church had never produced an authoritative doctrinal statement on the Church. There was indeed no significant monograph on the subject between Cyprian's *De Unitate* and Wycliffe's *De Ecclesia*. But with the Reformation the whole picture was altered and the doctrine of the Church as the community of believers vitally united to Christ as his Body through the Spirit received its first great formulation since patristic times.

Then a problem arose for Protestantism—in the stress upon the saving acts of God in the being and person of the Son, reaction from the static ontological thinking of Rome led Protestants to find their special principle in the dynamic aspect in contrast to the ontological. Unfortunately a detachment of the Acts of God from his Being-in-his-Acts, and a consequent estrangement of Protestantism from patristic theology and historical dogma, resulted in the loss of the doctrine of the Spirit. Detached from the Being of God the 'Spirit' became swallowed up in the spirit of man or the consciousness of the Church, and detached from the Being of the Son the saving acts of God became dissolved into 'eschatological events' indistinguishable from man's own existential decisions.

Is this the new 'Reformation'? Here once again it would seem to me that reformation can take place only on the Church's proper foundations, and that no real advance can be made until we learn to think together again the *Being-in-the-Act* and the *Act-in-the-Being*. I myself am convinced that it is this combination of patristic and Reformation theology which is our only real answer to the problems that Roman theology still presents to us, and that if we can undertake this constructive rethinking, as indeed Rome is now apparently undertaking herself, then we will be able to gather up the historical development of the whole Church in a movement of profound clarification which will enable her at last to make advances in theological understanding comparable to those which have been taking place in modern science. As far as I can see, this is indeed what is now going on. Surely the rapprochement of the Roman, Orthodox and Evangelical Churches in these areas of theological understanding is evidence of this advance into new reformation.

In this light I cannot but regard the passion for existentialism and anthropocentric theology which one finds in so many quarters as a retrograde movement, and indeed in theology as in science a flight from the hard and exact thinking that is required of us in genuine advance. One thing, however, seems certain, that the ecumenical movement means that for the whole of the future any permanent theological advance must take place within the dialogue between the great historical traditions of the Churches, and that means in the centre of the apostolic and catholic faith where that dialogue inevitably places us. No doubt pop-churchmen and pop-theologians may gather almost as great a following today as an Arius in the fourth century but unless their work is concerned with the kind of reconstruction that is rooted in the centre and grounded upon the original and eternal foundations it will also have only peripheral and passing significance. A new Reformation, however, is quite a different thing.

3. The Reformation can and must be looked at as a movement in thinking in which there was a shift from the priority of thought itself to the priority of being, or rather to the priority of truth. It was through the struggles of the Reformers with the Roman notion of tradition and the highly intellectual notion of truth that prevailed among the mediaeval schoolmen (whether realists or nominalists) that the principle of objectivity emerged which was to assume such a masterful role in the whole development of modern science. The Reformers had a passionate belief in the truth and were ready to sacrifice pleasant illusions and traditional preconceptions for the sake of the truth. They were determined to let the truth declare itself to them, the whole truth and nothing but the truth, irrespective of what it called in question in themselves.

A highly instructive statement of this principle is found in Calvin's letter to Francis I with which he prefaced his *Institute*. Wherever there is divergence of opinion appeal must be made beyond all ecclesiastical authority or biblical citation to the Truth of God himself for the Truth itself is the ultimate authority upon which we must cast ourselves and upon which everyone must rely. That Truth must be allowed to retain its own weight and authority, or majesty, and it is by reference to it directly that judgment must be passed on the truth or error of theological interpretation or statement. But this involves on our part a movement of the mind in which we refer everything to God in accordance with his absolute priority and nothing to ourselves, and this in turn means that we must allow ourselves before the Truth to be stripped of all our own prejudgments and feigned presuppositions. Unless in this way we are freed from ourselves and in a manner go outside of ourselves, as Calvin put it, we cannot know the Truth as it is in itself.

Calvin went on in the early chapters of the *Institute* to show that since true knowledge of God involves a movement of the mind in which we are cast upon the given Reality such knowledge requires of us obedience to God and to His own way of revealing Himself to us. We know Him only by serving Him and following the way He lays down in communicating Himself to us. It is not difficult to see the transition from this to the pursuit of natural knowledge in experimental science, especially in the writings of a Calvinist like Francis Bacon who deliberately transferred Calvin's method of interpreting 'the Books of God' to the interpretation of 'the books of nature'. Thus there arose the notion of scientific thinking as thinking that is obedient to its proper object, thinking which follows the clues supplied to it by the object itself, and therefore thinking which develops special modes of inquiry and proof appropriate to the nature of that object. Thus the scientist is not free to think what he likes. He is bound to his proper object and compelled to think of it in accordance with its own nature, as it becomes revealed under his questioning.

Now when Reformed theology developed its own scientific method along these lines, it rejected two primary principles in Roman theology.

It rejected the idea that the criterion of the truth is lodged in the subject of the knower or the interpreter. In all interpretation of the Scriptures, for example, we are thrown back upon the truth of the Word of God which we must allow to declare itself to us as it calls in question all our prior understanding or vaunted authorities. Reformed theology had to fight for this on a double front: against the humanist thinkers who held the autonomous reason of the individual to be the measure of all things, and against the Roman theologians who claimed that the Roman Church (the collective subject) was the supreme judge of all truth. What Reformed theology did was to transfer the centre of authority from the subject of the interpreter (Rome or the individual) back to the truth itself.

It rejected the idea that the definition of the truth belongs to the truth and is a necessary extension of it. This idea had long been developed by the canon lawyers and then by the nominalist theologians and remains inherent in the claim that whenever the Roman Church officially defines a truth, the definition becomes an extension of the truth and as such is so binding that acceptance of it is necessary for salvation. The Reformed theologians insisted, however, that definitions or formulations of the faith are only fallible human statements and are intended to point to the truth or to serve it and must never be confused with the truth itself. They can only be regarded as symbols which are always subject to correction in the light of the truth itself.

Thus in steering a course between arbitrary individualism on the one hand and authoritarian dogmatism on the other hand, the theology of the Reformation was battling for the principle of objectivity that now governs all branches of disciplined, scientific knowledge. At the Reformation this principle of objectivity was given vivid expression in two doctrines: (i) election or predestination, and (ii) justification by grace. Predestination means that in all our relations with God, in thinking and acting we have to reckon with the absolute priority of God. By his very nature, God as God, always comes first. Thus our loving of God depends on his loving of us, our choosing of God upon his choosing of us, and even our knowing of God depends upon his knowing of us, for it is only by God that we can know God. Justification by grace means that in all our relations with God, as moral or religious beings, we can never claim to have the right or truth in ourselves, but may find our right or truth only in Christ. Justification by grace calls in question our self-justification—for it tells us that whether we are good or bad, we can be saved only by the free grace of God, whether we are old or young we can enter the Kingdom of God only like little children who do not trust at all in themselves but only in their heavenly Father. When we apply justification by grace to the task of theology it means that we can never claim the truth for our own statements, but must rather think of them as pointing away to Christ who alone is the Truth. Theological statements do not carry their truth in themselves but are true only in so far as they direct us away from ourselves to the one Truth of God. That is why justification is such a powerful statement of objectivity in theology, for it throws us at every point upon God himself, and will never let us repose upon our own efforts.

It is not for nothing, therefore, that justification or election, i.e. the absolute priority of God's grace, has been regarded as of the essence of the Reformation in the sixteenth century, for it meant that the Church was reformed from beyond itself, and that it had to be freed from imprisonment in its own preconceptions, its own self-understanding, and its own immanent development in order to be renewed, and realigned to the truth of God, and before it could leap forward in fulfilment of its mission in the world. But if so, this is surely the essence of all true reformation, for objectivity is as essential now as then, and as essential in the great forward movements of the Church as it is in the most rigorous and progressive movements of modern science.

Now it is just here, I believe, that Protestantism is being sifted and tested down to its foundations today, and it is at this point that we *either* move forward into a great new Reformation *or* lapse back into the old errors that have dogged the history of the Church. The problem is perhaps most acute or at least most apparent in modern Protestantism's doctrine of the Spirit of God, for 'the Spirit' has come to mean little more than our subjective awareness of God or our religious self-understanding, and has very little if anything to do with the objective reality of the Being and living presence and action of God himself in the world. This is very distressing, for it means that the Church is suffering from a very serious malady: it has become so obsessed with itself and its own consciousness that it is unable to distinguish the objective reality of the truth and action of God from its own subjective states. In personal life, of course, this would be a symptom of serious mental disorder and confusion. Can we look upon it in any other light when it concerns the social or religious consciousness, or the Church itself? I cannot help but feel that failure to distinguish between objective realities and subjective conditions in modern theology is an alarming sign of irrational and indeed mental disorder in the life and soul of the Church. Thus I find it scientifically and theologically impossible to see in the so-called 'new theology' of Protestantism anything like a new Reformation, but rather the reverse, something revealing a deep-seated traumatic disturbance in modern Protestantism, in fact a diseased understanding of the Gospel. This revulsion from objectivity, and obsession for the reduction of the great Christian doctrines of the Incarnation and Atonement to forms of self-understanding for their explanation, indicate that religious man is in desperate need of some kind of deep spiritual psychiatry and therapy.

Nevertheless I am convinced we *are* in the midst of a real Reformation, even though we have today on the periphery of the movement, as in the sixteenth century, strange aberrations or anachronistic relapses. When we examine the history of Christian theology we can see that a positive advance has been taking place toward a coherent understanding of the Gospel. This is one that increasingly brings the teaching of the Fathers and of the Reformers to their full development and gives them expression in the modern dynamic style. This is the new biblical and dogmatic theology that is found in all the Churches, Roman and Orthodox as well as the Evangelical Churches, which cuts across the face of the old divisions and traditions and sets the understanding of the Christian Faith upon a scientific basis on its own proper foundation. Now at last this is beginning to reveal clear lines of advance in Christian understanding that has been going on for centuries, through the Middle Ages as well as the modern ages. One of the notable features of this is the common understanding between Roman and Evangelical theology that is leaping ahead at such a rate that it is often difficult to keep up with it—but one of the most tragic features of it is that just when the Church of Rome needs dialogue at a critical and profound level, involving the hard scientific thinking of pure theology, with the Evangelical Churches, she is so often met by a reactionary and anti-rational existentialism and a regress into obsolete speculations which have been tested and discarded as errors again and again in the long history of the Church.

There are at least two things here that are proving a help to the Church in steering it into the full stream of genuine and enduring reformation. One is the ecumenical movement which means that as all the Churches enter into dialogue they are flung back into the centre of the great historical development of the Christian Church and are weaned away from the side-developments into which they are tempted when separated from one another. The other is the fact that the whole of the future of the world will be mastered more and more by empirical science which can only force the Church back upon its own proper foundations and into more rigorous and objective thinking of its own proper object, the one Truth of God as it is revealed in Jesus Christ. Thus a way of thinking which was one of the great achievements of the Reformation and one of its chief contributions to the modern world now by way of empirical science can exercise a healthy pressure upon Christian theology and once again minister to its purification and clarification.

There are two other aspects of the Reformation in the sixteenth century that demand from us consideration today: the relations of Christianity to *nature* and to *nationalism*.

4. The Reformation in the sixteenth century certainly involved a profound change in the attitude to nature. To understand that let us return for a moment to the outlook of the Augustinian tradition which held sway in the West for nearly a thousand years, that is, the tradition in which Ptolemaic cosmology with a powerful ingredient of Neoplatonism and Christian theology had combined to produce the notion of the sacramental universe in which the visible and the sensuous world was held to be the counterpart in time to the invisible and eternal realities of the spiritual world. In this outlook nature was looked at only to be looked *through* toward God and the eternal realities. As such it had no significance in itself but had significance only so far as it reflected spiritual and heavenly forms and was moved by an immanent longing for them. In the Thomist modification of that the world of nature was meaningful only as it was understood to be impregnated with final causes, but that meant that the understanding of nature was inevitably controlled by prior understanding of the eternal ideas in the mind of God. This carried with it the difficult notion of the eternity of the world (*aeternitas mundi*) which gave St Thomas so much trouble and which only served to harden the sterile changelessness of nature.

This view came under the attack of Duns Scotus who held that creation was not causally related to timeless ideas in the mind of God but rather to creative ideas which God freely produced along with the created realities themselves. Hence all creation was regarded as contingent upon the freedom of the creative will of God. Unfortunately this was given a rather difficult interpretation by William of Ockham whose thinking drove a deep wedge between faith and reason and made nature repose upon the arbitrary and unpredictable will of an inscrutable Deity. It became clear with Ockham that so long as the mediaeval synthesis remained in its old form the notion of a genuine creation or the conception of what is really contingent could not be thought out without the threat of atheism—what was needed was a radical change in the doctrine of God. This was what was brought about by the Reformation, as we have already noted. With it the whole outlook upon nature changed. It is that change in the concept of nature that is so characteristic of the whole of modernity. The two Reformation doctrines that are of primary importance here are, *creation out of nothing*, and *grace alone*. We considered these at an earlier point, but now we must reconsider them in this connection.

Creation out of nothing means that the creaturely world is utterly distinct from God yet entirely contingent upon his will. Its actual contingency depends on its creaturely relation to God. Creaturely processes cannot be known by cognition of eternal ideas in the mind of God but only by examining the creaturely realities in their utter contingency and distinctness from God. On the other hand we cannot argue from nature to God, for if we are true to the contingency of nature we can only press our inquiry of nature up to the frontiers of creaturely being where it is bounded by nothing. This did not imply at the Reformation, as it had to mean within the mediaeval synthesis, some form of atheism, or a vast hiatus between faith and reason. Nature in all its distinctness is related to God by his creative activity and does not carry final meaning in itself, for in itself it runs out into nothing. And knowledge of God is gained not through abstraction from knowledge of sensible realities but by direct intuitive experience of God which we are given through his Word and Spirit. Here, then, as Francis Bacon expressed it, we have to give to nature what is nature's and to faith what is faith's: we study the books of nature in accordance with the nature of nature, and the books of God in accordance with the nature of God who discloses himself to us through them. This change released natural science from the domination of a rational theology and released positive theology from distortion

through a so-called natural theology. Along with the principle of objectivity which we have already discussed this gave rise to the notion of
positive or 'dogmatic science', such as pure physics or pure theology. But,
as Bacon himself realized, this position in natural science or in positive
theology depends upon the biblical and Reformed doctrine of creation
out of nothing—cut away that doctrine, and theology could only degener-
ate into deism, and natural science could only lead to atheism. Everything depends upon the active and creative relation of God to nature,
for that alone preserves the utter contingency of nature and obstructs its
divinization.

Along with this, however, goes the Reformation doctrine of grace.
That can be expounded in this way. In the Augustinian and mediaeval
outlook the whole focus of man's mind was directed *upward and away
from* nature to God, and therefore nature had only symbolic significance
as it was seen to reflect eternal verities and forms. This gave rise to the
kind of culture which we associate with the great Gothic cathedrals with
their lofty spires pointing upward into eternity. But with the Reformation the stress was upon the turning of God in all his compassion and
love *toward* the world which he had made and which he continues in his
grace to maintain as his creation. The stress here upon grace alone means
that man in response to the divine grace looks with God in gratitude and
wonder in the direction God himself looks, at the world which he has
made, and enters into that movement of his grace toward the world.
Thus Reformation man turned his eyes outward to the great world
which God had made, and as Francis Bacon expressed it, set himself to
exercise dominion over it, understand and occupy it in obedience and
gratitude to God. Natural science thus becomes a religious duty, for in
its pursuit man is gratefully and obediently fulfilling his divinely
appointed functions in relation to nature.

The validity of this depends, however, as Bacon was not slow to point
out, upon the distinction that must be maintained between the kingdom
of grace (*regnum gratiae*) and the kingdom of man (*regnum hominis*).
In the kingdom of grace man lives according to grace, in utter dependence upon God, by grace alone; but in the kingdom of man man is *by
grace* made to have a dominion over nature—yet this is a dominion
which he may exercise only as he is ready to be the servant of nature, for
he can know nature and control it only as he follows the clues which
nature itself provides. Thus it is only as a creature of grace and as a
servant in the order of creation that man is given this dominion. This
also means that man cannot transfer the dominion he has been given

over nature into the kingdom of grace, for man has no dominion over God. In relation to nature then man is a 'maker', one who fashions and constructs things, for the kind of knowledge he gains through serving nature is a form of power; but in relation to God man lives only as a child of the heavenly Father, by grace alone in utter dependence on God. Everything would go wrong in theology if man tried to exercise in relation to God the kind of power or mastery which he is called to exercise in the realm of nature; and everything would go wrong in natural science if he allowed theological presuppositions to control and direct his examination of natural processes, instead of seeking to know those processes out of themselves in their contingent nature apart from God.

How remarkably far-sighted Francis Bacon was, for he put his finger upon the very points where modern science and theology find themselves up against difficulties again and again, and where misunderstanding can only lead to disastrous confusion!

Let us return to Bacon's notion of experimental science as the putting of the question to nature, which in the field of determinate objects, necessarily takes on a violent form. We have to compel nature through experiments to answer our questions. Now Bacon himself granted that we can only control nature by serving it and following the clues it supplies us out of itself. Even when we have to 'disturb' it, we are not departing from nature but are still following it and developing its potentialities. We can achieve true knowledge only when we allow our minds to be obedient to the patterns nature reveals under our experiments. Many modern thinkers have tried to draw other conclusions from the experimental method of science. Because we force nature to answer questions in accordance with our own stipulations, we also, they claim, control the answers nature gives us. But this really means that it is we who determine the pattern that the universe takes as we apply to it our scientific questioning. This is the line taken by John Wren Lewis, who claims that in scientific knowledge we are not concerned with some order 'out there' in nature independent of us, but one that we ourselves create and impose upon nature. It is thus the technologist who, it is alleged, supplies us with the clearest example of scientific activity, in his inventions and in the imposition of his own artistry upon nature. According to Wren Lewis this transition in which the mastery is passing from pure science to technology is the great revolution in which the modern world is involved.

It must be granted that all human knowledge and not least scientific knowledge is reached through a compromise between thought and

being, but that does not entitle us to draw the conclusion that it is we
human beings who impart order to nature or rationality to the universe.
There could be no science at all if we were not up against an implacably
objective rationality in things independent of any and all of us. Certainly we do not find ready-made equations in nature. We have to frame
these ourselves, but we do so not by imposing patterns of our own
creation upon nature but by acting in obedience to a rationality inherent in nature itself. Number, as a calm and sober reflection surely
forces us to realize, represents something quite objective. Hence our
basic statements in mathematics and physics are made by way of *recognition* or *reflection* of what is there independently rather than by invention or imposition on our part.

Now when we relate the way in which Wren Lewis thinks of scientific
knowledge to the new attitude to nature that derived from the Reformation, it would appear to have far-reaching implications for theology.
Detach the view of nature that arises out of the doctrine of creation out
of nothing from God's direct creative activity, detach it also from the
doctrine of the renewal and redemption of the world through Jesus
Christ, and it follows that it is in man's control of nature through advance in technological science that the creative and redemptive patterns
of God come to view, for there is no other order or pattern in nature
than that which we impose upon it. Here man's creative activity is
identified with God's; or to express it in another way, here we have a
relapse into the old idea of *deus sive natura*. At the Reformation nature
was released from the control of a rationalist theology; after the Reformation nature lost its connection with God through his grace and an
extensive secularization of man's understanding of the universe took
place. Now, however, this 'new Reformation' appears to take the
form of an identification of the creative and redemptive activity of God
with the artistry and invention of man! One is, so to speak, the obverse
of the other; Christology is but a way of speaking of the immanent
processes the world manifests under the masterful control of scientific
and technological man! It is as he realizes this that Modern Man is said
to grow up!

There are elements of truth in this attitude to nature which we cannot
reject, for they arise out of a genuine Christology: that is, out of the doctrine that the Creator Logos of God has himself entered into his creation
as a creature and that all creation is somehow ontologically related to
Jesus Christ in as much as it coheres in him, the one Word of God
through which all that is made is made; and out of the doctrine that in a

profound sense all creation is affected by the redemptive activity of God in the death and resurrection of Christ, for in him who is the Head of all things visible and invisible all things are gathered up and renewed. But it would be a perversion and a distortion of the Christian Gospel to resolve Christology and soteriology without remainder, so to speak, into the processes and advances of technological science. But is this not the sort of thing that is being claimed for the 'new Reformation' that comes to view, for example, in the recent writings of the Bishop of Woolwich who relies so very heavily upon Wren Lewis? John Robinson is not a technologist like Wren Lewis but he is obviously a sort of artist whose thinking involves the imposition of his own creative and indeed pictorial images upon 'God', that is, not some Reality 'out there' independent of us, but one identified with the ground of our own being, infinitely near to us, yet helplessly involved in the toils of our own processes of life and thought, for he is unable by definition to stoop down to us and intervene creatively and redemptively in our need and condition. Like the God of Schleiermacher, he is a God without pity and mercy, and like the God of Bultmann he is present and active in the death of Jesus Christ in no other way than he is present and active in a fatal accident in the street. What is happening here? We have on the one hand in these thinkers a movement of thought which detaches nature from the Creator-creature relation, and so introduces the ancient radical dichotomy between God and the world, in which God is denied any active intervention in the world, and then as this leads to the secularization of the world and nature and even of religion (called the maturing of man!) the problem is met by finding God in the ground of being, and somehow identifying the patterns that become revealed under man's masterful technology and artistry with the creative and redemptive order. This is a sort of inverted Deism taking the form of *natura sive deus* rather than *deus sive natura*. People like Alasdair MacIntyre cannot be blamed for calling this atheism! It is certainly remarkably parallel to the 'atheism' which the Nicene theologians found in the Arian movement in the fourth century.

Several things may now be said. The root error here is a sin against the principle of scientific objectivity which we saw to be one of the great contributions of the Reformation and to belong to the essence of every genuine reformation. Whether in exegesis or in the interpretation of history or in theological formulation many modern thinkers have lapsed into a way of thinking in which they will accept as true only what they can form and fashion through their own imaging and conceiving. They think from a centre in themselves and not from a centre in the object 'out there' independent of them, so that their thinking is first by way of self-expression and then by way of projection. This artistic way of thinking in theology is parallel to the new technological way of thinking which does not think of technology as applied science but as the supreme form and indeed the very essence of all science. Everyone at work in the Universities knows that this tension between pure science with its rigorous principles of objectivity and a masterful technology is one of the most serious problems we have to face, but there can be no doubt that the whole of modern civilization will be destroyed and all the great advance of modern science will be brought to nought if this trespass upon the rigours of scientific objectivity is allowed to go on. Today pure theology is thrown into a new partnership with pure science, for *mutatis mutandis*, they are now seen to be battling for the same principle so far at least as their scientific methods are concerned, and the integrity of their relations to their respective fields of study. Theologically speaking, the root problem here is the sin of the human mind, in which man is still trying to be as God, and to impose his will upon the universe, and still insisting on a Christ who will subserve his own wishes and aspirations.

This is a much more difficult problem than naked atheism or materialism for it operates with a view of nature that has been produced by the Reformation understanding of Creation and Incarnation, but detached from the doctrine of God and from the high Christology of the Reformation and of the Early Church upon which it rested. We cannot let go for a single moment the insight of the Greek fathers or the Reformers as to the fact that all creation has been renewed in Christ and that he, the eternal Word and Son of God, the Creator and Redeemer, is in control of all things and will make all things serve the purpose of his saving economy. That includes the developments and advances of science for science is a gift of God. For this reason we have to engage in constant dialogue with those who explore nature and develop its resources which God has planted there for his own glory, but we must do it, as Francis Bacon expressed it, only as those upon whom God has set his grace and who, while they gain power over nature by serving it, can never transfer their God-given dominion over nature to the realm of grace or to the knowledge of the Creator himself. Let it be granted (and who would deny it?) that this is an area where we have still to do a lot of hard thinking, but let it also be clear that we can carry through the new Reformation or fulfil the on-going Reformation only by taking seriously the implacable objectivity of God, by learning to distinguish his objective Reality from our own subjective states and self-expressions, and by thinking on the basis of the Creation and Redemption of God in the Incarnation of his eternal Son. It is no service to nature or to science to lapse back into some form of monism or pantheism. Let me put the problem in a nutshell. When Paul Tillich claims that all theological statements are analogical except one, the statement that God is being, then he also insists that being is God. This is not reformation, for it cannot serve either the advance of science or the advance of theolgy.

On the other hand these modernist lines of thought force us to reflect again upon what happened at the Reformation when the great transition was made from an Augustinian to a Reformed view of nature. It would seem to me that something essential tended to be lost in that change, and that what we now require is a profound reconstruction of the whole history of Christian thought on this subject which gathers up the Augustinian and the Reformed attitudes to nature. We cannot afford to give up the outlook so wonderfully symbolized in the Gothic cathedrals. If the Augustinian looking away from nature to God required to be balanced by a looking out upon nature as God's good handiwork and the object of his grace, the Reformed outlook upon the world which is to be pursued and investigated for its own sake needs to be balanced by a recovery of the dimension of the 'heavenly' and the 'supernatural' and the 'eternal'. I do not mean to say that this was lost by the Reformers themselves (cf. the section in Calvin's *Institute* on the *meditatio vitae futurae* or *meditatio vitae coelestis*) but it is now clear that the Reformation emancipation of nature through the doctrine of creation out of nothing easily lent itself to secularization, to the development of Deism, and even to agnosticism. Nor do I mean that we must return to the Augustinian or the Thomist way of relating nature to grace, but I do mean that we have here on our hands one of the most important although one of the most difficult tasks: for the whole subject must be thought through in such a way as to do ample justice to the ancient, mediaeval, and modern insights, yet all on the basis of the biblical doctrines of creation and redemption. If *Honest to God* has any contribution to make at this point it is surely in throwing into high relief the tragedy that happens to Neo-Protestant prayer when it loses its relation to the transcendence of God, and when it allows Neo-Protestant subjectivism to smother or suppress the objective Reality of God in his own divine and eternal Being and majesty.

5. We have finally to consider the relation of the Reformation in the sixteenth century to the rise of nationalism. The Reformation was not intended as a movement of schism but on the contrary a movement to integrate the on-going faith and life of the Church in the fulness of the catholic faith as it came to view in the great ecumenical councils, but it failed or was retarded as a unity-movement through two principal factors.

First, the Western Church had become geared into a process of development in which it was governed ultimately by popular piety, that is, by a massive subjectivity coming to expression through the Papacy. Reform proved far too difficult, for it called for a logical and theological reconstruction which was too costly: it would have meant a profound reorientation in its traditional way of thinking and a rejection of appeal to its own consciousness as the ultimate court of appeal. Hence the reforming elements were ejected from the Church, and the old Church barricaded itself securely behind its own self-expression and tradition. The upheaval in the Roman Church that is now going on really means that at last this reorientation is taking place, slowly but steadily, for the pressure of objectivity has driven it back beyond its own traditional formulations of the faith to the substance of the faith. The distinction the late Pope John drew between the substance and the formulation of the faith at the outset of the Vatican Council now appears as a great turning-point in the history of Rome. Who can say what will come out of it? It certainly seems at the moment as if the new Reformation may well come in its most formidable form from the Roman Church rather than from the Evangelical Churches which are still so entangled in the swamps of subjectivity and relativity.

Secondly, and this is the point we are concerned with at the moment, the Church Reformed emerged at the same time as Europe was breaking up under the pressure of nationalist movements. Thus instead of there emerging *one* Evangelical Church there emerged *many* Evangelical Churches which inevitably became geared into the hardening cleavages between the nations (*cuius regio eius religio*), and so the Church Reformed absorbed into itself the divisions of the world into which it had been sent to preach the Gospel of reconciliation through Christ. This became a more difficult problem because of the new attitude to nature and its exploration which began to abound in the Protestant countries and to affect social and political relations as well as experimental science. Thus the development of a modern culture in the dynamic Protestant style was inseparable from the new appreciation of nature and the advance of empirical science. This began its rapid advance toward the end of the eighteenth century with the rise of Romantic idealism but it was in the nineteenth century that Protestantism yielded a brilliant and magnificent culture comparable to that of the Middle Ages. Meantime the Evangelical Churches in various countries had developed highly distinctive traditions of their own and had been passing through further internal division, with the result that the patterns of faith, worship and order became more and more determined by non-theological factors, and the barriers of division became harder than ever. In every country the Protestant Church tended to become a servant of public opinion, an expression of the national and cultural consciousness of the people, instead of the manifestation of the one Body of Christ entrusted with a revolutionary message of reconciliation that cuts across all the divisions of mankind and through proclaiming one equal love of God gathers all men without respect of colour or race or class into the one fold of the one Shepherd.

Thus the nineteenth century threw up an immense problem within Protestantism: the integration of the self-consciousness of the Church with the culture that developed out of the new attitude to nature. This led finally, especially in Germany, to the logically understandable yet quite un-Christian attempt to reduce the Christian Church to a socio-religious expression of 'blood and soil', to integrate grace with nature, on the ground that grace does not destroy nature but perfects and completes it, that is on the ground of a doctrine of *deus sive natura* or rather *natura sive deus*. There is no need to trace the story of this development, but we note that it did serve to shake the Church to its foundations, not only in Germany, and to put its faith to the test, and it also served to sharpen the issues between it and a movement of reform that had been going on steadily all through the nineteenth century and which has at last come to the surface in the great biblical and dogmatic theology of our time, and not least in the new theological developments in the Church of Rome. We have already spoken of this advance, one of the most significant and formidable in the whole history of Christian thought, but part of it, and alongside of it, there was a parallel movement which we must consider.

This is the ecumenical movement which owes a great deal to the concentration upon research into the historical Jesus which served to throw Christ and his Gospel back into the centre of the picture once again, and owes more to the attempt to give full theological interpretation to Jesus through his atoning and saving work. This has resulted in a steady attack upon the nationalist and cultural divisions into which the Evangelical Church has become fragmented. Here we see Christianity showing its ancient power to cut across the divisions of mankind, to preach a Gospel of reconciliation that must be lived out in such a way that the deep cleavages that have grown up among men are overcome and healed. At the same time this falls more and more under the objective way of thinking which presses on us from the side of empirical science. The principle of objectivity means that there cannot be more than one science in any field; faithfulness to the object carrying with it detachment from unwarranted and unchecked presuppositions, imports unity. And it must import unity where we think as we are compelled to think, not out of our own subjectivity but as the facts force us to think in accordance with their own nature. This is the kind of objectivity that is now making itself felt again, not only among the Evangelical Churches but among the Roman and Orthodox Churches, so that the movement for unity is being driven steadily deeper and deeper. And yet it is by no means mere method that is playing this forceful part, but method that arises out of content, order that is determined by inner substance, for it is the Atonement itself, the at-one-ment inherent in the nature of the Incarnation and Redemption, that is at work vanquishing the divisions that emerge out of nationalist and cultural roots and the devastating effect of sheer human sin.

Without doubt we are in the midst of a vast new Reformation—it shows a steady and ineluctible advance in spite of wilder and more extravagant theologies and movements which appear on the flanks of the Church's forward march. No doubt they may serve a purpose, if they draw the attention of those who are only concerned with worship or order in the Church to the impossibility of separating the thinking of the Church from the thinking of the scientists in the world at large, for it is to the world that the Church proclaims its message, and it is with this world which more and more is being dominated by science and a scientific culture that it must live out the divine life. But the Church will fail and inevitably be flung aside if it takes the road of subjectivity, and offers a Christianity as some sort of self-expression of the human spirit, a poetic or mythological epiphenomenon to the real work of exploring and developing nature. I cannot see any reformation coming to its fulfilment and taking its place as it ought within the thinking of mankind, and among all the peoples of the earth, except that which is wholly committed to belief in the Creator and Redeemer God, and which takes seriously and realistically the stupendous fact of the Incarnation, and except that which develops its theological understanding not by means of its own artistic creations but through rigorous and disciplined obedience to the objective reality of the Word of God made flesh in Jesus Christ.

The Christian Church is confronted today with its Nebuchadnezzar and his dream of a vast image reaching up to heaven, the image of a technological empire in which man imposes his own will and the patterns of his own invention upon the universe. But like Daniel the Church must speak of the stone that is cut out of the mountain not by human hands, which will smite the image of human empire and break it in pieces, and will itself become a mountain that fills the whole earth. The new Reformation cannot do without its apocalyptic message which is a transference to the history of human achievement in all the empires of political, social and scientific endeavour of the Gospel of salvation by *grace alone.*

INDEX OF NAMES

INDEX OF SUBJECTS